Profit from Real Estate
RIGHT NOW!

DEAN GRAZIOSI

Vanguard Press
A Member of the Perseus Books Group

To my son
Brody Dean Graziosi
who was literally born the day after I finished this book. Until the
moment you were born, I questioned if I could love another child as
much as I love my firstborn, Breana. Then the second I met you, it hit
me. It's not one or the other when it comes to your children, there is
so much love that it's equally available for both of you.
I love you and your sister more than words could ever express.
You both inspire me to be a better man.
Thank you.

Contents

Introduction

If you are near a computer, take a few minutes right now and go to **www.deangraziosi.com/intro** and watch a short welcome video from me. I think it will help set the right tone for the success you want from reading this book. If you can't do it right now, then do it when you have a moment at a computer.

When I started writing *Profit From Real Estate Right Now* in October 2008, the financial condition of the United States was in turmoil. With record-breaking bank failures and massive government bailouts, our country was heading into a tough recession. There was volatility in the stock market, a credit crunch, a housing crash, inabilities to get loans, and uncertainty about Social Security. Economists even compared the economic crisis with that of the Great Depression.

By the time this book hits the shelves, things may even be worse. These gloomy and depressing circumstances can cause you to feel a sense of despair and leave you wondering what in the world can you do.

Here's the good news. You have picked up my book at the perfect time. These seemingly horrific days (and they are horrific—for anyone who has lost their home, their job, their security and their sense of self), have also created a window of opportunity to make this the greatest time in history for anyone, yes even YOU, to profit from real estate.

Right now, like no other time before, you can make incredible amounts of money in real estate, but only if you take action with what you are about to learn. With the information in this book, you can create wealth and abundance like you might never have imagined. If you are afraid because of financial uncertainty, or feel unsure whether you'll be able to continue your current lifestyle (let alone improve it), if you desperately want to find *some way* to just get REAL financial security into your life, this book is for you!

It is an absolute FACT you *can* start making money in the next 30 days, because of *today's depressed real estate market, with no money and no credit,* just by using the unique strategies you are about to learn. If you do happen to have some money to invest, that's great, because these strategies will work better than most anything you will ever find in the real estate investing realm.

Maybe you're like many other Americans right now and have lost your ability to trust in various parts of your life. What you could count on in the past, no longer seems trustworthy in the present. Maybe you've even lost hope in the American dream itself. Yet, no matter what your problems may be, America still offers unmatched opportunity to achieve success.

Today's immigrants know this, while so many others seem to have forgotten it. Immigrants are still flocking to the USA in record numbers. According to the Census Bureau our nation's immigrant population (legal and illegal) reached a record of 37.9 million in 2007. So, if opportunity is everywhere, like the rest of the world knows it is here in America, why do so few people take a chance and make a difference in their lives?

I believe the problem begins with our lack of knowledge and initiative. Not only do we not know what to do to make a change, many of us have lost the belief that we really can change our lives for the better. This book is first and foremost going to show you what you can do to make a difference in your life, using real estate. If you're feeling stuck, this book will give you the recipe to get unstuck. If you have lost part of your life and are struggling just to get through each day, this book can show you one way to get back on your feet, regain hope, and grab your share of the great American Dream bigger and faster than ever before. If you haven't achieved the wealth and freedom you desire, this book will show you how to use real estate to transform your life. It will give you the right knowledge, show you the right actions to take, and lead you straight toward the results you want in your life.

In this book, I'm going to show you real ways to make money in a down real estate market, whether you have no money, a little money or a ton of money to invest! I know that's a mighty big claim, but since I have been doing this for over twenty years and have helped thousands of people like you achieve the goals they desire, I am more than confident about making such a bold claim. I want to give you the tools to think big, so you can turn those big goals into reality. It's time for you to listen only to your inner cheerleader, that voice that tells you, "I can do it," and turn the sound off on the inner critic and all those real, live, walking and talking naysayers around you.

At the time of this writing, I have over 30 real estate deals in the works. I'm also blessed that my other real estate book, *Be A Real Estate Million-aire*, was not only a New York Times, USA Today, and Wall Street Journal bestseller but was also one of the best-selling real estate books in America for over a year. While I am grateful that my company's products and services generate a great deal of money, I'm more excited for the opportunity to help people, just like you, change their lives with one of the most reliable and lucrative methods for creating wealth—real estate.

Throughout this book, you are going to hear real-life stories from people just like you, who decided they wanted more out of life, used my techniques, and achieved all they desired and more. They will also be sharing their unique strategies and secrets to get wealthy. I have also decided to go in depth with the story of one of my students, Matt Larson.

You will see his real-life progression, hear his strategies and learn how he went from a life of fear, insecurities and a dead-end job to a life of confidence and abundance. Oh, and did I mention he's now a millionaire? Be prepared, this is the real deal and with some action on your part, you could be in my next book as another one of many success stories.

One very important thing to remember when you are reading this book is that I'm not some "out-of-touch" guru who did a few deals twenty years ago and then became a teacher. I'm an active real estate investor, who loves sharing what he knows. What I have uncovered is a way to give you an unfair advantage to gain the fast track to success. I don't just theorize about it, I don't just talk about it; I make money with real estate every day. That's why this could be the single most important book you may ever read in your life.

Two things could happen right now.

You could read a few pages, decide that this is all a bunch of baloney, put the book down and go back to your everyday routine. You can allow all the naysayers (the same types who have always trampled all over your dreams) to convince you that you can't do anything extraordinary, that you just can't try anything new and win. That would be a travesty in my eyes, and it could be the biggest mistake in your life.

You have a choice. Five years from now, will you kick yourself for not taking action during this historic time, or will you look back and say I was there, I jumped at the chance to profit like never before in real estate? This is like having the chance to buy Microsoft stock for $5 a share, knowing that in a few years it's going to double or triple. You will probably never see Microsoft stock at $5 again, and you will likely never see real estate prices as low as they are right now again. People and banks are desperate to sell, interest rates are at an all-time low, and you have the perfect opportunity to get rich investing in real estate using none of your own money. I promise, if you don't step out of your comfort zone and take action with real estate right now, you will regret it for many years to come.

To do this, it may require you to be counterintuitive. To go against your fears and what other people (most often underqualified and overopinionated people) may be telling you.

Take action with these proven strategies that will allow you to profit with no money and no credit. This unbelievable opportunity can give you immediate results, and create tremendous wealth over the next 1, 5, and 10 years. It's your choice—stick with the uncertain, unfulfilling status quo, or keep reading and start living a life without the stress of worrying about money. Living the life you truly deserve is NOT a pipedream. You just have to give yourself the chance to try, gain the confidence you know is inside of you, and break free from the norm and provide the type of environment you want for yourself and your family (or the family you hope to have someday).

Let me be your guide over the next few hundred pages and I promise that if you do everything I say, by the end of this book you'll come out with the confidence, wisdom and capabilities to live the life you know you deserve. It's your choice, make it or don't, but keep this in mind . . . If not this book now then what and when?

Now is the moment. Seize it!

Part One

CHAPTER 1

Yes, You Can Cash In on Real Estate Now!

Literally, within one month from now, you could be depositing money in your bank account. Good money! I'm going to show you my step-by-step method to make money today in this depressed real estate market. With my method you can make $5,000 to $20,000 or more, in less than 30 days, even if you have no money! That's just the beginning—it gets even better. There is no limit to what you can make once you learn and apply what I'm going to show you. But first, I want to do all I can to make sure you are ready to become wealthy from real estate. You'll need to take action and follow what I'm going to teach you. Most important, I know it's not easy to step away from your normal routine, even if it is not working for you or actually causing you pain. I hope to help you overcome that through this book, with just enough inspiration mixed in. So before you start learning, let me share how I got the inspiration to write this book and where I began.

La bella Italia (Beautiful Italy)

As I write this, I am sitting on a balcony of an 1,100-year-old castle, converted into a 5-star hotel that overlooks the Mediterranean Sea, in Calabria, Italy. Calabria is also called *il cuore* or "the heart" of the Mezzogiorno region. It is a place of spectacular beauty, rich in history, which can be traced back to antiquity when the Greeks created dozens of settlements along the coast.

I'm here because I brought my dad to Italy to celebrate his seventy-second birthday and create lifelong memories for both of us. Before we left the States, I also hired someone to find family members on my mother and father's side, who were still living here. Although our family's bloodlines are close, we had never met, or even contacted one another before.

First, we saw the birthplace of my grandfather and great-grandparents on my father's side in the city of Sturno. Then we visited Potenza and Calabria to meet my relatives on my mother's side of the family. We acquainted ourselves with our newfound family over a dinner of local fish dishes. It was an amazing evening, sitting under the stars, overlooking the sea, next to the same historic castle whose balcony I am on as I write. To call it breathtaking would be an understatement.

Along with the banquet for the eyes that traveling the Italian countryside provided, Dad and I have eaten the greatest food of our life. I made Neapolitan pizza by hand at a local pizzeria; devoured succulent home-made cheeses, prosciutto, *supersade* (a hard Italian salami), and drank homemade wine with homemade pasta. It's been like something you see on one of those cool Travel Channel shows.

While I sit on this beautiful property that looks as if it was personally crafted by the hand of God, I realize that this could never have been a reality for my father if I had not taken action by investing in real estate.

You see, my father is one of ten children, from which countless cousins and second cousins have been born. None of them ever had, nor probably ever will have, the money to make the trip we have just made. As I reminisce over the last few days, I realize that had I not taken action with real estate, I probably would never have gotten involved in anything else that would have allowed me to prosper in such a big way.

I tell you this story not to brag but rather to spark your emotions and let you see what is possible. I'm a guy who never went past high school, lived in a trailer as a kid and only dreamed of things like I just explained. Yet real estate made it possible for me, and I want to make it possible for you.

If you are ready to take action with something that could propel your finances to the next level and allow you to have the life you and your family desire, please pay attention to what I'm about to tell you.

We are in a unique time right now. It won't last forever, but while it's here, the average person, who is willing to follow the information provided in this book, can gain massive wealth far faster than you would believe possible.

To prove it, allow me to read you some headlines and I'll explain why they are here in just a moment:

HOUSING PRICES FALL SHARPLY: REALTORS GROUP ATTRIBUTES SLUMP IN COUNTY AND STATE FIGURES TO FEARS OF RECESSION

AUCTION DRAWS BIG CROWD TO BID ON PROPERTIES

COMPTROLLER ASSERTS BANKS FACE GROWING REALITY WOES

REAL ESTATE WOES SEEN WORSENING; COMMERCIAL VALUES EXPECTED TO PLUNGE IN NEXT 2 TO 3 YEARS

HOUSING SLUMP IN CALIFORNIA SEEN WORSENING

REALTORS HEAR GLOOMY PRICE, SALES FORECASTS

BIG SLIDE IN HOUSING PRICES IS LATEST WORRY ON WALL STREET

CONSTRUCTION OF HOUSING FALLS 4.7% IN NOVEMBER

ONCE EAGER FOREIGN INVESTORS ARE SUDDENLY NERVOUS

You've probably seen headlines like this, and recently, some even more frightening, haven't you?

Well, guess what?

Those headlines are from 1988 to 1992, when this country had its last big recession and down real estate market. You see, history repeats itself and we are about to repeat history in a much bigger wave. If you know what to do, there's an absolute fortune to be made in today's market. Take it from someone who luckily stumbled into real estate investing during the last down market.

It's true. I actually started my real estate investing career during a time when the market was falling and everyone was telling me that it was impossible to make money, especially since I was a kid, broke, with no experience and only a high school education. Even people close to me were horrified that I would even consider investing in real estate. My dad, whom I love dearly, was against it. My neighbor, several good friends, and even my uncle all told me that it was impossible.

Even though I was deeply in debt, I was naïve enough to think that I could still buy property and make money. Thank God for being a little stupid sometimes, because the results were more then I could have ever anticipated. It's time for you to think big thoughts, set big goals and make them a reality too.

The "depressed" real estate market is what allowed me to become a millionaire in my twenties and a multimillionaire in my thirties. Even more astounding is that I did it by going blindly into a field where I had NO training or experience whatsoever. Imagine what *you* can do with me guiding you, and showing you not only the exact strategies that I used, but piling on the 20-plus years of strategies that I have learned since then. Oh, and another thing. I'm not going to do a brain dump here and try to download EVERYTHING I've learned into your head. I'm going to be as streamlined as possible, and focus on telling you what you need to know to make money now, in this market, starting from wherever you are.

You see, even in a down or depressed market, people are still buying and selling homes. Some want to sell, and some NEED to sell, creating opportunities for creative financing and other kinds of deals that you will soon learn. In this book, I'm going to teach you the "no money down" techniques of today that will show YOU how to profit from this current real estate market right away. And yes, this is the type of real estate market that makes millionaires out of people who are ready to take action. I hope that includes you, but I'm sure you wouldn't frown on earning an extra $20,000 in the next 30 to 45 days either (wink). One thing to know right now, the no money down strategies you're about to learn are not old-school, outdated, recycled techniques that simply don't work in today's changed environment. They are new, cutting-edge strategies that work NOW.

Looking back, I realize that one of my keys to success was being naïve and uninformed. If I had been more informed and as some have said "smarter," I might never have risked my time and energy in a real estate market that everyone said was horrible. Starting in a down real estate market was actually a huge blessing. If I had started in a booming up-swing or top market, I might have had too much competition and never would have gotten started. One reason my first real estate deal worked was because I never thought it wasn't going to work. My youth and in-experience kept me focused on winning and nothing else. If I had been older, when life had beat me down a bit, and overanalyzed the situation, I may never have done it. I know that I still repeat a phrase that I heard and live by in many instances of my life: "Watch out for paralysis caused by overanalysis." There is also a great quote by Wayne Gretzky that I live by: "You miss 100 percent of the shots you never take." Love it!

I tell the story of my first real estate investment in *Be A Real Estate Millionaire* but since I don't know if you've read that book, I'll retell it here to give you the right perspective on what I've just said.

My First Real Estate Deal

To tell this story, I want to preface it with a quick snapshot of my early life. I wasn't born into money or position. My dad and mom had troubles, and eventually divorced when I was three years old. While all of our relation-ships are different today, back then not only was this heartbreaking, it was ugly too. I lived with my mom in a trailer park in Marlboro, New York (the only trailer park in town). We were so poor that my mother had to work two jobs to earn a measly $90 a week. I grew up wearing hand-me-down clothes, and endured a lot of teasing from other kids. Needless to say, it wasn't fun. With changing jobs and my parents' new relationships, I moved more than twenty times before the age of eighteen.

In my early teens, I went to live with my dad and started working at his auto repair garage for a little spending money. Even though I worked very hard physically for long hours, I wasn't able to save any money. There was an apartment house in town, which had once been a decent place, but over the years the owners had let the wrong tenants in and the place had severely deteriorated. There were broken-down cars in the yard, garbage piled in the hallways, a broken front door, and some busted windows.

This apartment house was for sale, but in its horrible condition, no bank was going to give anyone a loan to buy it. The building wouldn't have been able to get a certificate of occupancy, and in most cases, you can't close on a piece of property unless a certificate of occupancy[1] exists. Now remember, I'm a broke teenager here, just picture me going to the owners of this property with no experience, no money and no clue what I was doing to negotiate a price. I did, however, have a plan, and for it to work, I needed to buy myself some time. So after some negotiations with the sellers on the price, I told them, "I'd like forty-five days to clean that place up, but then you have to sell it to me. To keep you from selling it to anybody else, I'm going to give you a tiny down payment. But in forty-five days, I will start pursuing a bank loan. Then I have sixty days from that point to close on the property."

With no other prospects in sight, the seller agreed. Now here is the part of the story that shows how naïve I was. Once the seller and I had a deal, I immediately went to work on the place before I even knew whether I could get a bank loan—I think even before I had a signed the contract. So in blind faith, I poured my heart, soul and elbow grease into cleaning up the place. First, I called around until I found a junk dealer who agreed to haul away everything in the front yard for free, so he could sell it for scrap.

With permission from the current owners, and then later in my contract, it stated that I could evict some of the worst tenants, so I got rid of the ones who were unwilling to be part of the massive cleanup. Then I got together with some friends and, with the tenants, hired the cheapest laborers I could find. Together, we fixed all the broken windows, the front door, and the porch.

We planted flowers across the front, manicured the lawn, trimmed the hedges, and painted the front of the building. Then we went inside and painted the hallway and cleaned up a couple of the apartments that we had evicted people from. They were nice apartments; they just needed to be cleaned. In forty-five days, the building looked gorgeous. I then went to the bank and was fortunate enough to get a loan because the property

[1] A certificate of occupancy means the property is livable—and this place wasn't, especially with the front porch ready to fall down, with an eight-foot drop to the ground.

was now appraised for much more money than I was buying it for. In fact, I got a loan for 100 percent of the money I needed! I kept that apartment house for many years, and while I lived in the best apartment for free each month, I also enjoyed great positive cash flow from it. Then I sold it during a peak cycle and made a huge profit. How much? Well, it was many years ago and although you might think I'd remember every penny, kind of like one remembers their first kiss, I don't remember exactly. I think it was over $100,000, which back then may as well have been a million dollars to me. Those profits went right back into more real estate and helped propel me to being a millionaire in my twenties.

What a great learning experience and what a great sense of accomplishment! To this day, I can remember standing on the front lawn, looking at the apartment house after I purchased the property, and feeling the sense of accomplishment that came from knowing I did everything I said I was going to do. My confidence started to grow at that very defining moment in my life, giving me the power for the next deal. That's how it all started for me.

How Could I Have Done This?

Looking back, I was so determined because I knew what I wanted and I wasn't going to let anything stand in my way. There was no "what if" option—only "when."

If a naïve kid who came from no money, had no mentors, and never went to college can do it, you can do it too. This book will give you the specific tools you need to get started. You just have to take action.

See, anybody could have done what I did all those years ago with that apartment house. Physical obstacles didn't stop other people from doing what I did. Mental obstacles stopped them.

If you want to succeed in real estate, or anything in life, the biggest obstacles to remove from your life are the ones between your ears.

I don't know how many problems or obstacles you may currently have. But here's what I do know: Everyone has obstacles, some much bigger than others. We all have them and they will never go away. Some problems are annoying while others are downright life-threatening. But no matter how big and scary any of your obstacles may be, they all share a common characteristic: You can choose how you respond to them. Sure, it's easy to say, often tough to do, but it doesn't make it any less true!

We may never eliminate all of our obstacles, but we can always learn how to work through them. It doesn't matter who you are, where you live, or what experiences you may have had (good or bad, pleasant or painful), you should remember this: You are worthy. You deserve to be happy. You can achieve your goals. You are special. You can do anything you want to do. You deserve to be who you want to be.

Surround yourself with positive people and fill your mind with positive information, which will encourage you to be enthusiastic and pursue your dreams. These people may not be able to provide advice that directly helps you reach your goals,[2] but they can provide encouragement when you feel frustrated and offer advice when you feel you can't go on anymore. Motivated people push you closer toward your goals through their encouragement and advice while negative people will always tell you why something will not work.

I'm not saying you need to start listening to motivational audios or take on any extra commitments. It might be as simple as dropping some current negative time-wasting activities from your life. Maybe spend less time with the most negative people in your life, or ask them to change the topic of their conversations.

An Off-the-Wall Challenge

In preparation for learning my greatest techniques and secrets for creating massive wealth right now in this down market, I am going to challenge you to free your mind and be ready for success. Go on a "news diet" for a few weeks while you read this book, and if you love it, do it longer. What does that mean and why do I want you to do this? Just as friends, relatives and other people can destroy your dreams through negativity and criticism, so can negative news and information. Because what we focus on, what we think about, can determine our future.

If the news is the only thing you read, watch or listen to, you'll be focusing on *negative* news, which can shackle your personal progress, growth and ability to make money. So a "news diet" simply means stop reading news, watching, listening to it or talking about it for the time period you set.

---

[2] A great place to find supportive people who can help you reach your goals is online at my real estate investors' community, **www.deangraziosi.com**, as well as in my Real Estate Success Academy.

Don't get me wrong. I believe you should know what is going on in the world, but when *so* many things seem so bleak all at once, it's easy to fall victim to a sense of despair, and it's highly unlikely you can do much feeling like that. If you somehow avoid feeling a sense of despair, you still may end up using the "sad state of affairs" as a crutch . . . an excuse about why your life's not going as good as it "should" be.

So instead of focusing on how *bad* things are, take a break from it. Just focus on what will encourage you. That means NO newspapers, TV, or talking with friends about such news. Instead of watching, reading or talking about negative events that are out of your control, do something really simple and spend time being grateful for what you already have. Then take advantage of the things that are in your control, like your successful financial future.

This exact exercise of focusing on what I should be grateful for in the face of adversity has gotten me through countless down spots in my life, as well as simply helping me reach new levels of success when things were going okay.

So what about it? For the next two weeks, wake up and take a quick walk before anyone is up, go downstairs or into your living room, outside on the porch, the garage, anywhere that suits you, and simply say out loud what you are grateful for. Sound a little silly? I thought so at first, but it got me through my toughest times when I felt depressed due to my surrounding circumstances.

So please stick with me here. You are only hours away from learning real-life skills that will put cash in your hand. But let's do a little more preparation so you can stick to it and create the life you deserve.

So what do you have to be grateful for? Need some ideas?

Okay, maybe you're grateful for your spouse, maybe it's your children or your health. If your health is bad, maybe you can be grateful that you aren't starving to death in the middle of West Africa because you live in America. Think about your friends, parents, past successes, and even the ability to read (hey, 867 million adults worldwide are reported as illiterates). Dig deep and be grateful. I challenge you to really experience gratitude.

I know at first I didn't experience gratitude; I was simply saying it. But when you truly can be grateful and say it out loud, the hair on your arms will stand up. You may even start saying it so loud that neighbors will think you are crazy. Let them! Remember, we all have problems, some much more severe than others, but set them aside (at least for the next two weeks) and be grateful.

"What does being grateful have to do with real estate investing and making money?" I believe that if you take a break from the news and other negative information, and focus on what you are grateful for, this exercise will open up a new window of energy, excitement and time so you can focus on a bigger future for you. A bigger future that involves cashing in on today's real estate market in a big way.

Much of our time is eaten up by focusing on what's wrong with the world. If you can focus on what is right and the opportunities you have, then your future success is unlimited. The fact of the matter is that RIGHT NOW is the greatest time in history to profit from real estate.

The only person who can allow you to achieve the future you desire and deserve is YOU! Imagine going on this news diet and turning all your focus on you and your family and your future. Instead of wasting time worrying, you can spend your time focusing on your dreams and learning the skills to achieving them.

NOTHING can propel you from debt to wealth, or from stagnant money in a savings account to having your money work for you, as real estate can, especially in today's market.

You may be working forty or more hours a week, earning just enough money to slowly keep sinking a little deeper in debt every month. Maybe you have a few dollars stashed away in a 401(k) or savings and realize it will not be enough for your retirement. You could be like lots of Americans, relying on credit cards to keep paying your bills, but you know that can't last forever. Even worse, do you even know whether you'll have a job next month? Next year? Working a job is no longer a secure way of making a living.

If you don't take action right now, you will undoubtedly have more of what you already have. If you have stress and worry, or just unhappiness with job and income, then you can expect to have more of that next year.

But here's the good news. You have taken your first step by deciding to read this book, and I am going to do everything in my power to keep you engaged, give you clear concise steps, boost you full of confidence to take action, and help you change your life and your future right now. Have faith in me, have faith in yourself and together let's create a bigger, brighter future for you and everyone you care for.

More important, don't you *dare* let anyone talk you out of your desire for a better, more prosperous life! DO NOT let anyone cripple your future with their own insecurities or unwillingness to step out of their own rut. You have the desire; you have already taken action by getting this book in your hands, and now is the time to make it happen.

· Let me make this promise. You are about to learn proven strategies that work right now, not regurgitated strategies that worked in the past but fail miserably under today's market conditions. This is the real deal.

However, I want to be brutally honest at this point.

Reading a chapter or two, getting pumped up and then slowly drifting back to your current life will never give you the life you deserve or desire. It takes work, but I have the recipe for massive success if you are ready to *get in the kitchen*.

If I asked you how to make *crème brulée,* most likely you would not be able to do it. Yet if you got the exact recipe from a master chef who won awards for his *crème brulée* and you followed that recipe line by line, you could make award winning *crème brulée* too.

What you hold in your hands right now is a recipe for creating massive wealth in today's real estate market. Follow what I share with you and get award-winning results. It's that simple.

Do you have a little bit of money but not a lot? Are you barely scraping by or, worse, broke? That's okay. I'm going to show you how to find properties that you can sell to others without a dime of your own money and make a profit, right now in today's market. I'm going to teach you a unique system to find properties at huge discounts, deals that no one else can find, how to locate a buyer who is perfect for it, and sell the equity in the amazing deal you found and make a profit!

You will finish this book and be able to do so much more than just survive a recession. You can get out of any debt you may have and create a life of abundance and wealth. You can get control of your finances, you can afford the things you want and need, send your kids to the finest schools, provide the best food, shelter, health care, help others in need, and anything else you want for your family. Life, as you now know it, is on its way out.

In my last book, I said that as we get older, having hope for our dreams or trying something new becomes harder because we get stuck in our ways. I ask that you read this book with a childlike enthusiasm. Picture me over twenty years ago as a skinny teenager, determined to buy that apartment building, and thinking of no option except that this will work for you too, if you apply my proven principles and strategies.

Taking action always outweighs overanalyzing. But the right combination of knowledge and action is even better, and that's what you're going to learn in this book.

In fact, as you learn throughout this book, I'm going to weave in a true story of one of my students, named Matt Larson, who faced almost all the obstacles we've discussed in this chapter. Matt's story will provide more real-life proof that you too can become financially independent u   s   i   n   g real estate.

I chose to include Matt's story as well as the stories of many others throughout this book because of a question I hear so often: "Dean, I know you can do what you teach but can the average person do it as well?" Hearing that question over and over sparked the idea of letting some of my students teach you how they did it. In their own words, with the strategies they developed from what they learned from me and what they discovered for themselves. You may sympathize with Matt's situation: he was in a dead-end job, broke, stressed, worried about his future, and surrounded by everyone who told him it would never work. Or you may have more in common with other stories you will read of people who were not broke, yet wanted to simply secure their future and make more money than they currently did, and went on to secure their retirements and build huge wealth. Remember, even if the person telling the story is not exactly like you, there is always wisdom to gain from what they share, so read it all and take it all in. They did it and now so can you.

On the next page Matt will kick off his story in his own words, and believe me, his story just gets better and better, especially when you realize that just weeks before I wrote this section, he used the strategies in this book to make $20,000 in an hour and a half with no money and no credit. YES, HE DID! But that is only one of about 35 deals he has done so far with another 10 in the works at the very moment I am writing this section. Did I mention that he is now worth over one million dollars starting with almost nothing? Okay, I'll let Matt tell his own story.

How I Went From Being Broke to Banking Big:
The Story of Matt Larson, Part 1

Like many of you reading this book right now, I knew nothing about real estate. I did have one belief, though; real estate was too complicated and too confusing for someone like me. I grew up in a small town of about 3,700 people where my parents had a farm. We couldn't afford to hire workers so my brother, my sister, and I always worked for free to help out whenever we could. I still remember turning eight years old and helping my father by driving a tractor around the farm.

Life never got easier as I grew up. I was always the kid in high school who got picked on for wearing old, worn-out clothes and driving a beat-up car. At one point in time, the only way my parents could afford to feed all of us was by relying on food stamps.

After I graduated from high school, I didn't have the slightest idea what to do. I tried to go to college, but after one semester, I couldn't afford to stay. At nineteen, I wound up working in a machine shop, in the town I grew up in, putting in ten-hour days and only making $6 an hour.

One day I confronted my boss and asked him point-blank if it was possible to make $25,000 a year. I picked that amount because my parents never made that much and I felt if I could make that much in one year, I would be happy. My dad always taught me that the only way to make a lot of money was by working a lot of hours, so I was willing to work as hard as I could to get rich.

Needless to say, working in a machine shop never did get me rich, so I eventually got into sales where I sold machine shop equipment. This job took me to St. Louis, and at the time, I was dating a girl who lived four hours away. To keep the relationship going, I would drive those four hours just to see her. One day, she gave me an ultimatum and told me that I either had to move back or the relationship was off. I decided to move back.

So I wound up right back in the town where I grew up, working at the very same machine shop I was at when I was nineteen. The only difference is now I'm older, and I'm working thirteen hours a day. On top of that I had a thirty-five minute commute, one-way, to this job. Every week, six days a week, I spent nearly fifteen hours of each day working this job.

My job forced me to stand on a hard concrete floor all day. There was no air conditioning in the summer and I never saw the sun on any day I was at work during the winter. Obviously, I wasn't happy. My relationship with my girlfriend started to fall apart. It got to the point where I was spending every night listening to audio CDs to teach me how to handle the stress in my life.

Every night I remember thinking, "This just cannot be what life is all about." To reduce my stress at work, I started streamlining my work process, and when I found that it made my job easier, I tried to present my ideas to my boss. To my surprise, he blew up in a rage and told me that I had to do exactly what I was told to do.

That night I went home, thought about it, and showed up to work the next day just to tell my boss that I quit. I didn't have another job lined up and I didn't have much savings. Without replacing my income I knew I wouldn't last more than a few months. But I did it and the moment I quit, I felt this huge burden drop off my shoulders. For some reason, the first person I decided to call was my friend Willie Herath, who lived in Los Angeles.

When Willie heard that I quit my job, he asked me, "What are you doing tomorrow?" I told him that I didn't have anything planned so he invited me to stay with him for two weeks and see what Los Angeles was like.

The next day, I bought a plane ticket and flew out to spend the next two weeks with my friend. What shocked me wasn't how different Southern California was, but how my friend Willie lived. He was managing an apartment complex. Not only was he living there rent-free, he was getting paid to do it while working about five hours a month. He had also bought a condo, fixed it up, refinanced it and pulled $75,000 out tax-free that he put in his bank account.

Willie kept telling me how great his life was and how much free time he had. Then he told me, "Matt, you've got to get into real estate." For two weeks, all day long, all he talked about was how great real estate was. I kept arguing with him that real estate was the worst investment you could make since that is what my family had told me ever since I could remember.

Willie persisted up until the very day I left. He continued to tell me that real estate was a good idea. More important, he kept saying, "One, you can do it, and two, it's worth it."

I hope my story isn't boring with the "before" details, I just want you to know where I came from so you'll see what I faced to get where I am now. Believe me, I am going to share how I went from those bleak beginnings to a millionaire and truly the happiest I have ever been in my life. In fact, beyond happy, I am living a life because of Dean and what he taught me that I did not know was possible. Willie inspired me to take action with real estate and I am eternally grateful. When Dean asked me to write this section, I was excited to do it because I hoped maybe I could be to you what Willie was to me, and through my story inspire you to take action and experience the life I now live.

To get back to my story, when I got back home, all I could think of was real estate. I still didn't have a job and I didn't care. I was now trying to figure out how to get into real estate. Then, as if it was sent to me by divine intervention, I was watching TV late one night right after the California trip and Dean's infomercial came on. I immediately ordered Dean's system, but I was still feeling unsure of myself. In fact (this is funny now, but at the time it was how I felt), I hid Dean's program whenever my friends came over because I didn't want anyone to think I was interested in real estate.

Every night, I read and studied Dean's program and thought it was awesome. I loved all of Dean's stories about the deals he had made and then learned the strategies on how I could do the same thing. I kept thinking, "This all makes sense. I think I can do this." What made this more surprising was that I knew nothing about fixing up or repairing houses. I had never even painted a wall before in my life.

While this was going on, the inevitable happened. My money ran out and I wound up getting a job outside of Detroit. I picked up all my belongings and moved seven hours away. I was still so excited about real estate that I got a real estate agent and started looking at properties without knowing anything more than what Dean had taught me through his program.

To learn more about real estate, I called my old landlord back home and asked for his advice. For two and a half hours, my former landlord told me that real estate was a terrible idea and that although he owned over twenty properties, he hadn't bought anything in the past nine years because there were no good deals left. That taught me to be careful who you listen to. Dean was great about teaching me that in advance.

Worried, I called my friend Willie in Los Angeles, and he told me that there were always good deals and to stick with real estate. About this time, I got a call from Dean's company, asking if I wanted additional coaching. When I learned that I could have a coach to help me learn real estate investing, I immediately signed up for it. It wasn't cheap; in fact, it was the biggest investment I had ever made in my life. Then again, I had really never invested in anything or myself up until that point.

To encourage people to jump into real estate investing right away, Dean's coaches offered a money-back guarantee that if I did five deals within a fixed amount of time, I would get my entire investment back. (He still does this.) When I heard that, I knew immediately that I could do five deals and get my money back. By the way, you will learn later that I got all my money back. Dean's the man!

After I sent Dean's company a check, people starting telling me to get my money back, fast, that I had made the biggest mistake of my life. Even the girl I was dating called me a loser for the investment I had made. Worried, I called Willie, who just laughed and said, "Don't worry. Ignore everyone. Just go for it."

I still wasn't convinced so I called Dean's company back and asked for my money back. They said, "Sure, you can have your money back, but tell us why." When I told them how I was afraid and what others were saying, they simply asked if the people talking me out of my goals and future real estate investing were qualified to do so. I said no. They asked me if I would try it for another thirty days and if I still wanted my money back, they'd send me a check at that time. All I can say is thank you to Dean's team for opening my eyes and getting me to go for it.

Now, please note that all the information I needed to be successful was in Dean's program. But personally, I needed someone to keep me accountable and on track. So working with Dean's coaches and being a part of his Real Estate Success Academy is not something you need to achieve success, but for me it was the greatest investment of my life.

Still not really knowing what I was doing, but using the knowledge in Dean's program and his coaching to guide me, I bought my first three rental properties by selling everything I had to get the down payment. I sold my truck, all of my prized motorcycles, and anything I could find and sell on eBay. It took me two months to buy those three properties, and though those properties were earning me rental income, I had no more money left to buy additional properties.

At that moment, a lightbulb went off in my head, when I realized that I could buy more properties with no money down, by following what Dean had said right there in black and white. Within the next twelve to thirteen months, I wound up buying fifteen more properties without using a single dollar of my own. My net worth was heading toward a half of a million dollars, and I had over $1,000 a week in positive cash flow. That's when I knew I had made the right decision to begin my career in real estate. I am so glad I didn't let anyone talk me out of this. Any one little thing would have stopped me from realizing the life I now have.

At the beginning of my real estate investing career, I had little money and lots of negativity around me. Fortunately, I also had a lot of hope and a few voices of encouragement, so if you're starting out where I began, with no money and people telling you that you can't do it, let me be your inspiration to let you know, "Yes, you can do it too."

Just think, if you're not desperate like I was, and you do have some money or a job that creates decent cash flow for you, think how much faster you can achieve wealth with Dean's techniques. If you want to become wealthy because you know your current job will never get you where you want to be, or your 401(k) won't make for the retirement you want, or you want more out of life than being average, then trust me. Dean's strategies work. Wherever you are in life, real estate can take you wherever you want to go.

In less than three years, I went from knowing nothing about real estate and having nothing in my bank account, to completing over thirty real estate deals. Today I have a net worth of over one million dollars. I've even made as much as $20,000 in less than two hours on one deal. If I can do it, you can too, and if you keep reading, you'll see exactly how I did it.

To see Matt's video go to **www.deansmedia.com/matt**

Summary

I'm guessing that I don't have to tell you how different Matt's life is today. Things have changed for him, and thousands of others who have taken action with what I'm about to show you.

Are you ready for your change? Then let's make it happen! Here's what I want you to remember from this chapter:

- Anyone can earn money in real estate.

• You can make money in any real estate market, but this current down market could be the best we will ever see in history to create massive wealth for the average person.

• The biggest obstacle to real estate investing isn't money or knowledge, but fear of something different. Don't let fear cripple your future.

• Go on a news diet and focus on the things for which you are grateful. This will inspire you to take action with the proven steps in this book to get wealthy.

• Whether you have money fading in a stock or savings account, have a lifeless job that will never allow you financial independence, or are in debt with bad credit, the strategies in this book can get you making a great deal of money as soon as 30 days from now.

• Matt Larson did it and so can you.

Action Steps

At the end of each chapter, I want to give you specific steps you can do to get started in real estate right away. I don't want you to wait one second longer than necessary because there are killer deals on the market, and the sooner you get started, the sooner you can start making money faster and easier than you ever thought possible.

Identify all the positive people in your life and make a plan to spend more time with those people.

Identify all the negative situations in your life and make a plan to spend as little time as possible in those situations.

Make a list of all the things in your life that you are grateful for. Spend every day reading this list. Read it once in the morning and maybe once at night before you go to sleep.

Stop reading, watching, or listening to the news. Substitute your usual time with the news by writing and thinking about what you really want out of life and how real estate could help you get it.

Success Story #1: Lorina K.

Location: South Range, Wisconsin

Experience before Dean's strategies: Owned and rented three houses.

Net worth increase since starting: Approximately $500,000. YES, a half a Million— Waaahooo!.

Additional monthly income: $1,880 positive monthly cash flow.

Best deal using Dean's strategies: Bought a house for $74,000 that was later appraised for $184,000.

How do you feel about Dean? Blessed the day that he and his book came into my life.

I never knew much about real estate. Growing up, my family didn't have much at all. My dad brought in enough money as a teacher, but then he tried starting a business with a partner who promised to back him with money. However, the partner backed out and left my dad struggling with the business until he eventually had to declare bankruptcy.

I grew up in poverty, without any of the benefits like food stamps, but we had a good family that we loved, so it was awesome. We moved around a lot as my dad was moving up the ladder in the school system. Every time we moved, my parents bought a house and every time we had to leave, they sold and always lost money. Everything I learned about real estate was about cutting your losses when you go so I knew about buying and holding, but I never knew anything about making money.

When I was 19, I got married to my husband, who was 20. Both of our belief systems were that you buy or build a house, live within your means, and work hard to pay off your mortgage. We paid $18,000 to build the shell of our house, which we paid within six years, but we always struggled. I still remember digging through couch cushions and car seats just to look for enough change to buy a pound of margarine or a loaf of bread.

Fortunately, my husband worked in construction so we decided that we could work our way to financial freedom. I had always heard that real estate was the way to go so we bought some property with my husband's brother-in-law and built a home. Unfortunately, we didn't know much about how to sell a home so it sat for a year. By the time it finally sold, we estimated we had all made about $4 an hour.

I still told my husband that real estate was going to get us ahead, so I started dragging my four little kids around, looking at different houses. Soon we bought three properties. One cost $11,200, another cost $16,000, and the third one cost $8,000.

We got renters in and used the rental income to send our kids to a Christian school, which was one of our goals. Then in March 2008, my husband and I were watching TV late at night, which we usually don't do, so I don't know why it was even on. I had never seen or heard of Dean before, but when I saw the numbers and profits that Dean was showing, I immediately thought, "Hey, that's something I could do!"

I always knew of the possibilities in real estate, and we were making a few dollars from what we had done on our own, but watching Dean's infomercial, learning about his background, was so eye opening that I had to order his book right away. I wound up reading it the first day I got it. Reading the motivational stories, mixed in with real life techniques that I knew I could do, was such a huge, life-changing, eye-opening experience. I never knew about motivated buyers/sellers, lease options, no money down deals, or any of that stuff. I knew life was about to change forever. Then I got a call from Dean's coaching program. I went online to research the program, talked my husband into doing it, and we decided to go for it. Hands down, it was one of the best decisions of my life.

Dean's book *Be A Real Estate Millionaire* has changed my life! I have gained knowledge, but most important, self-assurance, confidence, and a network of individuals from whom I can get a boost every day. I don't know if even Dean and his staff realize what a blessing it was for him to create **www.deangraziosi.com** where like-minded individuals can come to encourage each other on a daily basis.

Both my husband and I come from generations of what would be considered poor to middle-class families (although no one would admit to that and would NEVER accept a handout). I was determined to make things better for my family. I used to keep a ledger when the kids were little of where every cent went (I'm not kidding!), and there was NOTH-

ING extra for the kids. I realized that in order to get ahead one needed not only to "cut" costs (you can only cut so much), one needed to INCREASE income. I already believed Real Estate was the way to go, but seeing Dean and successful students on his infomercial was the POSITIVE BOOST I needed to make it a TRUE reality, to get past the limited way I was going about it!

After reading Dean's book, I found a real estate agent, and the next thing I knew, a listing came across in an automated e-mail from my realtor. This little one-bedroom was listed at $59,000 for months, but the picture in the listing did not do it justice. When I realized WHERE it was located, I did a little research and called my realtor. I looked at it the next day and immediately offered $40,000, thinking the seller would meet me halfway. My realtor called the next morning and said we got it!

I had noticed on the county website that the seller owned several homes and had back property taxes due in three weeks. I was offering a quick closing, so I'm sure this had a lot to do with them accepting my offer. (Fair market value now for this property is $57,000, so we have instant equity of $17,000.) Well, we closed with no problem and they already had a renter in place, but he was leaving in a month. So we raised the rent, advertised, and had someone else in less than four days. We have a $300/month positive cash flow on that property, and at the same time the value will build and build over the years.

The other bonus with this house is that it came with two lots (total of 100' x 140') in the nicest neighborhood in our city, where the newest homes are going up (the other half of the block ours is on is cleared now, and 50' lots are for sale at $30,000 each. We'll be able to cash-flow while we hold the property, long enough to make a nice chunk of money from anyone who wants to build a home on the lot. A bonus that we gave the seller was to buy the stove, refrigerator, and the riding lawn mower that were on the property. It was a good deal for us, and they were happy with a little extra cash: WIN/WIN.

The obstacles I have had to overcome are my fear and my ignorance. As far as the ignorance part goes, there is just so much that I never KNEW about Real Estate and the strategies/techniques that a person can use. Everything about bird-dogging, wholesaling, assigning, lease/options, lease purchases, seller-financing, hard and private money lenders, tax lien sales, pre-foreclosures, etc., was a new world to me. I had never heard these terms before. It has been a great experience trying so many of these new things this year. I grow more every day! My fear held me back from trying things at first, but with the help from Dean and the people on deangraziozi.com (HUGE ongoing PART), I have totally overcome that sick butterfly feeling in my gut. It's just not there anymore, when it used to control me! Ever heard of Frozen With Fear? That was me. You'd never know it now.

The biggest help that Dean's book has been to me, and what I've referred back to it for, more than anything, is the encouraging words about over-coming obstacles both exterior (from other people) and within yourself. Because even with ALL Dean's foolproof techniques, a person will achieve NOTHING if they cannot make themselves DO IT!! Even though down deep I am a person who really loves a challenge, I have always been one who does NOT like to take risks, especially when it means making some-one else mad at me. I like peace. So I am very proud of myself for learn-ing how to do this and not only convince myself that I can succeed, but convincing others that it will work, too.

My real estate strategy is simple. Since my husband can do construction, I look for houses that need cosmetic work or minor repairs that we can fix ourselves. I have my realtor e-mail me listings straight off the MLS (Multi-ple Listing Service) so I can keep my eye out for good deals. If the prop-erty is an REO, (Real Estate Owned) my realtor will suggest a price that she thinks the bank would take. Otherwise, I'll talk to the owners and get a feel for what they might need rather than just throw a price out there. I'll also research how much the owner still owes on a property, and that gives me a rough idea what they'll accept.

I know that Dean's strategies work and will work for me in the future. My only regret is not having come across his program long before I did. In-stead of buying one house a year, I am able to do one house a month. Every year I know I'll look back and say, "Wow! Look how far I came again THIS year!"

Lorina's Success Secret: You can do anything you set your mind to. One of the biggest things that I had to overcome was fear. I had to overcome fear of the unknown, fear of losing money, and fear of getting someone mad. You have to learn to overcome the fear or obstacles within yourself and surround yourself with positive people. I know being positive will al-ways win out in the long run because you always get what you ask for. This is like a lifelong dream to me because as a kid my favorite game was Monopoly, where I could buy up all the properties. It's like my whole life is a game that I love now and I get the benefit of the money too. Oh and one more thing. Trust Dean, he is the real thing.

To see Lorina's video go to **www.deansmedia.com/rina**

CHAPTER 2

How to Profit From a Down Market

In 2005, Matt Larson was just another guy living in a 300-square-foot apartment with a pile of bills, a job he hated, and no money in the bank. Then he decided to take action, like you're doing right now, and learn my strategies for profiting in real estate. Fast forward a few years and Matt is now worth over $1,000,000, has a positive cash flow of over $6,000 a month, owns his own home, and quit working in the rat race. Even better, in the few weeks before I wrote this chapter, Matt made over $70,000 in literally just hours of his time using the exact "No Money Down" strategies you are about to learn in this book. Sound impossible? It's not, and as you journey with me through this book, you'll see that it's well within your reach too.

What you have in your hands is a powerful tool that will let you create real estate wealth with little or no money of your own, no matter what your credit score may be. If you have limited funds to start real estate investing, or if you're a little hesitant to buy property, then this method is the perfect way for you to make money right now. Even better, it's one of the best ways to get into real estate in today's current economic conditions with little or no risk. You can become independently wealthy from real estate, and I'm the guy to show you how to do it. First, let me explain how you can take advantage of today's changing real estate market.

The Current "Economic Opportunity"

Before we get into the nuts and bolts of profiting right now, you need to know a little history on why the market is so far down and why that is a good thing for you.

It's no secret that we're in a state of economic and real estate recession (or depression, depending on your point of view), so you may feel my use of the phrase "economic opportunity" is misplaced, but stay with me and

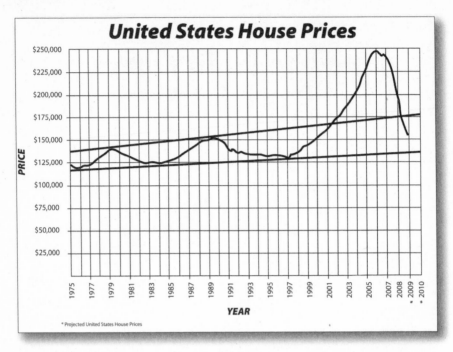

United States House Prices

*Projected United States House Prices

it will all make sense. The single, biggest reason for the decline in our economy is the irresponsible loans made by banks starting around 2002. Based on the last forty years of history, we should have started a natural downturn in the market right around 2002. In fact, take a quick look at an actual chart adjusted for inflation of the last forty years.

As you can see from the chart, that didn't happen. The innovation of unconventional loans, such as ARM (Adjustable Rate Mortgages) with enticing interest rates, combined with interest-only loans, at 100 to 106 percent financing (and artificially lowered lending standards), allowed anyone with a not-so-decent credit score to get a loan. Unfortunately, too many Americans got sucked into the buying frenzy and purchased a more expensive home than they could realistically afford. The multitudes of such people, armed with these unconventional loans, drove real estate prices straight up. You can see that on the chart happening around 2002.

Of course, the banks contributed by making mortgages far too easy to acquire, and exercising little to no scrutiny over loan applicants, which led to bad mortgages running rampant. It is easy to understand how this could happen when you take into account that charging applicants high fees, high pre-payment penalties, and the maximum allowable interest rates was all part of the lenders scheme to make as much money as possible from so many borrowers.

Further fueling this real estate frenzy were people, without any of the guidance like you are now getting, speculating in real estate. They saw home prices appreciating and decided to jump in for a quick buck. They joined the groups of renegade "home flippers" and used unreliable data, (if they used ANY data at all) to make their decisions. With certain markets driving prices up tens of thousands per quarter, these inexperienced investors would buy new homes during pre-construction and even put together financing for sight-unseen real estate purchases—all with the intent of selling before they ever had to make their first mortgage payment.

Banks would make poor loans and then sell these loans to other financial institutions and investors for profit. Can you see how the incentive was to keep making more loans as fast as possible? Risky mortgages were bundled into securities and sold on Wall Street. Big funds, obsessed with getting a higher rate of return, ignored the risks. These factors, followed by a lack of attention by the Federal Reserve, resulted in the creation of a "perfect storm"—and when that storm finally hit, it was like an economic tsunami.

All of these "creative loans" by large financial industries to produce the quick buck and perceived profits backfired. To date that is the main reason there are about 50,000 foreclosures a week hitting the market at the time of this writing.

In March of 2007, the United States' subprime mortgage industry collapsed due to the higher–than-expected home foreclosure rates. More than two-dozen subprime lenders declared bankruptcy. The stock of the country's largest subprime lender took an 84% nosedive, and it was a chain reaction from there on. Welcome to the economic "happening" of 2007 and 2008 that brought us to where we are today.

Tick–Tock–Tick–Tock–Boom!

Most large banks and financial institutions knew (and if they didn't they should have known) this was a time bomb waiting to explode, but the lure of the almighty "immediate" dollar won, as easy money proved irresistible.

Now that you know how corporate greed and irresponsible loans has created this economic turmoil, you have two choices.

One: You can buy into the uncertainty and panic that you read and hear about in the news, and remain paralyzed with fear so you do nothing. Whatever you are feeling right now will only compound in years to come.

If you have debt and worry, you can expect more of that. If you're worried about your 401(k) or stock investments today, you can expect more worry and anxiety tomorrow.

Two: You can open your eyes and see that this real estate market has actually created a huge window of opportunity to make incredible amounts of money right now. Combine this once-in-a-lifetime opportunity with this book's unique no money down system along with my twenty years of experience, and there are no limits to the amount of success you can achieve.

The Real Secret to Real Estate Investing with No Money Down

I know the term "No Money Down" may be a bit worn out, since so many self-proclaimed real estate gurus have been using it while pitching their real estate ideas for years. Traditional style, no money down strategies are nothing new. In fact, I have used many of them to succeed in my investing career. The difference is that I learned my no money down strategies through trial and error rather than being smart like you and learning from someone else's effort.

Unfortunately, most no money down techniques that have worked for the last twenty years, and even just 12 months prior to my writing this book, simply don't work right now, and they may not work again for quite some time, if ever.

Here is what I know at this point in time. Banks won't lend 100 to 106 percent of appraised value mortgages anymore. Stated income loans are harder to get than ever before. Subprime lenders have mostly dried up. Finding anyone who owns his or her home with no mortgage and is willing to finance you or hold the mortgage is rare. Most Americans not only don't own their homes out right, many are upside down—they owe more than their home is worth. Using credit card cash advances for down payments is hard, since most people already carry an average $10,000 balance on their credit cards.

If you have it, using retirement money is just straight-up scary. Those are some old-school strategies that worked well in their time. Yet in times like these, you can't keep trying what used to work. Instead, you have to do something different, and that's what my new no money down system is all about.

Let me tell you how this unique no money down system came to life. Back in 1998, I wanted to share with the country how I started out as a broke kid and was able to become financially independent with very simple techniques starting with absolutely nothing. I have always shot for the stars, so I figured the biggest and best way to share my message was on TV. Probably like many of you trying something new, I too had no experience in promoting myself through TV ads. But like everything in my life, I just took action and went for it. I spent many early mornings creating a program that could help people. When I was done, I hired a crew and filmed a show in my front yard. Over ten years has gone by since then. In that time I have experienced a boatload of failures and disappointments, but I learned a lot through trial and error, especially what "Not to Do." In the process, I soon learned to become a terrific marketer. Today, I'm even considered to be one of the best. Along my journey of creating wisdom products to share with others, I never stopped investing in real estate. In fact, many times when my marketing career was actually losing money, I poured in profits from real estate deals I was doing to keep my marketing business going.

I share this with you because that experience of working my tail off to understand marketing allowed me to think WAY outside the box and create the revolutionary no money down strategies that you are about to learn, which you can only learn in this book. That's a fact, because no one else has the unique process that I developed through my life experiences to get to where I am, and now you get all the benefits.

What you are about to learn is how to find deals that are 30% to 60% off the current and already reduced market price for homes. Even better, I'm going to teach you **automatic marketing processes** that not only will help you find killer deals, but bring them to you quickly and easily. These could be for sale by owner (known as FSBOs) properties, pre-foreclosures, REOs, (Real Estate Owned) short sales, homes being dumped by struggling investors, and more. I'll teach you the differences between these properties, along with how to negotiate deals that will make you wealthy.

Don't even think or worry if the market goes down further. With my system, you'll find houses at prices so low that your downside risk is minimal and your upside potential is enormous. If you're worried about buying properties without money and poor credit, relax. You'll soon see how easy this really can be. Without any money at all.

What I want you to study right now is this graph, which is current at the time I am writing this book and adjusted for inflation.

Notice how the market has taken a sharp nosedive recently while rising nearly as fast back in 2002. What this means is that we're at or near the bottom of this real estate market, which translates into an incredible opportunity that you may never see again in your lifetime.

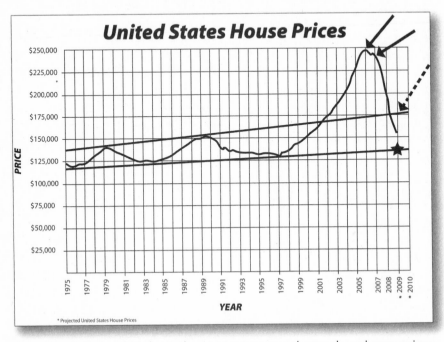

As you can see on this chart, the top two arrows show where home prices were selling a few years ago. The dotted arrow is where prices were when this book was released, and the star is where you'll learn to buy properties. Incredible as it may sound, I have students doing this everyday and now you will have the secrets to buy properties cheaper than anyone, including real estate agents or even other highly experienced real estate investors.

This is where you can see how profits can start pouring into your bank account. First of all, if I simply taught you how to find properties at 30% to 60% off, I'm confident you could immediately start making killer money on your own. If a home sold for $200,000 just two years ago, it might be worth only $110,000 today. If I showed you how to find it and lock this property up on contract for $55,000, do you think you could find a buyer for $65,000 and put $10,000 in your pocket? You bet you could, because most people don't have the skills or know-how to find such a killer deal on their own, but with this book, you will.

Of course, I'm not going to leave you on your own to find a buyer, or even how to create the proper paperwork to make a deal like this happen. I've created a proprietary system that will allow you to find "Motivated Buyers" in any real estate market, especially a depressed real estate market like today's. There are plenty of motivated buyers who want to find great deals, but most people don't know how to find them. We do!

Maybe you're telling yourself, "This sounds a bit complicated." It would be if you didn't have a book like this one or had to try to figure it out on your own, but you don't have to. In a simple step-by-step format, this book will show you exactly how to structure a deal, what paperwork to use, and (more important) how to get paid for your newfound wisdom and capabilities. In fact, just like Matt Larson and many others across America, you could be spending less than three hours on each deal to make significant amounts of money, once you know how to do it. In fact, Matt's last three deals alone have put over $30,000 in his pocket using no money and no credit—all in less than 6 hours total. It's all documented and a true reality for you to follow. Later in this book you will hear more about Matt's deals in detail so you can follow exactly what he has done.

What you hold in your hands today is the result of my desire to help others achieve financial success like I did. I've combined my twenty years of real estate experience and my ten years of marketing experience to create the Ultimate No Money Down Cash Machine for today's market. You'll be able to find deals on homes that are 30% to 60% off current selling prices. That's when you'll lock that deal up on a contract as a prospective buyer and, within 14 to 30 days, you'll assign that contract or sell the equity in that contract to a motivated buyer who will gladly grab such a killer deal from you. In return, you'll make a profit of $2,500, $5,000, $10,000, $20,000 or more for making all this happen. From this book, you'll have the techniques, wisdom, capabilities and confidence to do this over and over again. You can then roll those profits in to other deals that you can learn about in my *Be A Real Estate Millionaire* book or from our highly experienced coaching staff.

Best of all, it won't take a dollar of your own money or require a certain credit score. What it will take to put money in your pocket is for you to keep reading this book and never let anyone tell you that you can't do it. If you need assistance on a deeper level, you can always call a consultant (1-800-315-7782) and see if being a member of my Real Estate Success Academy will work for you. We have helped countless people just like you take their real estate skills and profits to a whole new level. Matt Larson was a student as well as thousands of others. So feel free to call us anytime.

One last thing, if you do have money to invest, this is still the greatest strategy for today's market. Once you find killer deals and lock them up, you can decide if you want to keep the deal, rent it and have positive cash flow and maybe sell it for a significant profit when the market improves, or simply flip it now for fast cash right away. The choice is yours!

Okay, here's a little more of Matt's story and then we will jump right in and start finding those killer deals.

Matt's First Steps

Like most people, I had all kinds of questions about real estate, but rereading Dean's books and with Dean's coaching; I was determined to make real estate work for me. Although I was living outside of Detroit, I decided to focus my real estate investing in a smaller area, which was over 450 miles away. Since I had grown up nearby, I felt more comfortable buying real estate in an area I knew. Plus, I had plans of moving back there and I wanted my investments to be close to me in the future.

For eighteen months, this was my typical day. I'd work all day and come home around 5:00 p.m. Chill for a little while, then for a few hours each night starting at 7:00, I'd put on a pot of coffee and concentrate on real estate, which I called my "second shift." This was the time where I was reading about and studying real estate, looking at real estate on the Internet, or talking with my real estate agent. By focusing on one area, I soon got to know every important detail I needed to feel comfortable. Even though my chosen area was 450 miles away, with a phone and the Internet it was very easy to learn that area from an investor's point of view. On weekends, I would pack a lunch, jump in the car and make the 7-hour drive to the area I was investing in. On Saturday, my real estate agent and I would walk through about twenty properties. On Sunday, I would work on whatever properties I owned, painting or fixing them up, and then Sunday afternoon I'd drive back to Michigan, get home around midnight, catch a few hours sleep, and then be back at work at 8:00 that Monday morning.

This was my routine for a year and a half. It was a bit exhausting, and I went at it harder than most people will, but the truth is, I was having a lot of fun and making money. When I compared the hours I put into real estate investing to any other job, maybe even being a doctor, lawyer or rocket scientist, I could see I was making more per hour for every hour I worked. Talk about motivation! My future never seemed so bright as it did during those busy days.

Obviously, I started with almost nothing, but I bought over twenty properties in those eighteen months. What made a huge difference for me was revisiting Dean's books and his coaching. Whenever I had a question, I would reread the section in the book that fit or simply call the coaching department of Dean's Real Estate Success Academy and they would tell me what to do next to overcome any problems, and, being the naïve person I was, I'd just go out and do it. As long as they told me to do something, I always believed it was possible. I'm glad Dean's coaches were the real deal.

After gaining confidence from a few profitable deals when everyone else said they would not work, I gained the attitude that if I ran into problems, I'd figure something out and it would work. Throughout this whole time, I always thought it was possible, and it was. It made me feel good, I felt like I was accomplishing something. I was sick and tired of being beaten down in life and I didn't want anyone to ever tell me what I had to do. In three years, I went from nothing to being financially free, thanks to real estate.

Now I have streamlined my real estate buying system so that I buy real estate without even looking at the houses. I know exactly what I want. In less than an hour, leveraging the time of my real estate agent (I'll share this secret soon) I put in 25 to 30 offers, and I'll usually wind up with one or two properties that I'll buy at 50% of their value so they'll will earn cash flow immediately, or I can pass that deal off to another investor or buyer and put $5,000 to $20,000 in my pocket in hours. Really, hours. Now that I've put in the time to perfect this system, it seems truly so easy, and in this book, for all that Dean has done for me, I am sharing every detail of how I did it and continue to do it.

Summary

The important thing to remember from this chapter is that you can make money in real estate no matter what the market is doing. Here's what I want you to think about:

• Real estate markets always go in cycles from boom to bust and back again.

• Right now, we may be in what will be remembered as one of the most depressed real estate markets in history, yet it's the perfect opportunity to make money now.

- Previous "No Money Down" techniques may be tougher to use, or may not work at all, in today's depressed real estate market.

- The "No Money Down" techniques you'll learn in this book will work in any market, especially today's depressed market.

Action Steps

In this chapter, you learned how the current real estate market crisis happened and how you can look at it as a complete disaster or an incredible opportunity. Just remember that every problem is just an opportunity in disguise, so this is what I want you to do right now:

Look in the newspaper or drive around your neighborhood and count the number of For Sale signs you see. Think of every For Sale sign as a big flag waving POTENTIAL OPPORTUNITY in your direction.

Before we tell you how to actually pick a great spot to invest in, take an educated guess based on your own knowledge, of an area you think may be best to invest in. Then later we can qualify it or not. Scan the newspapers to calculate the average monthly rent in different areas. I want you to learn how much rental income you can expect from similar properties located in different neighborhoods.

Success Story #2: Carol G.

Location: Honolulu, Hawaii

How much did you make on your first deal with Dean's strategies: $135,000 in less then 2 months.

What you will say to Dean when you meet him in person: Is "I love you" too strong? How about, "Thank you for helping me see my full potential."

Great quote: "I made almost twice as much on my first deal than I do working all year long in a 9-to-5 job and had so much fun doing it."

Raised net worth: $181,000

My husband and I were watching TV late one night and when Dean's infomercial came on, I told my husband to turn it off. He said, "No. I've watched lots of these guys and bought books and tapes that have always given me additional insight and knowledge." My husband had made a small fortune in real estate so he encouraged me to order Dean's book, and that's when I decided that my next career would be that of a real estate millionaire.

When I started reading Dean's book, I got really excited. In the beginning of his book, Dean explains how you can do some research to find good deals like distressed properties and then how to look up and contact the owners. What made me excited was that I was already working as a real estate appraiser so I had all the data sources, city and county information that I needed to look everybody up. Every time I walked the dog or drove around, I'd look at all these distressed properties and make phone calls or write letters to the owners.

My husband is a realtor, so he kept looking on the MLS to help me. I told him that you can't find a deal on MLS because everyone else is looking at it too, and the next thing I know, he found me a deal on the MLS.

It was a duplex home that was listed for $330,000 and owned by a man who had lived there for the past twenty years and never fixed or cleaned anything. Water was leaking from the tubs and soaking into the walls, creating wet rot and attracting termites. I offered $305,000 and had a termite and home inspector go through it. They couldn't believe how poorly maintained the home was, so I withdrew my offer and, following Dean's advice, I included a personal letter explaining why.

Based on my research and estimate for fixing up the home, I put in another offer for $250,000 and to my surprise it was accepted. Based on similar homes in a nearby town, I knew that the property was worth at least $500,000, so I felt safe buying at 50% off.

Although the renovations cost $65,000 and went $15,000 over my budget, I still managed to sell the home for $450,000 to make a $135,000 profit in less than two months. At the time, I was only making $75,000 a year at my full-time job as an appraiser and I didn't have nearly as much fun.

Probably the biggest mistake I've made so far is quitting my day job. The reason you don't quit your day job is because then you can't get a loan. Since I no longer have a full-time job and getting a subprime loan is no longer possible, I have to learn how to approach and negotiate with owners and get more creative about financing.

Because the cost of living in Hawaii is so high, many people can't afford to invest in real estate. However, they've found another way to grow their money, and that's by pooling money for an investment. Even if you're living somewhere else, if you don't have much money, find other people, go in together, and make it profitable for everybody. When you use Dean's techniques to find properties at insanely low prices it is so much easier then you could ever imagine to find the money to profit from it, or find a buyer. Don't let lack of money or bad credit stop you from getting started—you will regret it, I promise.

Carol's Success Secrets: I think the secret to my success has been a lucky combination of reading Dean's book *Be A Real Estate Millionaire* at a time when I was ready to make changes in my life combined with a strong desire to succeed. I've found that people who want to do better in life usually find a way, and Dean's books can help them find their way. I encourage people to just keep trying. Dean made it sound like anyone could do it, in any market, and he was right!

To see Carol's video go to **www.deansmedia.com/carolg**

Special Section:

Quick Start:
Pick Your Own Path

There is no doubt that the best way to learn all the techniques in this book is to read it from start to finish, and then reread the areas or strategies that interest you the most. For heaven sakes, you could read the entire thing in just a handful of hours.

I say that out of one side of my mouth and then on the other side I realize something else. Some of you are like me, have a little ADD and want to skip around or learn one method right away and go try it. Okay, even though I think you should take the time to read it all cover to cover I have created this Special Section for those of you whom I may lose if you have to read the traditional way. And I want this to work for everyone.

So what I have done is create three different paths you can follow for three different objectives. Again, I am only doing this with the caveat that I'm STILL expecting you to promise that you will eventually read the whole book. Because the truth of the matter is, the book is not really written to be broken up like this. It was written for a cover-to-cover read, and therefore you may miss helpful information that may reside in sections you might skip.

For example, the next chapter (chapter 3) goes into detail on robotic marketing strategies that will attract the perfect sellers for you to get properties at 30% to 50% off. These are techniques you can't find any other place on earth. In the first part of the chapter, I wanted to take the time to teach you how it works, why it works and give you lessons that will last a lifetime. Some of you may want to skip ahead to the actual ad you are going to run and read about how to create that ad at a later time.

You will soon learn how to find killer deals at 30% to 50% fair market value. Then how to lock those deals up with the proper strategy and paperwork, then how to find a motivated buyer, pass that deal along to the buyer, and profit $5,000 to $20,000 or more for making it all happen. There are a few paths you can take to do that. One uses robotic marketing strategies to drive the deals to you. You will also learn traditional ways to find great deals that have made me millions. Then, just when you think you've heard it all, I'll give you yet another amazing way to find insanely profitable deals. This is the Matt Larson Method of getting a real estate agent to follow your lead, do most of the work and make a profit that way. Both work amazingly well when you get houses locked up on contract so cheaply and create a flood of buyers, but both are a little different. I know that some of you will be dying to jump ahead to find the chapter or section that best fits your current circumstances. So here are three paths you can take (but don't forget my recommendation to find the time and read this entire book from front to back).

Path #1

The Matt Larson method of having a real estate agent make many offers at a huge discounted price and averaging getting 1 out of 25 accepted. For this route, you need to know how to find the right Real Estate Agent/Realtor® [3], how to determine a good deal, understand how it all works and how to lock up the property on paper, and how to find a motivated buyer to pass it along to and profit. To get started on this path, I suggest you read chapter 6 on finding a great real estate agent, then simply move on through the rest of the chapters in the book. You may get a little confused if there is a section that I mention that was explained earlier. So you will want to skim back to make sure you understand. But reading Matt's explanation alone of how it works will surely fire you up.

Path #2

If you are like many Americans today and have a piece of property that you want or need to sell or have tried many things and it is simply not selling, then you should read chapter 10 and 11 first to get inspired, but then go back and read chapter 3 so you understand the entire "Robotic" marketing strategies in detail.

---

[3] Realtor vs. Real Estate Agent—In this book I may use either of these terms synonymously, but they are NOT the same. Much like people incorrectly use the term Xerox®, which is a brand, to refer to a photocopy, people use Realtor® to refer to Real Estate Agents. All Realtors® are Real Estate Agents, but not all Real Estate Agents are Realtors®. Realtors® are agents who have joined an industry association that, for a fee, gives them the right to call themselves Realtor®, which is supposed to give them "status" above non-association Real Estate Agents.

Path #3

If you are like 25% of my current students, then you don't just want to flip and hold a house; you also want to know how to buy homes dirt cheap and keep them, rent them out for positive cash flow, and then possibly sell them when the market goes up for a huge profit. Or maybe you want to buy a cheap house for yourself. Either way, if you want to get inspired fast and learn how to get these great deals then read chapters 3 through 8.

Remember, you can choose one path or multiple paths; it doesn't really matter. The important point is to choose any path and take action to make it work for you. Depending on your circumstances, you may find one path is easier or more fun than another one. That's fine. Just pick a path and start making money.

Eventually, you should read the entire book, because you'll pick up valuable tips that can boost your real estate career in ways that you may never know about until you try them.

CHAPTER 3

Make the Great Deals Come to You

The first part of this exciting moneymaking process uses proven, yet non-traditional strategies for finding properties that will make money for you now (and keep making money for you, year after year). These techniques will blow your mind when you see how easy they are for anyone to apply.

I'm giving you proven tricks to find killer deals,[4] which other investors simply do not know exist and could never figure out on their own. This is a main ingredient for the recipe to make big bucks with little or no money in today's down real estate market, with very little effort once the system is set in place.

This and the next two chapters are going to teach you things you may not have thought to be ingredients to successful real estate investing. You are going to learn advertising and marketing techniques that are proven to get people to take action, and do what it is you ask of them. Some of these techniques cost me millions of dollars to learn, and marketing consultants will charge an arm and a leg to reveal them.

So trust me as you go through these chapters that we are laying the foundation for your long-term success in real estate. To better understand what the next two chapters are going to teach you, let me first give you a brief explanation and then we will get to learning.

Strategically Written Ad That Attracts Motivated Seller Unlike Anything Ever Created

You are going to learn and get real examples of strategically written advertisements and ads that you will place to attract the exact seller you are looking for. You will also learn about free and inexpensive places to put these ads to attract eager, even desperate, sellers.

---

[4] Killer deal—superior to the properties easily located by other investors, as well as the majority of other available options.

Your presentation will get people to call you, choosing yours over other ads or options when they are in pre-foreclosure, foreclosure, for sale by owner, property on market for 90 days or more, and other motivating circumstances. Soon you will learn how an ad is crafted and why people will call you.

Specially Crafted Recorded Message To Automatically Assist You in Sorting Out the Great Deals Before Ever Speaking To A Single Person.

Your ad will drive the right type of people to a specially crafted recorded message that will be like a full-time employee sifting out the good deals from the bad automatically, or as I like to say "robotically." This message will give people enough free, high-quality information to make them trust you and feel comfortable. It will let them know they may have an option other than they previously thought, and it will capture the RIGHT information so you can decide if you have a possible killer deal. You will be doing all of this before you ever talk to one single person live.

Killer Deals Delivered To You Robotically That Will Give You The Opportunity To Profit On Each Of Them

You will end up with quality deals, being delivered to you, through a direct-response marketing campaign. This is automatically designed specifically to kick up motivated sellers. I have generated over $150 million with direct-response techniques and now have created this unique system for you to follow.

Here's how it looks all together.

Using this method, you can find killer deals before anyone can. This system will do all the work once you set it up. You will simply call the people who have the properties you know could put cash in your pocket. (Soon you will learn all the determining factors to know if it's a profitable

Your Ad

↓

Specially Crafted Recorded Message

↓

Killer Deals Delivered To You

deal.) But in the next two chapters you are going to learn about direct marketing [5] so you can get a constant flow of killer deals coming to you, like a wave of financial opportunity that literally does not ever have to stop once it is set in place. So let's get started. What I'm going to share with you will allow you to:

• Capture the attention of the right individuals (sellers and buyers).

• Drive them to an informative resource (it does all the work for you).

• Educate potential buyers and sellers on what you want so it builds trust in you.

• Strategically and automatically screen all potential deals.

• Collect the information and make it available to you automatically.

• Strategically make the right offer.

• You will learn the steps to put cash in your pocket from the killer deals that have come to you without using any of your own money.

The best part about what I'm going to show you is the element of automation. Like everyone, you have a limited supply of time and energy at your disposal so this method uses techniques that will work for you 24 hours a day, 7 days a week. Just as setting the thermostat in your home keeps it at a constant temperature, setting up these techniques keeps attracting deals. Yes, people actually seek you out, instead of you having to go find them.

This is a tremendous advantage!

What you are about to learn may seem out of the ordinary. But trust me when I tell you that all my life, the only way I made the big money was by doing the opposite of the crowd or doing things out of the ordinary. In fact, whenever people I cared about, like my parents, my sister and some good friends, told me I was crazy, I knew I was on to something.

---

[5] The focus of direct marketing is to send your messages directly to your target consumer via direct mail, e-mail, telemarketing, etc.). An additional component is focused on driving responses/calls/purchases that can be attributed to a specific "call to action." If the advertisement asks the prospect to take a specific action, for instance call a toll-free phone number or visit a website, then the effort is considered to be direct-response advertising.

Along with these automatic techniques, in chapter 5, I'll also teach you simple and reliable traditional ways of finding properties. Plus, in a later chapter you will learn a brilliant method Matt perfected, to have a real estate agent gladly do most of the work—and get you deals over and over at 30% to 50% off.

Yes, Matt has 9 deals right now averaging 40% off fair market value locked up, on contract—and all of them took him less than four hours. Yeah . . . it's killer, and you will learn all about that. These various techniques will ensure that you can maximize your profits with no limits to what you can achieve. Once you know that you can buy property at 30% to 60% off from today's already reduced prices, your profit potential is astronomical.

With that said, let's jump headfirst into the process for finding motivated sellers. Start by taking on the mindset that you are going to make money by relieving sellers, who are eager or even desperate to sell, of their properties. Basically, that's the problem you solve. Most sellers rely on real estate agents or try to do a "For Sale By Owner" listing, yet that is no guarantee of ever finding a buyer, especially in a down market. The majority of Americans trying to sell their homes in today's market already know this. With this fact in mind, let's move on and learn how to find motivated sellers with my unique system.

The "marketing" process you'll need to understand is simple:

Use different ways of "advertising" to get your "message"

Which is—(I want to buy properties) . . . to your "target market"

Who are—(people willing to sell for a discount) . . . and get them to "respond"

That is—(contact you or your message so you can set up the transaction and profit)

The Automated Approach for Finding Motivated Sellers

You will start with simple, no- or low-cost advertising that these sellers will notice. Think about what captures your attention. Do pretty people catch your eye? If you answered "Yes," consider also that beauty is in the eye of the beholder. Have you ever seen a snazzy new car that left an impression on you? An Amish person might not have noticed it at all. What about seeing a building on fire, or an accident on the freeway, a searchlight in the night sky—do those things make you stop in your tracks? My point is that while these certainly are compelling examples, they don't apply to everyone. People don't all respond to the same things in the same way.

The simple definition of advertising is this: "the act or practice of calling public attention to one's product, service, want, need, etc." We are going to call attention to your "want." You want to find a seller who is motivated to sell and who owns a property that you can make a profit on. To attract sellers, you must be as compelling as possible in your advertising and target your message to the kind of sellers you want. Anyone can wait around for a property to go on the market or go up for foreclosure, but you will be finding the deals automatically before anyone else knows they exist, which eliminates your competition completely.

Becoming Irresistible

You are going to get some specific advertising examples you can copy and use very soon. You may be thinking, enough already! Get me to the section on profiting from real estate section! However, I feel it is really important that you first understand the thinking and strategies behind good direct-response advertising.

So let's take the time and educate you on things that could make you money for the rest of your life, which is the foundation for the robotic "Killer Deal Finder" system.

No matter what type of advertising outlet you use (flyers, signs, e-mails, classified ads, websites, business cards), the headline is the most important part of the message. If you're using an audio/audiovisual medium like TV or radio, the opening and closing statements are most important.

It doesn't matter how important the rest of your message may be if your target audience (potential motivated seller) doesn't NOTICE and read your advertisement.

Imagine an article on the front page of *The New York Times* that explained how each U.S. citizen could get one gold bar free, but the headline said something like "Most People Think Gold Is Shiny." Some people would read it, but others would ignore it. On the other hand, a headline like "FREE GOLD BARS FOR U.S. RESIDENTS" would get everyone reading that paper!

Headlines Capture Attention

The headline is what grabs people's attention, and pulls them into the advertisement. The reason you need a headline is to get the seller, your target market, to go straight to your ad over everything else and then read the other important material you have created.

There are basically eight main styles to writing headlines:

1. Be Direct—I Buy Houses.

2. Be Indirect—She Failed to Sell Her House Too

3. Give a Command—Sell Your House Today

4. Tell How To—How to Sell Your House This Month—Guaranteed!

5. Give a Reason Why—Close on Your House in 30 Days or Less

6. Include a Testimonial—After 6 months on the market, Dean showed me how to get my house sold in less than 14 days!

7. Announce News—Owners Sell Homes Fast Even Now

8. Ask a question—Want to Sell Your House This Week?

Within the eight main styles, there are other tips I have found to work extremely well. For example, people like specificity:

"The #1 Way in America to Sell Your Home Fast"

"What to Do If Your Home's Been for Sale 90 Days or More"

Those are two samples of the structure in the best headlines. As I mentioned, later in this chapter you'll see examples of great headlines in actual ads you can take right out of this book and use. But here's a hot tip to create your own unique ads: look for headline ideas in best-selling magazines on display in any grocer's impulse aisle.

Okay, I think I've made it clear how important the headline is to attract attention. Next, you need to make sure your advertising keeps them interested in your offer.

I want to remind you of one thing here. If you think this is Advertising 101, think again. You don't learn this stuff in college or even at a regular 9-to-5 job at an advertising agency. These are true-blue "out of the box" tested-by-me techniques that will get your results far past what most people can even comprehend. So trust me that it all fits together at the end

People who are motivated to sell their homes are obviously interested in one major thing—selling their home NOW! But there are other concerns and hot buttons that lie behind their motivation to sell such as:

- Facing foreclosure
- Work-related relocation
- Retiring and moving south
- Job loss for any reason
- Divorce or separation
- Death of one spouse
- Other tragedy
- Needs have changed
- House too big/small
- Disaster
- Overextended
- Took on too much debt
- Medical bills
- Disability
- Inheritance

These are things to keep in mind when creating your advertising. If you can zero in on and address the real concerns of people in your ads, the numbers of qualified sellers that will notice and respond to your ads will always increase.

Remember, your offer has to be interesting to sellers. One of the strongest points about the method I'm teaching you is how fast it is. You'll attract people who have been trying to sell their homes for months. Maybe they haven't had any offers, or maybe they're on the path to foreclosure, and then you show up offering to possibly complete a sale in 14 to 30 days—that is huge for them!

Another advantage is it costs the seller nothing out of pocket and nothing if the transaction is never finalized. They really have no risk! Those are the points to emphasize in your ads. (If it seems like we're jumping ahead a bit with the days to sell a home or no costs to sell, don't worry. I'll explain it all shortly.) The entire purpose of creating the specialized advertising pieces is to promote the pre-recorded message. It will do most of the work for you when it comes to finding and sifting out profitable deals. In chapter 4, I will teach you why people are 80% more likely to call a recorded message, what to record, what to ask for, and heck, give you the exact scripts and even the company that can host the message for you. But before we get to that let's get to all the places available for you to advertise for motivated sellers. Remember, the entire point of this strategic advertising is to drive the right people to your phone or to the message that will be a hardworking machine for you.

Advertising Outlets or Promoting Your Recorded Message Via Different Media/Mediums

Okay, before you ever post ads you will have your 24-hour recorded message ready to be heard by the people you want to hear it. As I go through these different techniques, I ask that you withhold any judgment or preconceived ideas about what you know, or think you know, on the subject. Keep an open mind and see which methods might work best for you in your situation.

Using Flyers

Flyers are one of the most cost-effective marketing media you can use. They are quick to make, inexpensive to print, and versatile enough to go almost anywhere. It's important to remember that your flyer is an advertisement. It needs to convince the person who will see it that he or she MUST call and listen to your informative message.

The people you are trying to attract aren't really interested in your name on a flyer. They're not even really interested in what you do . . . only in what you can do for them.

They're interested in their own needs and wants, so hit them with a headline they can't ignore, because it addresses their wants and needs.

Think about all the problems, both real and potential, that could arise from not calling you. Put yourself in your prospect's shoes. Learn what their concerns are, and identify things that will make a difference in helping them relieve or overcome their problems.

There are many different themes to grab the attention of motivated sellers. The following are some of the different themes for flyers you may want to consider:

• Financial distress situation theme—this flyer focuses on their stress related to their home not selling.

- Educational approach—addresses what other approaches are available to sell a home. I've spoken with many people who thought the only way to sell a home was through a real estate agent or a realtor. These professionals often don't explain all the options available to the seller, so it is important to educate them on other methods.

- Fear and anxiety—this approach focuses on letting them know that you understand their fears and anxiety, and how you can help with a solution.

(STATE) HOMES FAST

I buy all types of homes in good or ugly condition for any reason. I will make you a fast, fair offer on your house and provide you with a number of options including staying in the home. Call me today! I'm a professional (State) home buyer – get a cash offer for your home today!

7 Reasons to Call Me Right Now

- I can pay all cash for your home in X days
- I can close quickly and friendly
- I can take over your existing payments
- I can help you sell your house faster
- I can stop bankruptcy or stop foreclosure
- I can buy your property as is
- I can save you thousands on commissions and fees

CALL JOE: XXX-XXX-XXXX

The important element of your flyer is to offer free, no-risk information to people. You are offering a Free Help Line or a Free 24-hour Consumer Alert message depending on your approach (educational, preventive, or dealing with fears and anxieties).

You should trigger a sense of urgency, stimulating a call-to-action to get them to act. Essentially, your message is: "We can help you if you contact us now; otherwise, we may not be able to help you. With financial-distressed situations, pre-foreclosures, or foreclosures, time is of the essence. You need to do something right now to solve your challenging situation."

As for getting your flyers seen, there are probably many businesses in your local area where you can post flyers on announcement boards. Grocery stores or the library are often an ideal place to do this. You can have them distributed in specific neighborhoods or simply post them in places where they are likely to be seen by a lot of people. Whatever you do, just make sure you find places to post your flyers that make sense.

Using Yard Signs

You can also create inexpensive corrugated plastic signs to stick in the ground at various high-traffic areas using the same style messages as you might put on a flyer.

Yard signs (also called "bandit signs"), with an effective message and strategic placement, are a cost-effective way to get your message in front of the right people. These inexpensive signs allow you, as an investor, to target specific roadways with your distinct message and get the attention of potential sellers.

These signs come in all different sizes, but the best size is usually 18" x 24" and made of strong corrugated plastic. The 18" x 24" size sign is the easiest to read as traffic is going by at 30 to 50 mph, or even at major intersections when stopped in traffic, because they can be seen from a fair distance.

A smaller 12" x 18" sign is less noticeable and should be used in areas where a complete stop is required, or inside regions of a neighborhood.

Your message should be short and simple. If you're driving down the road at 40 mph, you have about 3 to 5 seconds to read the sign. Keep the message simple and to the point.

Using your recorded information phone number on your signs is strongly recommended over using a website. This is mainly because people tend to write a phone number down, whereas with a website they try to memorize it, and by the time they get home they only remember part of it or none at all. Advertising your recorded information phone number works much better.

The recorded message info line that you will soon learn how to create and set up is also a great way to track the results of different marketing messages. You can set up different extensions or even different voice-mail messages though the service I will tell you about, and you can assign a different voice-mail number or extension to different signs. This way you can track which signs are working better and in which areas. For no additional money you could have an extension for road signs, an extension for flyers, another for free classifieds and maybe another for paid classifieds.

You will better understand this in the next chapter, but this is the true definition of direct-response marketing at its best. This will let you know where most of your profitable deals are coming from since you can track calls by each extension. Then once you start to see trends you can focus your time on the areas making you the most money. More on that soon.

Put out 20 to 25 signs in an area in which you wish to market. If you order 200 signs, do not put them all out in the same area, since many city ordinances do not allow that. After you put your 20 to 25 signs out in one area, begin rotating areas.

Put enough signs out so that people will notice them, but not so many that they ignore them because there are so many. People will notice these signs when the message targets what they need.

You can have signs made at a local sign shop or look online. There are plenty of vendors that you can find online by searching for keywords "plastic yard signs" "bandit signs" or "corrugated plastic signs."

You should place the signs in high-traffic areas, such as on corners where cars pass all day long, and near freeway on- and off-ramp corners. The best areas to target are major intersections and off-ramps from the highway. You can also use long stretches of 40 mph roads. Put the signs out on the side of the road, about 10 to 20 feet off the road, and a quarter- to a half-mile apart, going both ways.

Here are four examples:

TIP: In many cases handwritten road signs will pull many more leads than the preprinted ones, so you'll want to test both types.

Placing Classified Ads

Classified ads are another way to drive attention back to the 24-hour recorded message, consumer alert message, emergency help line, or even your phone if that's the route you decide. Reading or placing your own classified ad has long been a cost-effective method of finding great deals, but to maximize its potential, you want to place a classified ad that drives people to your recorded messages. Remember, this isn't your grandparents' classified ad. These are strategically written for maximum results at all times.

A tiny little three-line ad can drive highly qualified leads to your "sift, sort and screen machine" (explained later) where they will be presented with helpful information and begin the process of trusting you as a reliable source of possible relief from their situation.

Now, where should you place these classified ads? You can use local freebie newspapers when available. Often, when you place an ad in the freebie newspaper, these newspapers may include an online classified ad. *The Penny Pincher* is an example. You might look into the *Thrifty Nickel* or *American Classified Ads*.

There are many different freebies or "throwaway"-type newspapers people will pick up at grocery stores or elsewhere. Local newspapers end up being another great resource. It depends on the demographics, [6] and what the circulation is as well. Look at your budget and see what makes sense.

You want to determine who your target population is. So based on your target area, who are you focusing on? (Later you will learn exactly what target that fits your personal criteria you want to go after.) What do the demographics look like? What is the age range? What is the race or ethnic demographic? What is the average income of a particular target area? It's important to pinpoint exactly who you are targeting and know what the demographics of the circulation are.

Will it reach the right people? How will they see your ads? Does this age range typically look online for ads or are they going to be more inclined to pick up a newspaper of some sort and take a look through it?

You have your options with online free classified ads, just as you do with printed materials. Some examples would be craigslist (www.craigslist.org), Kijiji (www.kijiji.com), or the Lycos Ads (www.lycos.

---

[6] Demographics are statistical data of a population, especially those showing average age, income, education, etc.

com) where you have different free classified ads. All you need to do is go to Google—or a "meta-search engine" site that ties in multiple search engines in one stroke, such as dogpile.com, mamma.com, or metacrawler. com. Just type in "free classified ads" as your search criteria, and you're off and running.

Remember, the most crucial part of your classified ad is the headline. This is the element that will grab the person's attention and get him to read the rest of your advertisement. A PROPERLY crafted headline can even target specific types of callers. To get the most response from your ad, try to craft it using words like "free," "proven" and "shocking."

I've included a sample list of different types of classified ads for you to use as is, or take and modify to your own liking. Before we look at those examples of classified ads, let's take a look at just a few possible headlines.

- Sell That House!!
- Behind On Mortgage?
- Selling Your Home—The Facts
- FREE Facts for Sale By Owners
- Answers About Foreclosures
- Can't Sell That Home?
- I'll Buy Your House
- Free Home-Selling Help
- Facing Foreclosure?
- Foreclosure Clock Ticking?
- STOP YOUR FORECLOSURE

- No Equity? No Problem!
- Avoid Foreclosure, Sell Your Home!
- Behind On Your Mortgage?
- LATE ON HOUSE PAYMENTS?
- 7 Ways to Sell This Week
- 7 Secrets to Sell Your Home Fast
- "Whew!"
- "Hellllp!"
- "Realtor Giving You Empty Promises?"

There are many different styles in the above examples. They range from posing questions to creating curiosity, to making promises, to stating facts. You should test a few different headlines against each other to see what works best in your area.

Now here are some sample classified ads that could drive prospects to a recorded message that will sift, sort, and screen people, so you wind up talking only to those folks most likely to work with you.

These samples contain rich emotional text that you can mix and match to create dozens of unique, attention-getting ads.

How To Sell Your Home Fast
FREE RECORDED MESSAGE
Call anytime 24 hours a day
xxx-xxx-xxxx

•

Sell Your Home For Free
FREE RECORDED MESSAGE
Call anytime 24 hours a day xxx-xxx-xxxx

•

THE UGLY TRUTH ABOUT SELLING NOW
The banks want you to keep paying on
your house! Find out how to stop them!
FREE RECORDED MESSAGE
Call anytime 24 hrs/day xxx-xxx-xxxx

•

LATE ON PAYMENTS?
1 to 3 Months Behind and Have a Notice of Default Recorded
Learn 7 ways to stop your foreclosure! Call this FREE 24-hour
RECORDED MESSAGE HELP LINE xxx-xxx-xxxx

•

The Banks To Blame…
That Your Home's Still Not Selling?
Find Out How To Fix This
Free Recorded Info xxx-xxx-xxxx

•

Realtor Not Able To Sell Your House?
Here's a Solution 24-hour FREE HELP LINE
RECORDED MESSAGE xxx-xxx-xxxx

•

What The Bank Hopes You'll Never Know
Find Out How To Sell Your Home in 14 Days
24-HR Free Recorded Info xxx-xxx-xxxx

•

How To End Your Home Seller Worries
Free 24-Hour Recorded Instructions
Learn what to do right now xxx-xxx-xxxx

Again, each one of these ads would send people to your phone or a prerecorded message that fit the ad you placed. You can see how each message will vary in comparison to the ad you run.

Other Places For Your Classified Ad

Most investors generally want to place their ads in the classified sections of major newspapers, but that is not the only option. You should investigate community papers or smaller independent papers. Consider finding out if a certain community you are targeting has a community newsletter or an HOA (Home Owners Association)-sponsored newsletter.

You'll probably find more options than you will need. Do a little investigation and see what's out there, and then test a few ads to see where you get the best response.

You can also put ads online on craigslist. This free service allows you to target your ads to specific geographical areas that attract millions of online visitors each day. Craigslist.org is a great place to find sellers. (You will soon learn of a wonderful place to find motivated buyers and investors to pass these deals along to.) When you go to the craiglist site, find your city on the home page, and then click on your city. If you don't find your city, look for a nearby city. If you can't find your particular city, it doesn't matter, you can do this anywhere there are buyers and sellers.

Next, click on the "Real Estate for Sale" link. This brings up all the real estate offerings posted for the past 7 days. You'll notice postings from real estate agents as well as individuals. For example, as I am writing this, there are over 35,000 listings for Phoenix alone.

This is an amazing resource, and the best part it is that it is all 100 percent free! Read these ads and find those that look interesting. You can then e-mail sellers to see if they're interested in working with you.

EBay has just released a free classified program too, which is located at www.kijiji.com. You can use all the same strategies that I discussed above with craigslist.org. It has a nicer platform than craiglist, but does not come even close to the volume of classified that craiglist is currently doing.

In your e-mail, you can use the following script or a variation on it that suits you:

Hello—

I am interested in purchasing your property. I am a real estate in-vestor. I want to be totally transparent with you and let you know my motives from the start. Here is the thing, though, as an in-vestor I have to purchase properties significantly below appraised value. But if the deal makes sense I can move faster than most and we could literally have a closing in the next 30 days. If you are interested in speaking with me further, please e-mail me back.

It can be that simple. You can get as creative as you want. But that is as simple as you need to be. Not all people will be interested in working with you, but you'll find many who will ask for more information. Remember, you will want to do your research on these properties to ensure they are in fact listed at a reasonable price. (How to do that will follow soon.) Look through the site, pick out 25 to 50 deals, and see what type of response you get. This is a perfect place to look if you already have a buyer, because you can then target the specific type of property the buyer is interested in.

Using Business Cards

Your card is going to identify your key points, motivating sellers to take action, so I would recommend having a couple of different business cards, depending on the individuals that you are approaching. You might have a different business card for foreclosure-focused people versus your **For Sale By Owner (FSBO)** people. Or maybe even have cards for refer-ral resources. Use a different recorded message for each type of business card so you can track which card is doing the best and which types of people are responding. This can be easy to do with an 800-number service, since you normally have 100 extensions.

The purpose of the business card is to relay your contact information and establish your credibility. By condensing your information, your business card acts like a compact marketing piece that people typically hold on to and keep. A business card thus helps create a higher retention rate. It can be informative, contain a call-to-action message, and be a great icebreaker all at the same time.

Here are examples of business cards that contain condensed information with a call to action.

Taking Advantage of the Internet

Another option is online advertising. Using the Internet is an effective way to find sellers and buyers that fit your profile. You can make progress quickly since the Internet can cut your "running around" time down significantly.

You can have a website created and activated for you, but you need to determine a few things up front. Who is going to create it? What is it going to look like? What kind of text are you going to have on it? How many different pages? You can purchase a custom-built website where the work is done for you. All you need to do is change your information on the site as often or as little as you like.

Although your website is accessible to anyone with a computer, you still need to market your website and drive traffic to your site. There are programs called pay-per-click, often referred to as simply PPCs. (Google, for example, is where you can go to get pay-per-click services.) You can learn all about online marketing and pay-per-click by listening to a special audio I created with an online expert at **www.deangraziosi.com/ppcinterview**.

Reciprocal links are another way you can drive traffic to your website. You have a link on someone else's website and they have a link on your website. You will be able to basically springboard the visitor to another resource that is related to your site. Similarly, if someone goes to the other website, your website link will bring viewers back to your site. Basically links help to drive traffic back to your website.

Your website can have automated features. An auto responder is a great tool. Basically it works like this: when someone enters his or her information on your site, the auto responder can send back a welcome, thank you or follow up e-mail asking for more information or providing the person with more information.

This can assist you in gathering detailed information about the seller's property and prescreen individuals so that you can identify whether the property is of interest (such as location, how much equity exists, what the level of motivation is, etc.). Beyond anything else, the main focus should be the following:

• Directing sellers to your 24-hour recorded message line or having the recording right on your website for anyone to hear at any time

• Making sure that viewers understand exactly what you do and what you need them to do

• Offering education and information updates

• Providing a prescreening tool for you

A website can be a very effective marketing tool that will definitely reinforce your credibility to your clients. It provides information about your buying program and about how you are going to be purchasing these properties.

On your site, you can explain what you do and how you can help people who are facing challenging times. You can explain what kinds of options people have and the resources you can offer them.

This website can also work in conjunction with your foreclosure emergency line. Both work 24 hours a day, 7 days a week, and the great thing is that the website is working when you are not available, just like your recorded message line does. So when people are doing research online or placing the call to the foreclosure emergency line, both are working for you.

Your preference may be to focus more on foreclosures versus For Sale By Owner (FSBOs). Your focus may be on people who are frustrated with their realtor. Whatever target you want to shoot for, you can customize your website to do it for you.

I am a huge fan of marketing 24 hours a day and I have been fortunate enough to have tremendous success using many of these so-called robotic marketing methods. I encourage you to do the same.

If you can't or don't want to create a site on your own but would love to use the power of the Internet to help you make money then go to www.automatedforeclosurefinder.com/discount.

At this site we have a program we built specifically to attract sellers in some phase of foreclosure. It includes a great website and the ability to make money from an online presence.

So this is what we have learned:

That not regular but very strategic advertising, written and placed properly, can spark the attentions of motivated sellers to pick up the phone and call the number you tell them to call. That number could go directly to you, but as you will learn in the next chapter the best way to use this direct-response advertising system is to send prospects to a specially crafted pre-recorded message. That message will do almost all the work to build a relationship of trust, sift out the good deals, and capture information robotically.

Okay, since I am a very visual person here is a snapshot of what we have learned so far.

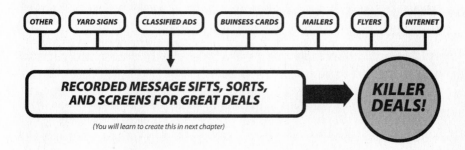

| OTHER | YARD SIGNS | CLASSIFIED ADS | BUINSESS CARDS | MAILERS | FLYERS | INTERNET |

RECORDED MESSAGE SIFTS, SORTS, AND SCREENS FOR GREAT DEALS

(You will learn to create this in next chapter)

KILLER DEALS!

Summary

Remember, not all advertising is created equally. Not even close! Once you get started investing in real estate, you need to let everyone know about it. That's where strategically designed direct marketing advertising comes in to drive potential sellers to your recorded message or website where you can sift, sort, and screen out the best deals. After having read this chapter, I want you to think about the following:

• The purpose of advertising is to drive the "right" potentially profitable deals to your door. Then your recorded message or website sifts, sorts, and screens out the best deals for you automatically.

• Automation is your friend. The more you can do to eliminate time-consuming, repetitive tasks from your process, the more time you have for other, more profitable or fun things!

• Free advertising can be just as effective as paid advertising. You can plant signs on the street, post notices on bulletin boards, or place ads on Internet sites.

• Let everyone know you're a real estate investor. You never know where or how a killer deal will show up, ready to give you a huge profit right away.

Action Steps

Remember that all Marketing and Advertising is not created equal. Having faith in what works and applying your own unique spin on it can have magnificent results. Create the mindset that killer marketing and advertising is a key to real estate success and therefore financial success:

• Practice writing one or two of your own classified ads, pencil out a design for your own yard sign, and try your hand at a mock-up of your own business card. Use the marketing principles you read about in this chapter. Remember, first identify the type of motivated seller you want to attract, then write a headline that will grab that person's attention.

• Think about all the places where you could place free advertisements to drive people to your recorded message. This might be your local supermarket bulletin board, signs you can staple to telephone poles, or websites where you can place advertisements at no cost.

• Write out a list of types of advertisements you'll use. Will you start with flyers and bandit signs, or something else? Make a plan for yourself.

• Make a list of all the places where you can place your ads where certain motivated sellers will be most likely to find it. For example, find places where you can post flyers or plant signs by the side of the road.

Matt's First Deals

Like most people who take Dean's course for the first time, I didn't know much about investing in real estate. I thought you always had to put a down payment on every property you bought, so the first thing I did was sell my truck. That still wasn't enough money, so I had to partner with a friend who put up the rest of the down payment I needed to buy my first property, a 4-unit building. This deal wasn't anything spectacular. I didn't really know what I was doing, but I found this property on a website and paid $76,000. Because I was still learning, I was afraid of making a mistake, so I brought in a real estate agent because she had the experience to walk me through the process and help me work the numbers. The property earned positive cash flow right away, so I made a little over $2,000 on the deal.

For my second deal, I sold all my motorcycles and bought a 2-bedroom (2 BR) foreclosed house for $28,300, but the house was worth at least $35,000. By now I was learning that most foreclosures are usually priced 10% to 20% below market value, so I put in an offer 20% below their asking price and ended up getting it.

The house only needed new carpeting and paint. I put $6,000 down, rented it out, and wound up with good cash flow and equity.

For my third deal, I found a 2BR house and paid $29,500, putting 20%

down for a little over $6,000 out of my own pocket. I knew this house was priced below value, so after a quick rehab, I built it up to $50,000 equity fairly quickly. After those three deals, I ran out of money.

Now, I knew I wanted to become a millionaire investor, but without any more money in savings or enough money coming in from my job, I was stuck. I wanted to keep buying properties every month and I didn't want to wait a whole year to save up a single down payment.

I basically wound up with three properties in three months. I just started small, put a little money in, and had fun owning property. By just owning those three houses alone, I already owned more property than the rest of my family.

I still wanted to play the game, so that's when I got serious. I went back and revisited Dean's No Money Down Strategies. I got with my coach and said, "I want to keep buying but I have no more money left—can we do it?" Between Dean's strategies that he shared in his book and my coach guiding me, I was unaware of the groove I was about to hit. Nineteen more deals in a row without using a single penny of my own money. YES, 19!

My family, my ex-girlfriend and most friends (except for one) told me it was not possible. My ex-boss called me a loser for quitting and not simply working more hours. I'm not mad at any of them. In fact, I actually feel badly that they are not willing to step out of a life they don't enjoy to try what I have learned. There are enough great deals for all of us to prosper.

I got started in late 2005 when the market was just starting to slow down. Many of my original no money down deals happened before a lot of the banking regulations changed. When they did, I started getting nervous that Dean's strategies for not using my own money would go away. Then, wouldn't you know it, he started teaching an all-new technique designed for today's down market when banks are much more strict. Again I hoped it was the real thing. I had no reason to doubt it for all the success I had so far. But could Dean hit on something just as good when things were so different? The answer is, "It Works!" Wow, does it work! Later on in the book, I will share with you how I am using the exact, yes the *exact* strategies you are learning right now to make faster and bigger profits then ever before. On my last deal, I literally made $20,000 with about 4 hours of work, and I just turned down a $50,000 profit on property I never even owned. I'll share both those stories and how I did it soon.

One last thing before my word count runs out and I have to work on another section for you: I bought many of my properties before the market turned and still did well, but not even close to the money I am making now that the market has hit bottom. The time to make a bundle of money is right now.

Success Story #3: Greg M.

Location: Booneville, Mississippi

Experience before getting Dean's course: Tried to buy and sell one house before, but barely made money

Profit since starting with Dean: $96,412.32 in less then 6 months

Favorite deal: $36,140.60 in 30 days with about 45 or 50 hours of my time

How many deals since starting: 10

Best quote: "Most people don't believe me when I tell them that by simply following what Dean showed me, I've never used a dime of my own money on any deal that I've done."

I've known for years that I wanted to do real estate, but I didn't know what I was doing, so when I did try to invest in real estate, I just struggled, barely got my money back, and got scared. As an electrical and plumbing contractor, I was working 60–70 hours a week, feeling stressed out, and just struggling to pay bills. I made a decent living, but I never got ahead. I was just tired of scratching to make ends meet so I bought Dean's course and started reading it, and thought, "You know, I could do this."

I got hooked up with Dean's hotline, but I was still working full-time so I had to squeeze in just an hour or two here and there. I had to do the best I could do since I didn't have any money and my credit was pure garbage, so I took one of the strategies that Dean suggested in his book for when you don't have money and started exploring and doing lease options.

My biggest obstacle was taking that first step and finding the time. After working for 8–10 hours each day, I'd go to bed at 9:30 or 10:00 p.m. and sleep for 3–4 hours. Then I'd get up around midnight or 1:00 a.m., go into my little home office, and start reading Dean's books. I'd do that for about two hours and then go back to bed around 2:00 a.m.

Even after making time to read Dean's books, I still had to find time during the day to meet people and return phone calls. For me, the two biggest obstacles were time and fear of failure. After juggling my schedule, I tackled the time problem and I eliminated the fear of failure issue by sticking with the lease option strategy because that technique's only risk is my time. Anyone can invest time, so that way they won't be scared. For me, lease options are about as close to being risk-free as you can get.

I did my first deal about 2 weeks after getting Dean's course. I was so anxious to get something going that I just wanted to get involved. I made $3,500, but it wasn't really just about the money because I also helped a family out. I bought their house to stop them from losing their house to foreclosure. Then I put someone in the house who couldn't get a loan from the bank.

The confidence I gained in buying that first house was worth much more then the $3,500 I made on the deal. In my head and heart I had become a real Real Estate Investor. That was the start of a whole new life and a string of very profitable deals.

Now I've got a system to advertise for both buyers and sellers just by using flyers. When I'm advertising to attract sellers, I use short headlines that go straight to the point like:

We Buy Houses
or
Behind on Payments? No Problem.

When people call, I explain to them that I have a unique program. I tell them, "I do debt takeovers." That always catches their attention because they're thinking, "Wait a minute? You're going to take over my debt?" I tell them, "Not only am I going to take over your debt, but I'll make your payments until I can sell your house, and fix it up using my own money."

If you're heading to foreclosure, how good does that sound to you?

In most cases, people are just tickled to death that you'll keep them from going into foreclosure. Then I line up buyers and ask for a down payment. For example, I found a guy who wanted a house so he put $7,000 down.

I used $2,000 to fix up the house, remodeling it with the other guy's money, and put $5,000 in my pocket.

After my first deal, I started putting out flyers everywhere, and that would catch a lot of people going through foreclosure or divorce. I would just lease out the property from one person and turn back around and re-lease or sell it to someone else. Basically, I just tied up the property on paper and never used a dime of my own money on any deal I've done.

This is a strategy I got from listening to one of Dean's live calls one month. What is even more exciting is that I am told that this entire book is about that strategy he has taught us only by e-mails and conference calls before. This strategy works like gangbusters and if that is what you are learning in this book, then read every single sentence and do exactly what he tells you. I love it.

Literally, when I need quick cash, I can turn around properties for as little as $2,000 to $4,000, but sometimes I can get as high as $12,000, even $14,000.

I get such a good response off my flyers that my phone keeps ringing every day. I've got 10–15 people on my buyer's list right now. To find buyers, I put my flyers in laundromats and apartment complexes. My flyers say:

3BR/2BA house rent to own.
If you got the money, we got the house.

I like keeping my flyers short and to the point. When people call, I tell them they can get into a house for just a down payment. Soon as they get in with a down payment, I'll work with a mortgage broker to get them a mortgage. I never need to run a credit check because the mortgage broker does that for me. You see, when you're broke you just have to figure out how to do things without any money.

All you really need is the time to put into this. I've got a laptop and a telephone. I don't even have a call system set up, but I might explore something like this later on to eliminate a lot of tire kickers. I'm after a different caliber of person other than a renter. I'm after a buyer. If they get a leaky commode, they fix it. They're buying the house, not me. It's a beautiful system. It's low-risk and safe as any real estate investing you can do.

Greg's Success Secret: When you're reading Dean's course, it's kind of like eating an elephant. Take it a bit at a time, just pick out one thing, and figure it out before you start jumping around. I tried short sales, buying foreclosures, and rehabing houses to flip them, but then I stumbled on the lease option.

That's why I say just pick out a little piece of the puzzle and make money. Once you get your money built up you might do something else, but this will let you get started and stay in the game. When you can buy with other people's money, it works. It's risk-free. All I've got invested is time.

To see Greg's video go to **www.deansmedia.com/greg**

CHAPTER 4

Using Automation to Cash Big Checks

I'm going to tell you everything you need to be familiar with using the recorded message strategy. I know, I know, you're saying to yourself, "Finally! Let's get to this magical pre-recorded message that we have been teased about throughout the entire last chapter." Well then, without further ado, here we go.

The recorded message is truly an amazing tool. It eliminates the need for you to manually deliver the same information over and over again. It will automatically play a message, specifically crafted, to cause the listener to take some specific action you want them to take. Think of a recorded message as a replica of you, giving out perfect information and capturing the caller's information, instead of you having to do it over and over again. What sparked my idea for this system was doing a TV interview for my previous book. The interview plays over and over again, informs people about my books, and sells them for me, yet I only recorded it once. Many authors do hundreds of interviews a year to sell their book. I do a handful, and just play them over and over again. I just figure out what is the best message I can share with people? This message is simple. I know in my heart I truly want to change people's lives, so I focus on talking about the things that will do just that. We roll the cameras, and shoot something that can play over and over. Does that make sense?

So now you can do almost exactly what I do. Instead of filming a show, you create your own ads and drive people to a recorded message. I'm going to show you how to create that message in this chapter. You will learn to create one that is uniquely your own, or use one we created for you. You will then record it one time, and it will play over and over and over again, to all the people who call the numbers in your ads. It will automatically be doing the job of screening out good deals from not so good deals. It will capture information and deliver profitable deals to your doorstep automatically. Did the light go on a little? I hope so. This is not easy to explain and it may seem like a lot of work, but that's only because it may be new to you. Like my TV shows, once your message is set up it can start bringing you deals and making you money. The best part is it does this while you are at a current job, asleep or even on vacation. That's the power of technology and replication at its best.

Robotic Messages

24-Hour Sift, Sort, and Screen, "No Money Down" Deal-Finding Machine

What follows is an example of the *type* of message you will create. Then you will drive people to that message with your advertising and marketing efforts. Each message can be modified to directly fit the type of deal you are looking for, or you can create a generic message that will work for all of your advertising efforts. (We will give you an example script for that as well.) As you start to read this, you may say, "This sounds intriguing, but is it worth the time to set this type of message up?"

The answer is an absolute yes. It is not hard at all to set up, and it becomes your full-time employee, doing amazing work 24 hours a day. You may be thinking, "Why incur the cost of having a voice mail like this, when I could simply drive people to my home or cell phone and talk to each person live?" That's a pretty common response from people the first time they hear about this, but my guess is, after this chapter, that won't be your first choice.

You'll learn how to determine the best types of sellers to find and how to set up a pre-recorded message. But first, the purpose of this type of system is a bit more involved than just saving you time. The system also will:

• Narrow down the callers to only the deals you can profit from.

• Validate sellers' fears and concerns (especially if they are behind on their payments) before you ever have to speak to them in person.

• Educate them about lending issues and explain their options.

• Capture their information robotically, allowing you to do research and decide on the deal before ever speaking with a single person.

The pre-recorded message technique is the key component to what makes this automated system function unlike any other method in the world. Instead of cold-calling people, or having them call you live, you direct them to a 24-hour recorded information line. Think of it as a sort of "Sellers Help Line." In a nutshell, it's like a longer version of a message you would have on your home answering machine, yet formulated with a purpose.

One purpose is to educate people who are desperate or motivated to sell their homes. Through simple education and sharing information you start to position yourself as an advocate, helping them in their quest. This encourages them to continue to listen. Your message will explain their real options and give them a true understanding of their current situation, and about selling in a down market. Second and most important, it helps you gain their trust while automatically eliminating those deals that will not work. By weeding out 99.9% of deals that will be a waste of your time, you can focus on the best deals from an investment standpoint.

Your 24-Hour Recorded Message for the seller does a lot of things all at once. It can be used to validate the seller's fears and concerns if they are behind on their payments. You can provide a lot of information regarding what the mortgage brokers and lenders did not tell them or predatory lending concerns, and the problems that could have caused the current circumstances for the seller (such as unemployment or unsteady employment).

You can provide some reassurance that you understand the issues callers are facing and comfort them that there could be a solution. In today's market, it can be difficult to sell a home and you want to educate them that you have the tools that could allow them to have a closing in 30 days or less.

Boy, that seems like a lot of effort to create the message. No worries, I am simply trying to get you to understand how it works. Below is an exact message you can use and tweak, and at **www.deangraziosi.com /24hourscript** I have included three more versions you can use or tweak to fit the type of sellers or deals you want to target.

Instead of me going on and on about how it works or how you can create it, let me simply give you a script below that I think will make any confusion simply go away and give you an "aha! I get it" moment. I have created a pre-recorded message script that is directed toward people currently facing (or in some phase of) the foreclosure process. Obviously, people would be driven to this message from ads that target their situation. So you can see in black and white how what we are talking about works in real life. The ad may be placed in a local newspaper, on craigslist, in a church flyer, at your gym, or local deli.

A number at the bottom of the ad will drive people to the recorded message below that will automatically, robotically, do all the work for you by sifting out the bad deals and allowing you to focus on the good ones, while at the same time building trust with the seller automatically. (Soon you will learn what deals to target, how to estimate a fair market value, and how to identify a killer deal that will put cash in your pocket without using a penny of your own money.)

Sample "Stop Foreclosure Information Line" Script

My name is (Your Name) and I want to thank you for calling my Stop Foreclosure Information Line. In just a moment, I'm going to reveal to you some tips and facts that most lenders and banks don't want you to know. Tips that can prevent the foreclosure process from ever starting—and—even stop it once it has started.

You may want to have something handy to take notes, as I'll be going through this material rather quickly. However, at the end of this recording I'll provide you with my contact information if you missed anything or have further questions.

Let's get started.

*What's going on right now in our country with so many homes going into foreclosure is due to **outrageous loans** made to almost anyone who could cause a mirror to fog up. In different parts of the country, many lenders even committed fraud by placing a higher value on homes than they were worth, simply to inflate the amount of the loan needed by the homeowner, and boost their own profits.*

The fears over the U.S. subprime mortgage market have triggered a global credit crunch, playing havoc with Wall Street stock portfolios and dragging down global markets.

In case you're not familiar with the term, subprime loans are offered at high interest rates, and usually on adjustable terms, to Americans who have a poor credit rating and might otherwise be denied loans. But as interest rates have risen, so do those adjustable payments, leaving many homeowners stretched beyond their means. You or someone you know may be facing this right now.

Here are 7 Ways to Stop a Foreclosure

If you have NOT missed a payment yet, but know you are going to, the first step you must take is to contact your lender and let them know your situation. If you've lost your job or have some other type of hardship going on let them know. They can give you time to help get your life back together, but you must call them as soon as you know you're going to miss a payment. The longer you wait, or if you wait until you actually miss your payment, makes it more difficult to ultimately get the problem solved.

Ask for forbearance. This allows you to delay payments for a short period of time, with the understanding that another option will be used afterward to bring the account current . . . for example, if you know you'll have the funds to bring your account current by a specific date because of a guaranteed sum of money you're

receiving.

Ask for a repayment plan. This is where the lender agrees to add a certain amount of the first missed payment onto each of the next subsequent two payments. These plans provide some breathing room for you if you only have short-term financial problems, such as a sudden expensive repair or a medical expense that makes it too difficult to pay your mortgage for one month.

If you have already missed two or three payments and owe a couple thousand dollars in lender legal fees, the lender of your mortgage may still try to arrange a repayment schedule. But you will likely have to pay a third to a half of the delinquent amount up front, and then pay off a portion of the remaining balance each month for a year or more. Also, never ignore the lender's letters or phone calls. Ignoring the problem won't make it go away— and if you're going into a foreclosure process, there are other fees and costs involved and ignoring them only makes these worse.

You may also be eligible for a loan modification plan, designed for people who can't afford repayment plans. In a modification, the lender actually adjusts the terms of the loan to make it affordable. It may lengthen your amortization schedule or lower the interest rate to cut the monthly payments, or roll the past due amount into the loan and re-amortize the new balance so you can pay the additional debt back over time.

Some companies may be willing to offer you a "short refinance" too. With these, the lender agrees to forgive some of your debt and refinance the rest into a new loan. This way, the lender still gets more money than they would by foreclosing on you.

A Deed in Lieu of foreclosure (DIL) is an option in which you voluntarily deed your property back to the lender in exchange for a release from all obligations under the mortgage. Unfortunately, there is no way to do this without hurting your credit, unless you get the mortgage company to report your mortgage account as paid in full. You may face income tax issues resulting from the lender forgiving part of the debt (which the IRS will likely treat as income to you, even though you don't receive any cash in the transaction), but you might be able to get yourself out of the hole and start over again sooner rather than later.

If you can afford your normal monthly mortgage payment, but can't afford to make up the delinquent amount and legal fees because your lender offered a really harsh repayment plan, you may want to consider filing Chapter 13 bankruptcy. Doing so temporarily halts the foreclosure process and can force the mortgage lender to accept a more friendly repayment plan. This is a last resort, and will still negatively affect your credit.

If none of these strategies work, there is still one other option.

As you may know, a foreclosure is devastating to your credit rating and can affect it for 7 to 10 years. What's more, buying or even renting another home in that time period may be impossible for you. But there is one more option where I may be able to help you personally.

Even if you can no longer afford your home, you can still protect your equity and keep a good credit rating.

Here's how:

Up until a few days before the bank forecloses on your property, you have the opportunity to stop that process by having someone purchase the property.

I may be willing to do this for you. I arrange creative, legal and ethical ways to buy property or assume mortgages from people who need help. I may even be able to let you stay in the house, *depending on your situation. The bottom line, though, is this: if your situation allows it, I can stop your foreclosure and often put money BACK in your pocket so you can start over in a more affordable home.*

So please consider what I'm about to say carefully. If you don't have the money to pay your lender off : . . . if you see no real chance of making up the payments and costs . . . and if you would be open to discussing opportunities that can relieve you of this burden, please do the following for me.

At the end of this message please leave as much of the following information as possible. Then I can see in advance if your property fits the criteria for me to step in and help in your situation.

I'll need to know:

- *How much is still owed on your mortgage and how many payments are overdue?*

- *Does the payment include the property taxes, and if not, are any tax payments overdue?*

- *Has a Notice for a Sheriff's Sale been sent?*

- *Has the bank sent you a list of additional expenses owed to them for the foreclosure process?*

- *Address of the property, or at least the closest major cross streets.*

- *Rate the house from Poor to Great condition.*

- *And, of course, your name, phone number (cell phone as well) and the best time to call you.*

That's about it. With just a little information and by spending just a few minutes talking, I'll be able to find out if I can help you— and your worries could be over.

Let me just say this.

I understand that this is not a pleasant thing to go through, and I truly hope my message provided you with information that can help you change your situation.

Please know that your situation is NOT hopeless. Your attitude and ability to keep it together during this time is crucial to getting through it with the best possible results.

Just remember, it's important to act fast. Time is of the essence in these situations.

If you resolve the problem and save your home from the information I shared with you, please let me know. I'll be positively delighted for you and we'll part as friends. If you can't resolve the situation, I could possibly be your safety net, because the last thing you want is to have a foreclosure happen.

Remember to leave your full name and your phone numbers so I can get back to you right away.

This is (your first and last name) thanking you for taking the time to listen and I wish you the best in your efforts.

(You can leave your number if you want people to call you as well)

Is all that marketing talk starting to make sense now? I bet it is! You can have this message be your full-time employee for pennies a day, sifting out great deals and allowing you to avoid the ones that are not so good.

This is a great message, targeting people facing foreclosure, and I include it here as an example. Of course, feel free to modify and tweak it to fit you and the properties you want to pursue. For additional help, feel free to use and copy the several sample scripts available at *www.deangraziosi. com/24hourscript*.

Did you see that we create in listeners a desire to reciprocate by giving them real-life techniques to possibly save their homes? In other words, we gave them something before we asked for anything in return. This makes people much more likely to open up and work with you, if the other options you gave them for free do not work.

How great would it be if you gave someone a technique to save his or her home? But if it does not work for them, you are the person they are going to turn to first. Understandably, you may not be able to help everyone who calls. That's the hardest part about all this sometimes. Try to remember that your goal is to find the people you can help!

This is only one type of robotic sift, sort and screening audio. You can create as many different types of messages as you want, to target as many different types of people, all of whom are desperate to sell. For example, if you wanted to target homes that have been on the market for 100 days or more, and in the price range of $125,000 to $175,000, you can adjust your ad and message to reflect that. These messages are meant to be out there, finding you killer deals automatically, and they will—once put in place.

Another angle to pursue might be handyman specials or people looking to move, or retirees who need to sell. That is the magic of this automated system. You can target whomever and whatever you want, and have the deal come to you. Then you can qualify the deal before ever speaking to a single person.

If you are thinking how will I know a great deal when it comes my way, or how do I negotiate the deal, or what about the fact I have no money or don't want to risk mine, trust me. You'll be learning all of that very soon, but we have to go one step at a time.

The message is pretty easy to set up. You create and record the message, then use the media/mediums I have listed in this chapter to drive people to call your number.

To set it up, you'll have to get a voice-mail box from a company that allows you to record a longer than normal outgoing message—your phone company probably can't do this so you'll have to use a company that specializes in voice mail.

I have arranged a special deal through the company I use, named COA NETWORK, for my clients. You can view their website and get set up through www.coaphonesolution.com. But if you have another option that fits you better or works better, then by all means use it. The important thing is to get it set up.

A note about recording the script: Unless you have a real-life difficulty with your ability to speak, I recommend that you personally record the message into your outgoing greeting. The message is meant to position you as an advocate, and what better way to do that than by having your real voice deliver the message? You'll want to practice reading through it out loud a few times, until you're comfortable with it.

The important thing is to speak normally. You don't have to be perfect. You are not voice-over talent, you are a real estate investor looking to help people and make money in the process. I have a message recorded that you can listen to at www.deangraziosi.com/previewmessage so you can see how simple it can sound and how effective it can be.

The content of the message is strong enough to stand on its own. You don't need to sound like a radio personality, just speak clearly and as you would to a friend you respect, with commitment. People will know you're real if you speak earnestly. Don't force it.

Once this message is set up, you can use as many of the strategies in this system as you want to drive people to it. And if you use a company like COA, you can set up multiple phone extensions and multiple messages and test many of them at the same time for no extra costs at all.

It's an amazing tool!

In short, you can assure people you understand how, in today's market, it can be difficult to sell a home. You want them to know you have the tools to buy or get their home sold quickly in this challenging market.

Your message can and should:

- Give real-world, valuable information and hope to the listener.

- Provide listeners with wisdom and list their realistic options.

- Cultivate the desire for reciprocity—they'll feel like they owe you one.

- Position you as an advocate, thereby building trust in you.

- Capture their information and a snapshot of their situation robotically.

- Make the listener feel encouraged, appreciated, and not alone.

- Make you money!

You can also direct your prospect to a website and provide more educational information there using audio or even video. You can also provide a printable version of the information for them to download, instructing them to call you when they're done. The recorded message strategy is the most effective and foolproof way to automatically educate your target and eliminate a ton of repetitive busywork.

After your prospects have been educated by your marketing system, the next step is to get them to take a specific action. If you use a recorded message, the action may be leaving their name and number so you can return their call.

It may be the option of pushing a number on their phone to connect with you directly, or leaving all the information about their home and their circumstances, such as in the script I showed you earlier.

Ask them to take the action that fits your needs. Whatever you choose, the goal is to create an opportunity to tell them, instead of sell them on, exactly what you will do and how that is important to them in selling their property.

Later, I will cover all the things you need to say, and what you need to find out once you actually make contact with a seller.

One more thing, as long as we're on the topic of educating people, you also need to create your own personal "commercial" that you can use to express your mission to others when you are face to face. It could go something like this:

> ***"My name is Dean and I specialize in investment deals that allow people to sell their homes extremely fast, even in a down market."***

Use a line like that whenever you have the chance to talk with people. You never know who may be in the market to sell. And never feel guilty, because if you make money, the typical by-product is that you also allowed someone to sell his home fast.

Here again is a "Big Picture" snapshot of how my system delivers deals to your door:

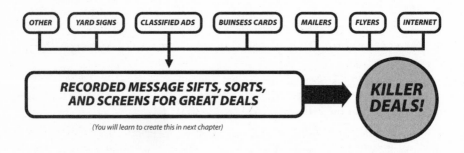

OTHER | YARD SIGNS | CLASSIFIED ADS | BUINSESS CARDS | MAILERS | FLYERS | INTERNET

RECORDED MESSAGE SIFTS, SORTS, AND SCREENS FOR GREAT DEALS

KILLER DEALS!

(You will learn to create this in next chapter)

The ultimate result is that you can wind up with tons of deals delivered to your door. Then all you have to do is go after the best deals and put big cash in your pocket.

It may take a little work and effort to get a system like this set up, but think about what it can return once you're done. All in all, between learning, setting your message up with COA and writing and placing ads you may have invested less than 5 hours in the entire system. Yet those 5 hours could create a potential flow of nonstop deals to your doorstep, for as long as you desire. It's like a full-time helper that never sleeps, and only costs pennies a day to bring you big returns. There is nothing like it. And if this still seems like a little too much work, ask yourself how much time you put into your current job or jobs in the past and if those jobs had the potential to make you the type of money real estate does. I doubt it . . .

What we have learned so far is that innovative, "out of the box" marketing techniques, applied in this down real estate market, can kick up killer deals and automatically drive them directly to you just by strategically placing ads in a variety of mediums and places. Your ads will drive targeted prospective sellers to your pre-recorded message. Your message will supply the criteria for what type of property you are looking to buy.

Now, you may be wondering, what do you do once you find a great deal? How will you recognize a great deal when you see one? I'm sure you have a boatload of other questions as well. I'll answer all those questions and many more shortly.

Also, you will learn a strategy from Matt Larson that will allow you to find deals at the same huge discounts by leveraging a great Real Estate Agent and using a unique strategy that Matt has perfected.

But first, I want to cover some more traditional effective ways to find incredibly profitable deals in today's down market. We'll cover those methods in the next chapter, so you have every possible option to make money, in what is truly the greatest time in history for you to become rich from real estate.

Matt's First No Money Down Deal

I found a small 2BR house that had been on the market for several months. It needed a little cosmetic work, but it was located in good area. The seller was asking for $40,000 while rents in that area were going for $350/month. If I had bought it at $40,000 and thrown in taxes and insurance, my monthly cash flow would have been negative. Apparently, other investors came to that conclusion too, which is why the house had been on the market for so long. However, I calculated that if I could get the house for $25,000 and get over $500/month for rent, then I could get positive cash flow.

I offered $26,000 and the seller accepted my low offer. I locked it up under contract and figured it was worth $65,000 after putting in new carpeting, paint, and general repairs. I then went to the bank, showed them the property I had locked up, and they told me to get estimates for repairs. Because I had to put in new windows, the repair estimates were $10,000. Despite this higher than expected repair cost, the bank still said that the house would have 30% to 40% equity. Then I asked the bank, "Since I already have that equity, will you give me the money to rehab the place and allow me to buy the house with no money down?" To my surprise, they said yes, and it all stems from buying houses really cheap.

Next, I put an ad in the paper offering the house for rent at $515/month. It rented immediately. Now remember, other homes were renting for $350/month, but I noticed this town was growing and money was being poured into the downtown area because businesses kept expanding. That local economy was doing so well I had a feeling that other investors didn't realize the opportunity. With more people moving to this area, I figured more people would need housing and I was right.

I went back to the bank and presented a plan to buy 13 properties in the next year and a half. My plan was to buy more houses below value and get positive cash flow from them right away.

The bank liked my plan but told me to take it one deal at a time, just as long as I could keep buying properties as cheaply as I could. I thought, "That went really well." I looked for other houses in that same price range ($40,000), made low offers, and rented them out for $500/month.

In one year, I bought 13 houses, rented them all out, and by myself increased rent in that town by over 20%. Property values immediately jumped for those houses to $60,000. I had found a little niche and jumped on it immediately, buying homes faster before anyone else could catch on.

The key to this strategy was that I showed the bank how they could make money instantly just by giving me a loan. Unfortunately, that strategy doesn't work any more since banks no longer do 100 percent financing. Despite never making a late payment and the fact that my bank had never had a foreclosure in its entire 100-year history, the bank examiners told the bank they couldn't do those types of loans anymore due to the mortgage meltdown.

Like I mentioned earlier, that's when I started looking into Dean's no money down techniques for today's changing market. But until I actually started using that strategy, I found another way to get 100 percent financing. I just had to be a little more creative.

My bank told me that if I paid cash for a house, I would have no mortgage and then I could refinance it. So that is when my real push for techniques to buy homes at 50% off really started. I started buying houses at 50% off, sometimes even more, paying cash for them because they were so cheap, and then refinancing the whole thing. Yes, they would refinance with a 100 percent loan, just not up front.

Now remember, a refinance loan is not like an original mortgage, which is based on purchase price. A refinance loan is on appraised value. Since I was buying properties so cheap, the appraised values were much higher than my purchase price. Thus the bank would refinance my properties, which would give me back all the money I paid for the house. Instead of doing a no money down deal up front, I'd pay cash, refinance, and get all my money back in 30 days. The same bank that refused to give me 100 percent financing agreed to refinance my homes. All this worked because I decided to use a different strategy—it's something anyone else could have done, including you.

Summary

I know we've covered a lot of information in this chapter, but I hope you see the powerful benefits of setting up this incredible automated system that can drive profitable deals directly to you "after" they have been somewhat pre-qualified automatically.

You need to use marketing techniques to find the motivated sellers others can't find. Plus, you must do it in a way that literally lets you replicate yourself. The end result is, find a motivated seller and you can find a great deal and make a huge profit.

• A recorded message can be your 24/7 robotic worker, helping you find killer deals even while you sleep.

• After you find a motivated seller, you need to educate the person on their options. You are there to help the motivated seller solve a problem.

Action Steps

I hope you're starting to see how recorded messages can take away much of the hassle in finding killer deals. Instead of hunting them down, a recorded message lets those killer deals come straight to you. What I want you to do now is the following:

• Find a place where you can create a recorded message. We have set up a special deal for you at COA Network at www.coaphonesolution.com. Of course, you can always find someone else to handle it for you. Look in the Yellow Pages or on the Internet to find a company where you can rent out voice-mail boxes to create your recorded message.

• Get your recorded message ready and test it to make sure it works. Identify the type of motivated sellers you want to target first. Maybe you want to go after foreclosed homes or For Sale By Owner properties. (Eventually you will target them all or find your niche.)

• Take the sample recorded message scripts in this chapter and tweak to fit your target area or the type of motivated sellers you want to attract.

• Take notes on the great information Matt shared. I will be expanding on some of those exact strategies later in the book.

Success Story #4: Dawn L.

Location: Gann Valley, South Dakota

Experience before Dean's strategies: None.

Net worth increase since starting: Approximately $100,000

Most money made on one deal: Purchased a foreclosure property for $17,500. The home is currently valued at $51,000 and the deal came to me using Dean's automated systems.

What you would say to skeptics: "Please, please, please, don't let anyone talk you out of reaching your full potential and real estate is one of those things that can help you reach it."

My life changed dramatically in 2006. In August 2006, my boyfriend broke up with me on the same day that my best friend's 5-year-old son passed away from cancer. In December 2006, my co-worker and his entire family died in a plane crash. Within three months, I went to five funerals. At the time, I was living by myself in North Carolina and suddenly felt very, very alone. I struggled for about a year, trying to deal with the sudden disappearance of so many people from my life.

That's when I really understood on a deep level that life is very, very precious. Right before Christmas of 2007, I felt that the only thing keeping me in North Carolina were the things I owned, so I decided to give away all of my nice belongings and move closer to my family in South Dakota while I figured things out.

South Dakota is soooooo different from North Carolina, especially when it comes to winter, but it is where I felt love from my family. No words can describe the power of real love.

Although I rarely watch television, I happened to catch Dean's infomercial on TV once. At the time, I didn't know what to do with my house in North Carolina so I decided that if I saw Dean's infomercial a second time that I would order his book. Well I did, and I placed my order just hoping it was really all it seemed to be.

I got Dean's book, and like most of you reading right now, as I turned each page I felt inspiration and at the same time a little fear. Can this really work for me? Am I smart enough, willing enough, motivated enough? Now I know the answer to all of those internal questions is a big fat YES for all of us.

After reading the entire book a few times, I knew it was time to get out there and make a deal happen. I also became a student of Dean's Real Estate Success Academy because I felt I needed a little extra helping hand to make sure I accomplished the goals I desired.

I remember the first days of beginning real estate investing very well. I began looking in the paper for other real estate investors and called one. I met for lunch and told this investor some of my ideas. It was obvious that the investor was skeptical toward me and my intentions. I was nervous inside and kept saying to myself that I am growing and learning and I have absolutely nothing to lose and possibly a lot to gain. We became friends, the real estate investor and I, and we began looking at houses. He actually found the house but he was wrapped up in a couple other projects and was unsure whether to invest in another project. He had already done inspections and spoken with the owner. He began negotiations and I finished his lead.

My major obstacle, of course, was financing! The property did not go through a realtor so I learned how to write purchase agreements. I then learned the importance of a lawyer to help with this process, to make sure everything is correct and get the seller to help finance it. I called Dean's coaching company frequently to get advice on different strategies. That's how I did my first deal of purchasing a home for $98,000, which was later appraised for $150,000. I did some improvements to the house with painting, landscaping, and changing the light fixtures.

My real estate investor friend has become very curious about the many things I am learning because my goals have gotten much bigger. He has now inquired about Dean's program, and he has been investing in real estate for 30-plus years.

My brother helped me find my second deal, which was land in a community near where my brother lives. I was able to find out that this city had a significant lack of homes and multiple job opportunities. I knew I wanted action and felt that this project would help me "get my feet wet."

The land was directly on the border of town and a farmer wanted to sell the land. I purchased the 6 acre lot for $14,577, using a zero percent interest credit card. It was of course a bit scary, but I knew the deal I was getting was amazing. I simply told myself that I have spent that much on cards over the years on useless things, and now I had a chance to make a huge profit, armed with Dean's information and his coaching staff, so I went for it.

My first plan was to rezone the land and make it into four lots, which would make it 1.5 acres each. I told my brother how to rezone for his purchases in nearby lots. He had no idea how to do this, never knew it was possible. He talked with the county commissions and they were very happy to agree to rezone due to the lack of homes. A new water line was put in place on the land and suddenly the value increased.

Originally, I was planning on keeping the property—I could easily sell each lot for $35,000 in a few years for a total profit of $140,000. However, I have a second exit strategy now. My vision and goals have expanded and I am looking only to purchase cash-flow properties. I have a passive income goal and deadline and definitely plan on achieving this. Although the profit is very large on this deal, it does not completely align with my vision. Therefore I found a buyer who will purchase the land right now. We are doing a contract for deed deal and will have it paid in a balloon in twelve months. The deal is set up with $3,000 per acre, which would be $18,000—10% down and 10% interest each month with a balloon payment on the 12th month.

I am ecstatic with this because I have learned on the project. It was very, very, very easy, and I am still making money. I am also learning how to do the contact for deed for future larger cash-flowing projects. I am understanding the process, which is essential for future projects!

By now my confidence is through the roof. I've found the path in life I was supposed to take, and Dean cleared the way for me. I found my third deal by networking. I am finding this is key and fundamental in my success. I went to a seminar and met up with other real estate investors and was able to make a purchase with this network.

I found a duplex in foreclosure, which I bought for $77,500 (its tax assessed value was $136,600). I had tenants in place before I even closed on the property by simply telling everyone I knew what I was doing. Minor repairs cost me $100 while my monthly rental income is $3,800, giving me positive cash flow of $550 a month. On this deal not only do I get tax benefits, but my tenants are paying off my mortgage and building my net worth. I also get to reap the benefits of the appreciation and net worth increase when the market turns and prices go way up again.

I found my fourth deal while on a "business trip," attending a "Master Your Mind" seminar. I did not know how I would pay for all of the trips and hotels, but I have learned that the details are not as important as maintaining focus on my vision.

When I checked into the hotel, I told the clerk that I was a real estate investor and she immediately said, "Oh, I know of a house that's being foreclosed." The house was valued at $51,000, but I only paid $17,500.

I transferred my Roth IRA to a Self-Directed IRA to bypass tax penalties and purchase the property. I'm working with a property management company that is getting the home ready for lease, possibly even with the same people who foreclosed in the home. This property management company works on helping people reestablish their credit and get their finances more stable so that everyone wins in an unfortunate situation. I plan on leasing this property out at a reduced rate and still maintain positive cash flow of $350 a month. My exit strategy is to sell in twelve to twenty-four months with a significant return on the property. More amazing is that I found all of my deals by people coming to me using some of the exact strategies Dean is teaching you in this book.

I am constantly finding incredible deals through other people and keep up ongoing great relationships with all of them. If you just ask questions, you'll get what you can negotiate.

Since starting with Dean's course and real estate investing, I now have a VERY clear vision of my life and direction. When I reach my goal next year of $10,000 passive income per month, I will celebrate by going to Nepal on a trek and volunteer in Kathmandu at a children's rehab hospital. When I return, I plan to begin my own training for teaching mind power/self-hypnosis techniques to health care professionals to help dramatically facilitate improvements toward how they interact with their patients.

I've now been able to invest in properties in North Carolina, two properties in South Dakota, St. Louis, and one in Orlando, Florida. I'm even looking at a six-unit apartment in Minneapolis, and I didn't even know what a foreclosure was when I first started.

Before I began real estate investing, I did not know where I belonged. Granted, I loved being a physical therapist, but I knew I wanted to affect more people and share my gifts with as many people in this world as I can. I have learned that we all have gifts and talents and that we should move toward the things we are passionate about. If we don't share the gifts that God gave us, it is greedy. These are lessons I have learned from different tragedies in life.

And because of Dean Graziosi and Real Estate I feel I have dramatically grown since I began in May. What a ride and experience! Real estate has given me the passive income that has dramatically changed my life and filled it with true purpose and passion.

Dawn's Success Secret: The greatest secret I can share for finding deals is to network. It really does seem like there are incredible deals all around, especially now in this economy. It also seems that time is often an incredible valued resource. Networking and meeting other like-minded individuals that will help achieve your dreams and goals are truly essential. People ask me, "Do you ever sleep?" And I tell them, "This isn't really the time to sleep." You can create your own reality, but you have to believe. It's all in your brain. It doesn't take money to create your own reality. You can just create whatever you want. It's just a matter of believing.

Miracles happen every day! This was one of the first visions I wrote down when I first started real estate investing. I reviewed my goal list a couple of weeks ago and said to myself, "Oh, I haven't achieved that yet." And just a few weeks later, it's happening...

To see a video of Dawn telling her story go to **www.deansmedia.com /dawn**

CHAPTER 5

Finding Profitable Deals the Old Fashioned Way

While the automated methods of finding properties are cutting edge and work like wildfire, there is no reason to ignore the power of more traditional ways of finding great deals. I could never turn my back on ways that have made me millions of dollars and neither should you. In fact, I suggest you use some of the robotic techniques in combination with traditional methods.

Whatever method you use, the goal is to keep it simple and leverage your time and energy. The only thing scarcer than money (before you become a real estate investor) is time, so I promise to always teach you ways to use both your time and money wisely.

First, let's review the common types of distressed properties where you are more likely to find motivated sellers and killer deals. Most people buy homes using a loan from the bank. In return for this loan, the homeowner must make monthly payments back to the bank. This payment includes the amount borrowed (the principle) plus any interest. When a homeowner can no longer make payments for any reason (such as medical bills, loss of a job, divorce, death in the family, or overspending), the bank notifies the homeowner that the foreclosure process will start unless payments are made. This period is known as a pre-foreclosure.

During this time, the homeowner can try to refinance or pay the amount due in order to keep the home. However, if the homeowner fails to pay or work out a new agreement with the bank, the bank will foreclose on the property.

Since the foreclosure process can be expensive and time-consuming, a bank may sometimes accept less than the amount owed, which is called a "short sale." If the homeowner cannot continue payments or the bank can't sell the property through a short sale, then the property goes through foreclosure, in which it's sold at a real estate auction or trustee sale to the highest bidder. If no one bids on the property, or if they do not bid enough, the bank will take ownership of the property. Such bank-owned properties are called REOs, or Real Estate–Owned properties. Banks don't like owning property since they make money by providing loans, not owning and managing properties. But this is the standard practice. In an up or strong market, banks don't really care because the property will sell fast. That is the complete opposite in today's market, which creates opportunity for you.

In addition, some other types of distressed properties are tax properties, probate properties, and divorce properties. Tax properties occur when a property owner fails to pay property taxes. When this occurs, the county will place a *tax lien* on that property, equal to the amount of taxes owed.

A tax lien prevents the owner from ever selling the property. To remove this tax lien, the owner must pay the back taxes owed plus interest. If the owner fails to pay the back taxes, the county can also seize the property and sell it, using the proceeds from the sale to pay the back taxes.

As an investor, you can either buy a tax lien or seized property, known as a "tax sale." If you buy a tax lien, the property owner must pay you the cost of the lien plus interest, to remove the lien from the property. If the property owner fails to do this, you can take possession of the property just for the cost of the lien alone.

To raise money from seized properties, the county will hold an auction where the highest bidder gets the property, even if the bid is way under the fair market value of the property. Whether you buy a tax lien or a tax sale, you can get property for literally pennies on the dollar.

When someone dies, they may leave property behind in a will, which is called a "probate property." Often the people inheriting the property live out of town and may never have seen the property. What's more, they'd rather sell it so they can easily divide the cash among all the inheritors. As a result, probate properties are often sold below market value just to get rid of it.

Similar to probate properties are properties jointly owned by married couples. When a couple divorces, they often want to sell the property so they can divide the cash. As part of finalizing the divorce, they often want to sell as soon as possible, which means they'll price it below market value.

To summarize, here's a quick list of the types of distressed properties that have motivated sellers:

- Pre-foreclosures

- Short sales

- Foreclosures

- REOs

- Tax sales

- Probate properties

- Divorce properties

As you can see, all types of distressed properties have motivated sellers, which is half the battle. Now let's go over different ways to find these killer deals.

Visiting the County Courthouse

Every county has a courthouse that publishes and stores public records that anyone can view. In many cases, you can even view public records over the Internet. The most useful public records for real estate investing include:

- Notices of default (pre-foreclosures)

- Real estate auctions (foreclosures and tax sales)

- Wills (probate properties)

- Divorce records (divorce properties)

To find your county courthouse, look in the phone book or search on the Internet for your county such as "Salt Lake County" followed by the term "county courthouse." Here is a quick snapshot of exactly what you would type in the Google search bar. I am sure you have used Google a thousand times, but I just want to be sure.

If you plan on visiting the county offices, call ahead and ask when they are least busy. That way the clerks will have more time to help you and answer any questions you might have.

By visiting your county courthouse periodically, you can find potential killer deals. Don't worry about finding the right office or files. Just ask for help! After browsing through these public records, you'll soon get a feel for what to look for and soon you'll be skimming through them like a pro.

Newspapers

Your local newspaper can provide a ton of information buried in the classified ads. In larger cities, you may also find special legal newspapers that also provide classified ads. Depending on the type of newspaper, you can often find the following:

- Notices of default (pre-foreclosures)

- Trustee sales (foreclosure properties)

- Auction notices (tax sale properties)

- For Sale by Owner properties

For Sale by Owner properties are great potential opportunities depending on the seller's reason for selling. Usually people prefer selling their house themselves to avoid paying a real estate agent's commission. Since For Sale by Owner properties aren't always listed on the MLS where every agent can find them, often For Sale by Owner properties have less competition, which means the homeowner may be more open to negotiating. Remember, if you find out what the seller wants, you can push his "magic button" and make a deal, in a win-win situation for everyone.

In most cases if you have this book, then you may also have my book *Be A Real Estate Millionaire*.

In that book I go really deep on how to learn the magic buttons of sellers. Also, I go into much more detail on the traditional ways to find sellers. I highly suggest you read that book as well, either before or after this one. Even if you skim or skip to parts that excite you or enhance your skills in an area you want to pursue. And, of course, don't hesitate to call one of our consultants to see if you qualify to be in our Real Estate Success Academy and have a faculty instructor work with you to reach your personal goals, answer questions you may have and keep you accountable for your own success. Okay, let's continue.

Internet Property Services

Browsing through public records at your county courthouse can be time-consuming, so that's why you might prefer subscribing to one of the many property-finding services available on the Internet. On those sites, you just type in the criteria you want in a home such as location, price range, or number of bedrooms, and the service lists all properties that match your criteria.

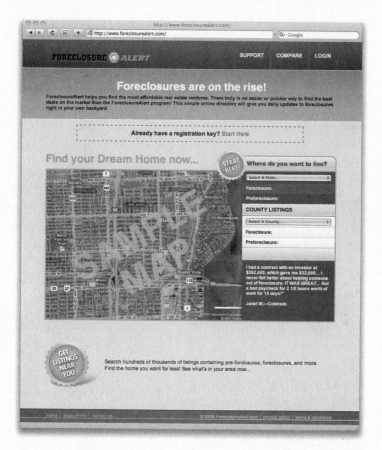

Typical fees for these services are $49.95 a month, which gives you access to listings that cover about 75 percent of the nation's counties. I'm a little partial, naturally, because I helped create the site, but by far the best value for this type of service is a site called Foreclosure Alert (www.foreclosurealert.com) or FAL for short, which is not only the most comprehensive service available, but as you can see from the comparison chart, almost half the price of its closest competitors. Consider that we pay tens of thousands of dollars each month to get the data that you can access for just $29.95 a month. We keep it priced as fair as we can so our students can easily take advantage of all its benefits.

The Foreclosure Alert service gives you instant access to nationwide pre-foreclosure and foreclosure listings that are updated daily. No matter what you're looking for, the deals are out there. This one-stop resource will help you find foreclosure properties without having to worry about scanning the filings at the courthouse or relying on real estate agents for foreclosure leads.

In addition, this service will allow you access to TENS OF THOUSANDS of properties containing pre-foreclosures, foreclosures, HUDs, VAs, FHAs and more across the United States. In many cases this includes recorded information regarding ownership, property characteristics, tax information, and more through map searching and directory navigation. Once you find a property of interest, you can access detailed foreclosure records on the property and surrounding area. FAL combines the detailed property information with the foreclosure record to provide the most comprehensive data available to help you make better investment decisions.

FAL also integrates with Virtual Earth® and Google Earth™—allowing you to quickly and easily view properties through your computer. See what's taking place in any area before you spend valuable time driving there! The mapping feature also includes many tools to help you execute other nontraditional methods of mapping.

The FAL Street Snapshot will display information on all of the neighbors surrounding a property of interest. There is also an Alerts feature that keeps you informed with pre-foreclosure and foreclosure (REO) properties by notifying you when new properties that match your specific criteria come available. This time-saving tool selects the properties from your predetermined criteria and returns the results to you daily.

If you are already signed up for this, then congratulations, and if not, give it a test drive when you are ready to get started. It's a great additional tool for your success toolbox.

Banks

Whenever banks loan money to someone for the purchase of a home, there's always a chance that the property owner will stop making payments. When this happens, the bank has to take the property back, which the bank considers a liability. Naturally, banks want to sell these properties off as fast as they can to generate cash or establish a new mortgage loan and turn the property into an asset.

Because the property is just sitting there, banks are usually eager to show you their lists of REOs—if they believe that you are a qualified buyer and are serious about purchasing it. When you call a bank, ask for the REO department. They will most likely direct you to a real estate broker who handles that bank's REOs. When you get the name of that broker, you're halfway there.

An easy way to obtain a list of these brokers in any particular state is to go to the REO Network's website (www.reonetwork.com). You can search through the site by city, state, or zip code to make a list of brokers in the locations that interest you.

Real Estate Agents/Realtors®

I mentioned earlier in a footnote that all realtors are Real Estate Agents/brokers, but not all Real Estate Agents/brokers are Realtors®. Realtors® are agents who have joined an industry association that, for a fee, gives them the right to call themselves Realtor®, a registered trademark reserved for the sole use of active members of local Realtor boards affiliated with the National Association of Realtors, which is supposed to give them "status" above non-association real estate agents.

In the next chapter you are going to learn how to develop a relationship with a great realtor and how important it can be for your success. A good realtor can help you search for all types of properties such as pre-foreclosures, short sales, foreclosures, REOs, tax sales, and even probate and divorce properties. In addition, a real estate agent can tell you the areas that are growing or falling, where the highest crime rates are, and the fair market value for similar houses in a particular neighborhood. Think of your real estate agent as your eyes and ears, keeping you in touch with your real estate market. Since your realtor is your partner, a good real estate agent is invaluable. Once you find a good one, you can both work together to hunt out and find great deals. When working with any real estate agent, make sure it's a win-win situation for both of you. I like to get my real estate agent involved in every deal I make, even if I find it on my own. That way my agent gets a commission for doing little work on her own. In return, my agent charges me a reduced commission and constantly looks for deals as soon as they arrive.

Again we will go deep on this topic in the next chapter and give you terrific ways to find a realtor if you don't know of any from word of mouth or experience. It will take a specific type of realtor to fit the criteria for making the money you desire.

Attorneys

Divorce and probate attorneys are the first to hear of properties that need to be sold for a divorce settlement or an inheritance. By establishing a relationship with these attorneys, you can often hear about properties before anyone else even knows they're available.

Bankruptcy attorneys can also steer you toward property owners who may be facing foreclosure. By offering to help these people, you can relieve their financial burden and protect their credit rating while getting a killer deal at the same time. Contact these types of attorneys in your area and let them know you're a real estate investor. You may simply be the one who can help clients in distress, so it is a positive thing for attorneys to have your name on file.

Government Agencies

Banks are not the only institutions that wind up with REOs. Two government agencies, HUD (Housing and Urban Development) and the VA (Veterans Administration) are government agencies that help people buy homes. If owners default on their loans, both HUD and the VA may wind up with REOs.

The HUD website (www.hud.gov) divides homes into owner-occupied listings (for people who want to purchase a home in which to live) and investor listings (for investors). If you sign up on their website and list yourself as an investor, you will be able to bid only on the investor listings.

Properties owned by the VA or HUD are sold through a bidding process. Whereas HUD prices can vary dramatically from fair market prices, VA properties rarely sell for less than 93% of the listed price. To find VA homes, along with other federal government properties, visit www.home-sales.gov.

Purchasing VA and HUD homes is popular among investors during an up market. But during a down market it is worth taking a look since the two agencies are excellent resources for finding affordable investment properties.

Of course, VA and HUD aren't the only government agencies that may wind up with properties they'll want to sell in a hurry. Some other government agencies you may want to look into include:

- Federal Deposit Insurance Corporation (FDIC)

- Internal Revenue Service (IRS)

- Treasury Department

- County Real Estate Tax Authority

U.S. Marshals Service

The Marshals Service (www.usmarshals.gov) administers the Department of Justice's Asset Forfeiture Program. Basically, that means when law enforcement agencies seize property due to illegal activities, the Marshals Service is responsible for managing and disposing of these seized properties.

The proceeds from the sale of forfeited assets, such as real estate, are often shared with the state and local enforcement agencies that participated in the investigation that led to the seizure of the assets. Seized properties are sold as is, so it's important to inspect the properties before you buy, though you can find some real bargains.

Public Auctions

The traditional way to sell property is to list it and wait for someone to place an offer to buy. Since this process can take time, many motivated sellers (banks, government agencies, etc.) prefer to offer property in an auction. Not only can an auction sell property in one day, but the bidding process can often drive the price higher than the seller might normally get by just listing the property.

You can often bid in person or over the Internet. Just make sure you don't get caught up in the frenzy of a bidding war and drive the price up so high you can't make a profit. By contacting auction companies directly, you can find when an auction will be held in your area. Visit the following auction websites for information:

- AuctionZip (www.auctionzip.com)

- Hudson & Marshall (www.hudsonandmarshall.com)

- RealtyBid (www.realtybid.com)

- Real Estate Disposition Corporation (www.ushomeauction.com)

- Williams & Williams (www.williamsauction.com)

Driving Around

I've found some killer deals just by driving around a neighborhood on a Sunday afternoon. By exploring different areas, you can see which parts of town are improving and which ones may be sinking.

Many realtors offer open houses on the weekends, but keep your eye out for any For Sale signs you spot, especially For Sale by Owner signs or even For Rent signs. If you call owners who are trying to rent their homes and tell them you're more interested in buying rather than renting, you'll be surprised at the response you might get. Many property owners are tired of dealing with the hassle of tenants, so they might be open to selling at the right price or at the right terms.

I also like looking for distressed properties in nice neighborhoods. Try to find the one house with the weeds in the front lawn, the fading paint, and overall worn-out look. By contacting the owners, you may find that they no longer have money to maintain their property and would be happy to sell it. Remember, it never hurts to ask—and you never know where you might find your next killer deal.

Word of Mouth

Once you make the decision to start investing in real estate, tell everyone you know. Ask that if they hear of any properties that go on the market, or of any friends or associates who are in trouble, to please send them your way or give you the information so you can follow up. I've made some terrific investments this way.

Remember, the more people who know you're a real estate investor, the more likely someone is to find you a deal. Many times, people will know of a neighbor, relative, or friend who wants to sell a property in a hurry, and if they know you buy real estate, they may offer it to you first at a great price.

Just through word of mouth alone, you can get people literally bringing you killer deals without having to do anything to find them.

Matt's Foreclosure Tip

When real estate brokers receive foreclosures to list for sale, they often receive a bulk of houses at one time. The process of listing a foreclosure includes getting a "broker's price opinion" (BPO). What I found is that many times the brokers rush through this process just to get all of the houses listed for sale. Most of the time they will list houses at around fair market price, but every once in a while they will miss something and list the house far below actual value. I always try to have my real estate agent find these types of houses for me by running an "average cost per square foot" analysis.

For example, one foreclosure I bought about a year ago was listed for $46,000, which was a HUD (Housing and Urban Development) home. Here is what my agent noticed. The house had over 1,200 livable square feet, but it was only listed at 800 sq. ft. There were 2 extra bedrooms upstairs that were not counted as livable square feet. The reason why is because there weren't any heat ducts running upstairs. I learned from Dean's book *Be A Real Estate Millionaire* that HUD will accept an offer of 93% of the asking price. So I put in an offer right away for $43,000, which was accepted immediately.

After looking at the house, it was just what I expected. The house was amazing and huge. It was just listed poorly or no one spent even a little money to get some heat ducts upstairs. Even though I bought the house at 93% of its value, it was an amazing deal, because my real estate agent and I are always on the lookout for things like this.

After closing I called a friend who installs ductwork and he came over and simply ran ductwork upstairs. The whole thing only cost me $500, but it raised the value of the house by $30,000. If that same house would have been listed by a homeowner, it would have never sold that cheap because a homeowner would have counted the upstairs as finished livable space. That type of inconsistency is why I love buying houses that have been through the foreclosure process!

Note: Due to the current housing conditions, HUD will now accept offers as low as 86% of the asking price if there are no other offers on the property at the time you put in your offer.

Summary

In this chapter, we've covered traditional ways of finding a deal, which require more footwork to hunt them out and track them down, but that's also what keeps many people from doing this too. By taking action, you'll always come out ahead compared to somebody who doesn't do anything at all, so don't you dare let your fear of browsing county courthouse records or bidding on auctioned properties keep you from snapping up a great deal. Just remember:

• You can find killer deals everywhere, everyday. You just have to take the time and effort to find them.

• Your county courthouse contains public records that can help you find pre-foreclosures, foreclosures, tax sales, probate, and divorce properties.

• Newspapers often list pre-foreclosures, foreclosures, tax sales, and For Sale by Owner properties.

• For a monthly fee, Internet property services can retrieve potential deals straight to your computer so you can do all your real estate searching from the comfort of your home.

• Banks, attorneys, and real estate agents are a great source for finding distressed properties.

• Many government agencies sell or auction off seized properties.

• Public auctions can be a great way to buy property for pennies on the dollar. Just don't get caught in the bidding frenzy and pay more than you should.

• Drive around different neighborhoods to find For Sale and For Rent signs and contact the owners. Also, look for houses that don't look as nice as the rest of the neighborhood.

You never know where your next killer deal may be coming from.

Action Steps

People often ask me, "If real estate investing is so easy and profitable, how come everyone doesn't do it?" The answer is simple. Most people aren't willing to take the time to learn what to do, and then they aren't willing to do the work needed to do it. Just by reading this book, you've taken your first step toward real estate investing. Now it's time to start taking action at each step of the way, so this is what I want you to do right now:

• Find out where your county courthouse is located and find out the times it's open and the times least busy.

• Visit your county courthouse and determine the proper procedure for finding notices of default, foreclosure notices, tax sales, wills, and divorce properties. Don't be afraid to ask the courthouse clerks for help. That's what they're there for!

• Sign up for a free trial with one or more Internet Property Services to see what kind of information they offer.

• Look on the Internet to find how you can buy properties held by government agencies in your area.

• Browse through your local newspapers to find out when and where they print default notices and real estate auction notices.

• Find out when the next public auction will be held for real estate in your area and attend at least one auction.

• Drive through a neighborhood that you like and look for properties for sale or for rent.

• Make at least one call a week to talk to a property owner and find out why he or she is selling.

• Tell at least one person a week that you are a real estate investor and make sure that person knows how to contact you.

Congratulations on making it this far! Right now, you're very close to getting started on your first deal! Knowing how to find those motivated sellers is the key to making big money in real estate.

But there are a few more things to discover. Like, how do you know for sure you have a motivated seller? How can you find out what properties are really worth? Who can help you get reliable facts? What do you do once people start calling and leaving messages after you find a killer deal using these methods? How do you buy and sell one of these great deals to make a bundle without spending a penny? All this and more still needs to be revealed.

So with that as our goal, let's take one more step and show you how to find a great real estate agent.

Success Story #5: Bob and Debbie B.

Location: Clarkesville, Georgia

Experience before Dean's strategies: Owned one commercial property and one rental home.

Net worth increase on first deal: $147, 000

Most shocking part of first deal: Not only did we buy 6 brand-new homes at a huge discount with no money down, we actually left the closing table with money.

Additional monthly income on first deal: $1,200 cash flow.

What you would like to say to Dean: "Thank you and God bless you. You opened our eyes and took away our fear, allowing us to see a whole new world of making money with real estate."

Best part: The newfound confidence we have in our financial security. I know our retirement is secure no matter what the economy does around us. We had a small rental home, but when we looked to the future, we realized that our rental income wasn't enough to provide for our retirement. Our stock portfolio barely made any money and we were fortunate enough to pull all our money out before the big stock crash near the end of 2008. When we looked at our options, we saw that real estate had always worked for us and we decided that we needed a stable source of income. When we saw Dean's infomercial, we knew that we needed to know more and had to learn from someone smarter than us. Dean seemed like the guy and he was.

Although we had some experience as real estate investors, Dean's course gave us the confidence and unique strategies that we didn't have before. In the past, our only idea behind real estate was to put 20 percent down, have the bank finance the rest, and make a profit from rental income. Dean gave us the boldness to ask and look for deals rather than just buy and sell real estate the conventional way. Basically, Dean opened the door with the knowledge he gave us and we just walked through it.

Once we knew we wanted to get started, we interviewed several real estate agents and settled on the one agent who was a real estate investor herself. Not only did she understand how to find a deal, but she was eager to share her knowledge about real estate investing. We knew what questions to ask now and knew what things to listen to.

At that point we decided to find low- to mid-priced homes because people who were losing their homes would need to downgrade and find a less expensive place to live. On the other hand, people upgrading would need an inexpensive home to move up from an apartment. By buying low- to mid-range homes, you can capture the market from both ends.

Our first deal involved six houses on the same street that had been foreclosed and left vacant. Although each house was worth approximately $92,000, the bank offered them for $75,000 each. We looked at the houses and saw that most were in good shape, others needed only minor repairs, and one needed major work, but still looked promising.

As you can imagine, this was a bit scary. Before getting Dean's information, no way would we have even considered it. The truth is we would have never even found this great deal without the knowledge that Dean taught us. But with a newfound skill set and Dean's voice ringing in our ears, we pushed forward with a newfound courage.

Initially, the bank offered to sell all six houses with a 20-year loan, but we told them that was too short, so they extended it to 30 years. They did this because we had the confidence to ask the right questions, which we never would have had before Dean's course. To make it even sweeter—because we asked—the bank covered the closing costs, gave us a 5.5% rate, and we left the closing table with $2,400 in our pocket, all with no money down. Yes, better than no money down—they gave us money back! This is exactly how the deal went, and I never would have thought these types of deals were possible, but they are.

If you had told me just a short while ago that a bank would go through a foreclosure process and then sell you the property for way less then it was worth, hold the mortgage at a low interest rate and do it with no money out of pocket, I would have called you a liar. But it's not only true, we are looking for lots more of these deals as I write this. It comes down to the old saying: *you don't know what you don't know.* Well I am surely glad we now Know! The way we were going, it would have taken us decades to increase our net worth as much as we did on our very first deal, if ever. We can wait until the market improves and then sell one or two of the houses, hold them all and earn rental income, or sell them all for a huge profit. I have to say this again, none of this would have been possible without Dean's teachings.

Bob and Debbie's Biggest Secret: The biggest secret is almost no secret at all. If you have the right information (Dean's techniques) and combine that with simply taking action— or as Dean would say, "Just do it!"—it's possible to profit from real estate during any market, especially now. Don't just blow past the inspiration Dean shares with you; those same messages got us through the tough times, onward to realize our profits. Don't let fear or anyone hold you back. Read the e-mails you get from Dean, watch the videos he sends, get on his conference calls—and absorb it all. Even if it seems a bit much at first, it will all sink in and come in handy when you do your first deal or a more efficient deal in the future.

To see a video of Bob and Debbie telling their story go to **www.deans-media.com/bobanddebbie**

Part II

CHAPTER 6

The Perfect Real Estate Agent = Huge Profits

One key ingredient to successful real estate investing is finding a very solid real estate agent who fits your needs perfectly, and is willing to help you use some of the strategies you are about to learn. In a down market, many agents are struggling, and to have an up-and-coming real estate investor like you is a major plus for them. You will not only learn here how to find a great agent eager to make you money, but also how to leverage the agent's knowledge and time to allow you to profit with minimal effort on your part.

The ideal real estate agent is different for everyone. An agent who helped a 65-year-old couple find their dream retirement home in a 6-month period may not be the type of aggressive go-getter you want as a strategic partner to help you make you a boatload of money as an investor. A good real estate agent can help you identify a great deal, take most (if not all) of the detailed work off your shoulders, and answer strategic questions, so let's take a moment and teach you exactly how to find a great one.

I am a huge advocate of real estate agents and feel that it is a must to have a great agent working with you. But I am also the first to say that there are a lot of incompetent agents out there. What bothers me even more than them being incompetent is that they will spread wrong or inaccurate information and sometimes rob people of their goals and desires. In many cases a real estate agent is a good salesperson, but never took the time to invest themselves or do a true analysis of the real estate cycle changes. So in an instant, they will voice "their opinion" as if it is fact or as if it is coming from a real estate expert. They may be experts at selling real estate, but that does not make them real estate experts.

Think of it this way. If you go to buy a new car, you talk with the salesperson. He makes you feel great, gives you the deal you want, shakes your hand, and you go on your merry way. But if in a month the car starts making a funny noise, you never go back to him. He is not a car expert, he is a sales expert. Makes sense.

Nothing makes me happier than when I hear that my students connect with an ethical, open- minded, and hardworking agent who wants to be a long-term partner in their real estate success. I truly believe there are more great agents or brokers out there than not-so-good ones. But on the other hand, NOTHING aggravates me more than when an unqualified agent talks someone out of their desires and goals. I have heard agents tell clients the exact time the market will turn with no foundational proof other than what they hope to help make sales better. You will soon learn a strategy that turned Matt Larson into a millionaire and made his Real Estate Agent Star a small fortune. But when you approach a narrow-minded "afraid of change" agent with this strategy, they may flat-out tell you "It Does Not Work"—they will say this based on no experience and before even trying it.

Before we go any further, I want to say it again, there are amazing agents out there and we are going to teach you how to find them. But don't you dare let the wrong agent, or in some cases a small-minded, afraid-of-change, so-called expert agent, talk you out of your desire for a better life. If they knew what I am teaching you, they would not be scared to death. Rather, they would be out working, opening their mind to new things and changing their strategy with the changing environment. I am going to teach you a way to find a good agent, and I promise you will know when you find that agent. Remember, negative people who never have a bigger future than their past will always tell you why something will not work. Whereas positive people, growing, heading toward a bigger future, will always be optimists, want to learn and want to try new things, finding the light at the end of the tunnel.

Here are some smart ways to find a great real estate agent. Absolutely the best way to find a real estate agent is by word of mouth. Despite all the online resources, the phone book and other tools, nothing beats word of mouth from someone who has had experience with that person. If you look up a website or open a phone book, you may as well shut your eyes and point. Every agent wants you to believe they are the one for you. Unfortunately, it's easy for any of them to overpromise and underdeliver. If you use this search method, you're just as likely to come across the village idiot as opposed to the neighborhood superstar.

Use other people's experiences, positive or not, to guide you regarding your choice. Real estate professionals are such an important part of investing that you have to be sure to go with someone with a proven track record and great references. Smart places to look for agents like this are real estate investing clubs. You can find a local investing club many ways. I would call different real estate offices and ask if they know of one, look online for a local club, or check these online resources:

National Real Estate Investors Association (www.nationalreia.com)

Real Estate Investors Club (www.reiclub.com)

This way you know you are working with someone who is used to investors and motivated to find good deals. You can also go to **www.deangraziosi.com/findarealtor** for a step-by-step tutorial on how to do this.

Once you have a candidate, interview him or her by asking the following questions:

- Time in the business

- Willing to work with new investors

- Worked with investors in the past

- An example of the best deal they ever made, how they took their expertise and allowed a client to profit or have a smoother/easier deal

- Worked with banks on foreclosures/short sales

- Ever successfully handled an assignment of contract

- Invest themselves (not always a conflict of interest)

- Willing to make low offers

- Willing to send property info regularly that matches your criteria

Make sure you are not talking to a "dud." When I ran ads for my staff, I would send the candidate to pre-recorded messages to leave their information. The ad would ask for motivated, high-energy people. I would get people leaving a message as if they were still half asleep or started the message off with "Yo!" Communication is key, so make sure the agent can communicate well. How they sound with you is how they're going to sound when they represent you to others.

Determine what you can expect of them and tell them what they can expect of you. Take notes during these conversations so you know exactly what type of relationship was established. Consider working with a few realtors initially to determine who actually does what they say they're going to do.

Automatically Finding an Agent

Here is what Matt Larson did to find his real estate agents. Matt used this method once to find deals and ended up not only finding deals but also a lot of real estate agents calling to represent him. (By the way, once you start having success, the best realtors in your area will hunt you down.) Now it is a system you can use to sift out the ones that can fit your desires.

Matt's Advice for Finding an Agent

The first thing I did to find a real estate agent, was to build a fax or e-mail sheet that listed everything that I was looking for. For example:

PROFESSIONAL REAL ESTATE INVESTOR
LOOKING FOR PROPERTIES

Hi, my name is Mr. or Mrs. (your name) and I am an investor in the local area. Due to the current economic conditions, I have decided to ramp up my existing operations. I not only represent myself, but I also have several investors in and out of the area that I help find, rehab, rent out, and manage properties. Because of the money backing me, I have set the goal to buy 100 hundred properties within the next 12–18 months. Some of these properties I will buy and hold myself, some of them I will sell to other investors and some I will buy, fix up and flip for myself. Regardless of the strategy I use on each property, I need to be very aggressive on the price I pay for the property, especially in the current market. I have not chosen a real estate agent to represent me yet. The agent that I choose cannot be afraid to offend other agents with low offers. The agent I choose also will have to be available at all times. I use several strategies to buy and sell properties quickly, including making verbal offers when permitted. I will also look at a lot of properties and buy only a few. So an aggressive work schedule will be required. The upside for the agent who gets accepted will be lots of commission. We will close on properties every month. I will pull in the agent on For Sale By Owner deals. At times I will write additional commission into the contract when we ramp up to full speed. All that aside, I am a professional and I expect to work with a professional. I want to make money and I want the agent to make money. Here are the type of properties I am looking to buy:

(Below you would replace these sample details with your own preferences).

Single family homes 3–4 bedrooms,
1–2 baths at least 1,000 sq. feet.
No mobile homes at this time
No home built before 1950
No vacant ground
Located in zip codes 12345, 54321, 43434, 23231,
only in low-crime neighborhoods

If you have properties that fit this description or would like to represent me please call me at 555-555-5555.
Thanks for your time,
Mr. or Mrs. (your name)

Just make adjustments to this sheet to fit what you want, and then fax or e-mail it to every real estate office in your area. Your phone will ring. I did this thing about six months ago and I still have agents calling me with deals and asking if they can represent me, but I already have the agents I want.

When you get calls, simply tell the real estate agent exactly what you are looking for and make sure they commit to the things that you wrote in your fax. You may even ask them to respond to your fax with a one page letter. From there, go with your gut feeling and pick someone you feel is easy to talk to and seems hungry to make a bunch of money.

• • •

That's a great suggestion isn't it? The only thing I would do differently is to direct the interested agents to call a recorded message that would tell them more. That way, when I finally talk to a prospective agent, I can be certain she has the right qualities for working with me. Like I mentioned earlier, you can also tell a lot from how someone conducts herself on a message. Remember, this person is going to be representing you to sellers, so you want to make sure she sounds professional when leaving messages. With the recorded message you will be able to sort through agents just based on this. (I am going to use "her" from this point because my two favorite real estate agents are ladies.)

Throughout this book I like to use Matt's real-life examples and his words. For years, people would think "Dean can do it, but can I?" Now there are countless people, just like Matt, who are making money RIGHT NOW all over the country, and they want to share what they have done with you. People like Matt took what I shared with them and ran with it. Knowledge + Action = Results. So the more I can share these techniques with you in real-life scenarios, with real-life people using them, other than me, the more I love it. If you want to see some more success stories from people who sent in home videos of their successes, go to **www.deansmedia.com.**

Matt had such a great handle on finding the perfect real estate agent to fit the strategies you are learning in this book that I am going to let his words continue to teach you.

More From Matt on Finding a Real Estate Agent

Most real estate agents don't like working with investors because investors put in low offers and most of their offers don't get accepted. When I'm looking for a real estate agent, I interview them to find the right one.

First, I let them know up front that we're going to offend other agents by constantly placing low offers. Next, I let the agents know that we're going to make a lot of offers, but very few of them will get accepted. However, we will close on a lot of houses so they'll be earning commissions every month.

Unfortunately, too many agents simply want "gimme" deals working with retail buyers. Some agents will tell you that they don't like putting out lots of low offers, so they'd rather not work with you. That's exactly what you need to know, because then you can sort, sift, and screen through different agents until you find one who doesn't have a problem working with you. The best agent is one who doesn't mind putting in low offers simply to close deals consistently. A real estate agent is your partner, so it's in your best interests to find the best partner willing to help make money for both of you.

In the last few years my agents have made well over $150,000 dollars working with me, and we have only just begun. I plan on sticking with them forever, making this a win-win relationship for both of us.

You'll be able to see how our relationship for making money together has evolved. And you can do exactly what I did in your area with the right person. I have asked my real estate agent Star for a letter on why agents should work with you, and also what to say to make them the most efficient—not only to make you money but to make themselves money. Later on in this book I'll share Star's letter, along with my 25:1 strategy. Believe me, it's killer and allowed me to become a millionaire. I know that I could not have done it so easily and so fast if it was not for my real estate agent Star. Create a win-win for you and your agent and the sky is the limit. And if your agent can't see your vision, then find someone who can.

I want to tell you Star and I have become friends who help each other make money. We have working together down to such a science that when I see her calling me, I simply say. "What did we buy today?" I know there are lots of Stars out there. Go find one of your own and start making money.

Crafting a Strategy with Your Real Estate Agent

As soon as you have chosen the right real estate agent, you can decide what price range you want to target. Ask your real estate agent a few simple questions to help decide what area and what price point you want to target. Of course, with the strategies you'll learn in this book, you can make money in all areas and in any price range. However, it's best to focus on one area first to dramatically increase your opportunity to make money.

Here are the two questions to ask your real estate agent:

- "Which pocket or area has homes selling the fastest?"

- "What price range of homes is selling the most or the fastest?"

Knowing the answers to these two simple questions will enable you to find homes that fit in those criteria so you'll have a much greater chance of producing cash faster. Soon you will learn other criteria to pick which are the "prime" deals for making money, and the answers to those questions will help you make your decision on pulling the trigger on a deal or not.

Now that you know what property areas are hotter than others and what price ranges are selling the fastest, you can get ready to start looking for amazing deals.

This information, along with all the other factors we covered, will let you sit down and create a full-blown strategy that you and your agent can use as a template for your success. And that strategy can always evolve as you find new areas that can be profitable for you both.

(Remember, in this book I'll be teaching you various no money down strategies for today's market. However, you can use these same principles to find an amazing deal, buy it yourself, and rent it out for positive cash flow. If that strategy excites you, or you would like to do both, you can get more information on this type of buy-and-rent strategy by going to **www.deangraziosi.com** or by calling 1-800-315-7782, to talk with one of our consultants about advanced training programs and my Real Estate Success Academy.

Once you have a real estate agent on your side, have pinpointed where you want to invest, the type of property you want, and the price range, it's time to start looking for killer deals!

Summary

A real estate agent is one of your most important partners, so this chapter gave you different ways to find a real estate agent who will be willing to work with you, answer your questions, and help both of you make a ton of money in the process.

• A good real estate agent is crucial to your success.

• Don't go with the first real estate agent you meet. Interview several to find the one willing to work with investors.

• Rather than look for a real estate agent, use Matt's technique of getting a real estate agent to come to you.

• A real estate agent can help you find the best places to look for killer deals.

Action Steps

Congratulations on getting this far in the book! I want you to keep moving forward each step of the way. Now I want you to take the following steps to make sure you keep moving toward the type of life you've always dreamed about:

- Ask friends for references to a good real estate agent.

- Contact several real estate agents and ask them if they'd be willing to work with investors.

- Interview different real estate agents until you find one who seems most helpful.

- When you find a real estate agent you want to work with, make a plan to stay in touch regularly so you can put your real estate plans into action.

Success Story #6: David L.

Location: Atkinson, New Hampshire

Experience in real estate before getting Dean's course: None

Net worth increase since starting: $213,700

Favorite deal: Increased my net worth by $109,000 on one deal without using a single penny of my own money. Thankfully, since I had no money to invest.

How life has changed: Went from huge debt, a job I disliked, and basically not liking my life to quitting my job, moving to a great area and getting to do something I love, be a full-time real estate investor.

Before I started Dean's course, I was renting a room in some lady's house that I found through an ad on Roommate.com. I had to live in her house because I could only afford to rent a room. I was drowning in $80,000 worth of credit card debt with no hope in sight.

When I bought Dean's book, I devoured it. It immediately gave me the confidence and desire to believe that it was possible. I'd seen people making money in real estate and never knew how. Then all of a sudden, after reading Dean's book, I knew how. I moved out of that lady's house and "upgraded" to a $500 month apartment.

I had gotten Dean's course in February 2007 and closed on a first house by November 2007. This house was a brand-new, bank-owned home that had been appraised for $615,000, but I bought it for $410,000.

At my salary, I had no business holding a $460,000 mortgage, so the only way I could afford it was to get a 40-year note and find a tenant to help pay part of the mortgage. Coincidentally, a friend of mine had just lost his home to foreclosure. He needed a place to stay, I needed a tenant, so he agreed to rent out one of the rooms for $700 a month.

I took a giant leap of faith, knowing that I was going to take on a huge note without having the income to afford it.

By using a $460,000 mortgage, I pulled $50,000 out to cover closing costs and used $40,000 to pay down my credit card debt. I then used this first house as leverage to buy my second property, a 3BR bank-owned foreclosure. This second house was appraised at $260,000, but I bought it for $155,300.

Since I couldn't get a mortgage for 100 percent financing, I had to put $2,000 down. If I couldn't find a way to finance the rest of the deal, I would have lost that entire $2,000.

I knew I couldn't rely on a bank for financing, so I started looking for individuals willing to lend money, otherwise known as "hard money lenders." At work, I struck up a conversation with a co-worker and told him I needed to borrow money. When he asked why, I told him that I bought a house, and once I had the deed in my name, I could refinance it. Then this guy said, "I'll loan you the money," and when I showed him the house, he said, "Wow!" I bought the house, fixed it up, and found four tenants by sticking signs all over town.

I refinanced the $60,000 loan on the two houses so the combined mortgage payments were $4,200 a month, the tenants were paying $3,500, which meant I could live in a half-million-dollar house for only $700 a month.

After these two deals, I decided to quit my job and focus on investing in real estate full-time. I met two investors who had sold their company and made millions, and they wanted to invest in real estate, but they didn't know how. They asked me to help them out, so all of us moved to Florida.

We're planning on closing on five houses and one of those houses will be mine. We're basically buying $250,000 houses at auction for only $50,000. Best of all, I'm not using any of my money; I'm using my investors' money. They provide the cash, I provide the techniques I learned from Dean, do all the work, and we split everything three ways.

David's Success Secrets: If I can do it, you can do it. I went from $80,000 in credit card debt up to my eyeballs with no hope in sight and thinking about filing for bankruptcy to buying Dean's course and learning to think a little different. Once I find a house with lots of equity in it, I try to get that house. I don't care how I finance it, because once it's in my name I can tap into that equity.

Don't let the lack of conventional bank loans stop you. There are people out there who lend money at a high percentage rate, but if it helps you get a deal, it's a win-win for everybody. When I was living in an apartment, I never realized that you could get houses without conventional mortgages.

In five months from November 2007 to March 2008, I made two transactions that took my net worth from minus $80,000 to positive $200,000.

Dean's course helped me do it and got me thinking, "There always a way." You have to think differently. Don't think about the obstacles blocking your way, think about the possibilities. It was that nudge, as simple as it may sound, that made it happen.

Now whenever I see Dean on TV, I tell people, "You've got to listen to this guy." You don't need a conventional mortgage. You have to think of what you can do, not what you can't do. Dean is very sincere and authentic, not just a guy selling a book on TV. His ideas are phenomenal. He's got it down. He's smart. He's been using his ideas for years.

You've just got to have faith. When you do, your world just opens up. Now I'm getting paid a salary to use other people's money to buy houses. Where do you think I'll be in five years? I'll probably be worth $5 million.

To see a video of David telling his story go to **www.deans-media.com/david**

CHAPTER 7

Identifying a Killer Deal

So far you've learned my unique way of attracting a steady supply of sellers who want to sell property. Along with my "marketing-based method" of attraction, we've also covered the traditional methods for finding potential properties too. Now that you have the smart marketing, know how to find the deals, the next skill set is to identify which deals are worth pursuing and how to communicate with the sellers you have found. Most important, you need to know the process for preparing and submitting an offer that is super low yet has a great chance of being accepted.

In this section, I am going to review the characteristics of an ideal seller and help you to identify the types of sellers best suited for little or no money down methods. I'll describe a typical seller profile; tell you how to determine the value of a potential deal, and how to sign an agreement with your seller.

Last but not least, you'll learn how to legally pass a property to another buyer and cash in on the transaction. These methods are powerful and proven to generate a great deal of money, so take notes and learn them both. Then you can decide which one, if not both, fit you the best.

By the time you're through with this chapter, you'll understand how to evaluate both the properties and their sellers, as well as how to submit only those offers with a high likelihood of getting accepted.

You'll have complete control over your options and your decisions. So fasten your seatbelts, and let's get started by exploring the Seller Profile. You already know there are a number of different types of individual deals that you can focus on. For now, let's look at pre-foreclosures, For Sale By Owners (FSBOs, pronounced "fizz bows") and sellers who have had their homes on the market for more than 90 days. These three Seller categories are typically the very easiest situations to use the no money down techniques. In today's market, they are extremely plentiful with enough amazing deals to keep you hopping as an investor.

I'm going to give you a brief overview of each of these sellers just to make sure you have a working understanding of their situations and the kind of emotional pressures they face.

Pre-Foreclosure Sellers

Most pre-foreclosure sellers find themselves in their situation due to the economic factors I covered in the first chapter. No matter how they got to the pre-foreclosure phase, they are going through significant changes in their lives. Their financial situation may have worsened due to any of the following:

- Job loss

- Poor economy

- Divorces

- Bad or wrong bank loan

- Death of one spouse

- Disaster

- Financially overextended

- Medical bills

- Disability

These sellers may also have delinquent property taxes that would cause them to be in pre-foreclosure status.

For Sale by Owner Sellers (FSBO)

In a slow real estate market, For Sale By Owner sellers are likely having problems selling their homes. They might have little or no equity in their property, which makes it even more difficult to sell because they don't feel they have much room to budge on their price.

They might be buying another property, or moving to another city due to a job transfer. They could have already started moving into another home and counted on their first home selling faster than it has, and now they're stuck with two mortgage payments.

These are unfortunate circumstances, but in a slow market, this is a common situation. As a result, this makes FSBO sellers motivated to sell.

Homes listed for 90 days or more

Almost anyone whose home has been for sale for 3 months or more is anxious to sell, more so than when they first put their home on the market in week one. The longer any house has been on the market, the stronger the seller's motivation may be. It all depends on what's at stake for them if they don't sell.

Pre-screening Sellers

Even though your automatic or robotic system does most of the work for you, eventually you will have to talk with potential sellers about how your program works. If you are not using a recorded message company like the one I mentioned previously (COA Network page 82), make sure you have a professional voice-mail setup so potential sellers can leave a message. However you get your sellers, you should try to have them go through your automated sift, sort, and screen process to avoid wasting any of your precious time.

Whether you talk to them via e-mail (my preference in the beginning), on the phone or in person, always treat your potential motivated seller like gold and handle yourself respectfully. Remember, they may be interested in selling their home to you. That can result in profit in your pocket, so treat them with kindness, honesty and respect.

Remember, the right real estate agent can also handle correspondence for you as well.

Let me take a moment and let you know that when I'm working with my agent, I have her get involved in almost all of my deals. I buy them so cheap that there is always room for her to work with me and do a lot of the heavy lifting. So even if I find the deal through one of my strategies. I will give her 1% to handle the offers, the transactions and running around. It's a win for everyone. Now, if she finds the deal or sells a property completely on her own, then of course she would get paid a higher percentage. So you can share with others, handle it all yourself, or simply know how you want to direct your kick-ass real estate agent to handle things on your behalf.

Once you start working with a great real estate agent, you can try to work out a win-win scenario for you both. Leveraging her time to do things for you can be awesome if the money is right for all. You can probably see now why I took the time to dedicate an entire chapter to making sure you find yourself the agent who fits your needs perfectly. Don't ever be shy about using your realtor's time. Remember, they are working with you and for you. The more you can pass off on them the more time you have to look at potential deals. Another reason I encourage using a realtor is that they have lots of experience in dealing with sellers and seller's agents. One thing to always keep in mind with real estate investing is leverage, whether it is your money, time, or resources.

Be prepared to offer sellers a brief but interesting summary of the help you will provide. When you speak over the phone or communicate by e-mail with sellers, you can provide them with information and answers like these:

NOTE: All of this can be done with a pre-recorded message, online audio, through your real estate agent or e-mail—this allows you the freedom of not spending so much time on the phone. But the method is something you need to know, and it's not the worst thing in the world if you need to say it in person or on the phone yourself.

> *"I am real estate investor. I'm not a real estate agent or broker. (If you happen to be one, you may say 'I am not calling as a real estate agent or broker.') I have a very unique and effective model that allows me to get homes I buy or work with sold fast, even in this down market. I do this to make a profit and I make it a win-win for everyone involved. Your home may fit in my criteria.*
>
> *Mr. Seller, I've got buyers with decent credit that could not get funded through traditional channels, but my connections can help get them a loan. I also have a pool of investors with cash waiting to buy.*
>
> *If we can come to an agreeable sale price of your home, all we need to do is sign a couple pieces of paper. One that tells you I am a real estate investor, and my exact goals. A second gives me some simple rights for 14 to 30 days. There is no cost to you at all to do this, no risk, and it is completely ethical and safe. Basically we will be drafting a contract that states I am buying your home. The entire contract can expire in 30 days or less if I don't buy it. During that time, if I find a buyer who wants to purchase your home I may pass off the contract to them or rip up our contract and*

have you work with the new buyer directly. If we do this, there will be a pre-set fee I will be paid for the equity I found, which will not come out of your pocket since you and I have already agreed upon a price. (You will learn how to price out a deal soon.)

Tell them you will want the ability to bring associates by the house, if necessary, to inspect it. Be certain to tell them that it will be scheduled at times when it will NOT disrupt their lives. You don't want them to think you are going to be bothering them ten times a day.

Tell them that if everything goes well, you can get a purchase and sale agreement signed by all parties, and then go to closing where they get their house sold and you get your profit as an investor. And in many cases this can all take place in that 30-day window.

Remember, some people will have had their home for sale for many months, maybe even a year, and are wondering, "What allows you to buy or sell homes so fast in such a horrible market?" Just tell them the truth—that you are using a revolutionary marketing system that kicks up buyers in a down market when most people can't find them. Express how you are doing people a great service, and you happen to get paid to do it.

Because you can do this, in many cases you don't have to negotiate all of the profit out of the deal for the seller. Your goal is a win-win-win approach for all parties. I know win-win is an overused term, but this truly needs to be one of your goals in the process. You want to help the seller successfully get their home sold. You want to attract a buyer who wants a home, and because you are smart or informed enough to make it a win-win for everyone, you make money when a transaction is successfully completed.

Remember, you are just trying to solve the seller's problem and profit from the difference that the seller would normally discount the house for anyhow. In this market, you can't be bashful. People need to sell their homes and, using my methods, you are going to kick up the percentage of people more than willing to sell at a huge discount and be happy to do it.

Sellers don't mind if you make $5,000, $10,000, $20,000 or more, just as long as they get their house sold fast. They typically don't care how it happens, as long as it does happen.

Determining a Seller's Motivation

Ideally, your recorded message can screen out all but the most motivated sellers. Such automated strategies can also give you a feel for what realistic price the seller considers the fair market value of his or her property. But of course the more motivated people are to sell, the better price or opportunity for profit.

When people get emotionally attached to their homes, they can lose objectivity and fail to grasp that what they perceive their home to be worth and what a willing buyer will actually pay—especially in a Buyer's Market—may be as far as the east is from the west. If you get a good sense that the seller is realistic, then, using the questionnaire that follows, you can get a feel for what their low-end selling price might be. When you ask the seller questions from this questionnaire, try not to sound rehearsed. Prepare yourself ahead of time to ask questions in a conversational manner.

This questionnaire is NOT a list to ask in order like a roll call. Some questions are redundant and some won't apply to every seller or situation. Just use this list as an example of the information you want to gather.

NOTE: Depending on the extent of your automated system techniques (described in previous chapters, many of these questions can be answered long before you ever speak to the seller. You can do this through your recorded message, a website, your real estate agent or even e-mail. Ideally, the goal of these automated techniques is to make sure that you only talk to sellers who have deals worth pursuing. You can e-mail some or all the questions below, or create a one-page fax sheet to be filled out.

Example Questions for the Seller

Hello, my name is _____. May I ask you what your name is? Can I call you by your first name _____ (Bill or Mary, for example)?

• Can you tell me a little about your home (how many bedrooms, bathrooms, etc.)?

• Do you know the square footage of your home?

• How many square feet does your home have on the main floor and in total if you have an upstairs and/or a basement?

- *What would you say are the best features about your home?*

- *What would you say are the worst?*

- *Is this a single-level home, or is there an upstairs or basement?*

- *How large is the garage?*

- *How old is your home?*

- *Do you know what the annual real estate taxes are?*

- *Do you know the names of the elementary, middle, and high schools for your neighborhood?*

- *Are there interesting attractions near your home (such as parks, shopping, public transportation, etc.)? If so, how far away?*

- *It sounds like you have a nice home. May I ask why you are selling?*

- *Why are you moving or where are you moving? Do you already have a house in mind? (This can be a question to possibly find a motivated buyer too.)*

- *How long has the home been for sale?*

- *How many offers have you had? Do you mind telling me what the offers were? Were they all cash, or did they offer anything special?*

- *How did you determine the sales prices?*

- *What, if any, were some of the negatives that potential buyers have mentioned regarding your home?*

- *Are there any outstanding mortgages? If so, how much is outstanding?*

- *What are you planning on doing with the money from the sale?*

- *How did you arrive at your asking price?*

- *Are you flexible?*

- *Would you mind if I use a couple of independent sources to assist in determining the market value of the home?*

- *Are you open to creative financing?*

- *If I bring you an all-cash offer, what is the lowest price you would be willing to accept? (The answer to this question is very important as it gets you closer to understanding what the seller's bottom line is.)*

All of these questions will help build your relationship with the seller and give you an idea of what the seller needs the money for, how soon they are looking to sell, and most important, whether they are a truly motivated seller. In most cases, the first answer they give you is not really the lowest number they would be willing or even happy to accept.

Once you have determined if your seller's motivation is right for you, the next step is to figure out the value of the property. At this point, you can simply tell the seller you will make an offer after you do your homework.

Determining the Fair Market Value (FMV)

Now that you know the motivation of your seller, you need to know the Fair Market Value of the property. Understanding how to determine current FMV is something you must understand since this will allow you to estimate the value of any home in just a few moments. In most but not all deals, you'll have to physically examine the property. For other deals, you may want to make the offer first and when the seller accepts your offer, then take a look at the property before you sign a contract.

Before you visit the property, I recommend completing a preliminary analysis first. This is important so you don't let your emotions or impulsive judgments cloud your thinking. Be as objective as possible. The fair market value needs to be realistic, since this will directly influence your ability to complete the deal and make a profit.

To determine the fair market value of a piece of property,

you can visit several websites that provide free home valuations. To get an accurate estimate, I suggest checking the results from at least three different websites:

- Zillow.com

- Homevalues.com

- Realestate.yahoo.com/homevalues

- Realestateabc.com/home-values

- CyberHomes.com

- HomeValueHunt.com

- Homes.com

- Domania.com

- Homegain.com

When you visit these websites, just type in the street address, city, and state, and in some cases, the number of bedrooms, bathrooms, and square footage, to determine a market value for a particular address.

By using multiple websites, you will come up with a range of preliminary property values. Unless there are unusually superior features about a home that increase its value, the recent sale prices and market timing of comparable homes in the neighborhood should give you a fair market value. Depending on the demand in the market, aim for the mid- to mid-low range for the market value. In a down market, use the low end of the range.

With so few sold properties nowadays, fair market value can be difficult to measure. In the past, investors looked to previously sold properties using resources like comparables from realtors, appraisers, and even the taxed value of homes. Gather addresses and phone numbers of homes in the area of your subject property and ask owners or their realtors the following questions:

- Reason for selling

- FMV

- Price

- Square feet (sq/ft)

- Beds/baths

- Amenities

Combine this information with estimates from online resources, your knowledge of real estate in the area, and information from your real estate agent. Remember, even though the market value of a property may have been $200,000 two years ago, you need to determine the accurate value for today's market. In Phoenix, where I live, I've seen houses drop by over 50% in a two-year period! Make sure the seller is aware of any such significant decrease in value, way ahead of time.

Your *killer* real estate agent can also help you determine a property's FMV. Just make sure you use more than one indicator to come up with the price. Great agents will use their own factors to get you an FMV, and if you want them to use a strategy that you come up with, they can do that as well. All of this stuff that is taking you a while to read and understand literally takes minutes in the real world to figure out. Yes, minutes!

Before you actually submit your offer, remember this. Like anything in life, from riding your first two-wheel bike, your first kiss, your first job, to being a parent, you were moving through unknown, scary, unchartered waters.

But once you did it a few times it became second nature. This is no different. This may be new and completely foreign to you, but I can assure you that for the right real estate agent this is common everyday business, and soon it will be a walk in the park for you too.

Physical Examination of the Property

There are two strategies for examining properties. One, you never look at the property until you have an accepted offer. This saves you time from looking at property for which the owner has unrealistic expectations and your offer may be turned down anyway. Two, you feel more secure looking at the property before making the offer. This lets you see ahead of time what flaws a property may possess. Either way, before we spell out exactly how to structure your offer and what price to give, we will go over how to examine properties.

Eventually, you need to walk through and evaluate the property to determine its value and physical condition. You need to see whether it's worth investing your time to get involved with this seller and property (both of which may have unusual characteristics that may cause you to think otherwise).

Take a notepad or a voice recorder during your walk-through and take detailed notes of unique positive selling features the seller may have neglected to tell you about. You may also want to note any maintenance items that might turn off potential buyers. Remember, seemingly negative items could make this the perfect handy man special and the reason you may be able to purchase the property for 50% off its FMV. Taking good notes and staying organized can only help you.

Use the following checklist as a guide for major items to inspect (or go to **www.deangraziosi.com/propertyinspection** and download a free, more complete list).

EXTERIOR

• Roof—check for discolored areas that indicate patches or areas that may need to be replaced.

• Foundation—look for cracks that indicate settling.

• Walls—check for dry rot, mold, mildew, or termite damage; look for crumbling or missing mortar between bricks.

• Chimney—look for crumbling, discolored, or missing mortar that could indicate an unstable building.

INTERIOR

• Windows—check that all windows open and close properly; check for leaks or signs of water damage.

• Doors—check the alignment of doors to make sure they close properly; out-of-alignment doors could indicate settling of the foundation.

• Walls—look for signs of discoloration or fresh paint, which could be used to cover up a problem.

• Plumbing—check all bathroom, kitchen, and laundry fixtures for leaks, corrosion, and cracks. Look under sinks for water damage or leaks. Check drainage of all sinks and tubs and turn on all faucets.

• Appliances—turn on all appliances and let them run to make sure they work properly (air conditioners, heaters, etc.). Turn on each stove burner, run the dishwasher, turn on the oven to make sure all appliances staying with the property work correctly.

• Electrical—check the "main box" for loose or burned wiring, which would indicate shorts to the system. Check each outlet to ensure it's working.

• Water heater—look for rust, water damage, or corrosion on pipes and around the unit. Check for gas leaks or "rotten egg" smells.

• Basement—look for mold and mildew.

It really does not matter if the seller is or is not realistic about his/her selling price, because you will know what the property is worth and what you want to offer. If the seller is stuck on selling his property for $250,000 and your independent analysis says the house is objectively worth $200,000, and you feel it needs some fix-ups that you estimate at $5,000 and there are no other mitigating circumstances (for example the house has an outstanding view or some other unique feature that adds value), then you might be wasting your time with this house. Or you may submit an offer in writing at the price you are willing to lock it up on under contract and move on.

Once you've had an opportunity to examine the property and have figured out its market value, you might want to share the objective data with the seller. The purpose of this discussion (without upsetting the seller) is to reach a common understanding of the true, objective market value of the seller's home

The sale price needs to be objective because the appraised value and mortgage loan will provide the ultimate reality check for all parties in this transaction, which can be especially critical when executing a no money down deal. Many sellers ask a price they "wish" to get based on emotions instead of facts. Being transparent in your finding shows that you are the expert and have a calculated way to come up with a fair value for what the property is worth.

If you make an offer but find there is not enough room to make the money you want, drop the deal and move on to the next property. In this type of down market, there are way too many properties to waste time on a deal that is doomed from the start.

If you can make an offer prior to looking at the property (with the condition of looking at it as a stipulation), you can find out if the seller will be flexible in price. You can find out whether it is even possible to lock it up on contract or if the seller is determined to sell for a price he or she will never get.

At this point, you can make an offer in writing, on the phone, or in person. Compared to just a few years ago, you can be extremely aggressive in your offer.

Don't be afraid to offer 20%, 30%, 40%, or even 50% off the current fair market value. Or you can simply offer $5,000, $10,000, $15,000, or $20,000 less than a price you feel you could sell to someone else in a hurry.

You may be asking yourself, "How do I know if this could sell fast?" Well, hold on for a moment and I'll give you some more information on knowing a killer deal.

Making Your Offer

Taking everything into consideration, you can create a system that will allow you to easily and always come up with an offer and price you are willing to pay that makes it profitable for you.

What I'm about to teach you is so simple that you'll probably read it and say, "Well, heck, Dean! I could have done that without reading this book!" The truth is that maybe you could and maybe you couldn't, but unless you did—you haven't! So pay attention and start making some money this week.

Once you have the fair market value, combined with all the other outside elements, you come up with your offer by subtracting a percentage from it.

Let's say you're looking at a cute three-bedroom, two-bath house (3BR, 2BA) that has an FMV of $100,000. Soon we will show you how to find a buyer in advance or feel confident that you could find a buyer fast because you found a great deal that other people want.

For finding this killer deal, let's say you want to make $5,000.

The equation is easy.

(FMV) <minus> (FMV x Percentage Off) = (Your Offer Price)

So in our example of the $100,000 house, let's say once you have this property locked up you want to sell the house at 10% off its FMV so that it's extremely attractive to buyers and sells fast. (I am being conservative. In a down market like today, you can get a lot more aggressive and get a much better deal at 20%, 30%, or 40% or more off.)

Plugging in a value of 10% or 0.10 into the equation calculates the amount at which you want to offer the property to a future buyer: $90,000.

$100,000 <minus> (100,000 x 0.10) = $90,000

Now, should you think that the house also needs around $2,500 in repairs like carpet and paint, which the new buyer will need to do, then that can be deducted as well.

$90,000 <minus> ($2,500 <minus> repairs) = $87,500

Subtract the amount of the profit you want, such as a $5,000 profit (if you get the house for a bigger discount or want to make more. This amount can be adjusted accordingly), and you get a price to make your offer. Such as:

$87,500 <minus> $5,000 (profit you want to make) = $82,500

So your offer in this case would be $82,500.

Or, go to **www.deangraziosi.com/fmvcalc** and calculate the profit, rehab costs, and offer price.

If your offer is accepted, you could make a $5,000 profit in 14 to 30 days, in a win-win situation for everybody. With an accepted offer, you can lock that property up on contract and make yourself money, just by being smart enough to lock a property up in ANY type of market. If $5,000 doesn't excite you, consider that this whole process can take only 1 to 8 hours of your time.

You could do as few deals as one a month and add $60,000 to your income over a year, and that's only if you make $5,000 on each deal. There is a lot more profit to be made in today's market if you lock up properties at an even steeper discount or sell the property at a higher price. Just weeks before writing this paragraph, Matt Larson did several deals like this literally in just a handful of hours, working hand in hand with his real estate agent and made over $37,500 net—net income that went into his bank account. You will learn exactly how he did it very shortly.

Tips on how to submit an offer to the seller

So, using the calculations and all the other "ingredients" you've just learned, you now have a solid system to come up with the amount you want to offer to the seller. When placing a super-low offer on a promising property, ask yourself:

1. Is the property in or facing foreclosure?

2. Has the property been on the market for over 90 days?

3. Are the taxes very low in comparison with others like it?

If the property shows low taxes on the MLS sheet, chances are good that an older person owns the property and has lived there for quite a while. When people have been living in one spot for a long time, they usually have more equity and probably never refinanced to pull the equity out. When that is the case, it makes it much easier for them to accept a lower offer, since they do not owe much or anything to the bank.

4. What are key words in the listing description? Such as "must sell, will consider all offers, handyman special, sellers moving, vacant" and so forth.

5. Is the property already priced below value? This shows you sellers are motivated and there is a good chances they will have equity.

Let's go over what you've learned and summarize it here to make sure you know all your options for making the offer directly to the seller or through their real estate agent (or yours).

- You identify the kind of the seller you want to find.

- You determine the seller's motivation to sell, the "reason why."

- You determine the Fair Market Value.

- You do adequate research to make sure your FMV is right.

- If desired, you do a physical examination of the property.

- When these requirements have been satisfied, there are three ways for you to make the offer.

1. You can make a verbal offer over the phone.

2. You can fax/mail a written offer to the seller or his agent.

3. You can have your real estate agent present the offer.

One of three things will then happen. The seller will either say yes, no, or counter your offer with a different offer. In this strategy, "yes" is almost always the only acceptable offer, but there may be exceptions.

You can find an offer sheet template that you can modify and use at **www.deangraziosi.com /contractoffer**.

This may have seemed like a lot of information, but believe me, compared to everything else you could ever do in your life, nothing can make money this fast with so little risk. If you have to read this book three times, take notes, practice, then do it. No one is going to change your financial future but you, and nothing can make you money like real estate, so don't you dare give up on me!

Now that you have digested all of that, I want to share a technique that I've been teasing you with throughout this chapter. I've already covered how to find a real estate agent, and once you find an agent to work with, you can use this formula that Matt has taken and perfected.

Matt Larson took the strategies he learned from my books and my coaching program and created an amazing yet simple system to get his real estate agent to follow his directions, do 95% of the work, and kick up deals unlike anything I have ever seen. What's so amazing about Matt's system is that it hardly takes any effort at all, yet consistently works to find killer deals faster than any other methods. In other words, you get twice as many killer deals with half the amount of effort.

With all you have learned in the previous paragraphs, I feel this is the perfect place to share this strategy with you because now it will make complete sense. If this doesn't get your heart racing, you'd better check your pulse.

Matt's Magic Money Making 25:1 Formula

Here's what you do in a nutshell:

• Have your real estate agent look for 100 properties that suggest a potentially motivated seller.

• Narrow this list of 100 properties to 25 of the most promising ones.

• Have your agent submit offers verbally or through e-mail at 30% to 50% off the asking price.

• Out of those 25 to 30 offers, you'll usually get one accepted offer— that's why we call it 25:1. Now is the time to look at that property to make sure it's in good condition.

• Get the deal locked up on contract and decide to keep the property for yourself or pass it to another buyer for cash (you will learn your options and how to do that soon).

• Buy the property or collect a check for finding this killer deal.

Before we go any further, I need to stress here a hurdle you are going to hit. This is not a hurdle in reality, yet one that is in the head of many real estate agents you may talk to. Many will simply say, "It won't work." Even if you explain it is working for people all across America, they may say, "Well, maybe it will work there but not here." The fact of the matter is that it will work ANYWHERE. It is that particular real estate agent who may not work.

Another successful DG student I met on www.deangraziosi.com told me that when he first started out and approached a real estate agent, the agent immediately told him it would never work. After the agent found out that he was taught this strategy by an "Infomercial Guy," he said it was all a bunch of baloney even though he never read a single page or knew anything about Dean. After bashing my strategy and Dean's books, the agent went on to tell him how tough the real estate market was and how it wasn't easy to make money, even though he had been an agent for over ten years. The DG student went on to make his first deal happen literally less than 20 days later and the agent he chose got to make a nice commission on the property. I am confident he has moved on to many more deals since then.

Before I give the 25:1 strategy, I want you to hear from my real estate agent, Star, on what she thought in the beginning and how she has become a believer.

I'll put this letter up at www.deangraziosi.com/agentletter and you can print it out and give it to real estate agents you are trying to get on board. It's proof, from one real estate agent to another, that the 25:1 strategy works.

Every time an investor approaches a real estate agent, the agent may get preconceived notions of their real intentions and if they are a real player. Luckily, I am just too eager to please and successful to turn anyone away. When Matt Larson walked into my office just three years ago and told me he wanted to buy enough properties so he could retire in 3 years or less, of course I was a bit skeptical. He said his strategy was to find properties that met his criteria and then offer 30% to 50% under fair market value. He said we would be making hundreds of offers, but at the end of the day we would be buying a lot. He said if I would trust him and stick with him, he would stick by me throughout his entire investing career. The stars must have been aligned for Matt, because I just trusted what he had to say and I was ready to step out of the normal routine and go for it. So we started our relationship.

Our process started a little slow. I got Matt's criteria and would submit offers in writing. Lots of them. It worked and we got a few homes. At this point, all my skepticism melted away and I was ready to help perfect a system and help Matt reach his goals while I, of course, got to make money. With a few deals under our belt, I went from submitting offers in writing to making offers through quick phone calls. When presenting such low offers, I would start by reassuring the seller's realtor that we were not trying to insult anyone; rather, I was representing a buyer who could close fast, ethically and honestly. He simply made closing easy for people who need or want to sell below what they originally thought they could get. This approach helped to not offend agents so they wouldn't be so defensive when we spoke.

At first, other agents told me I was crazy. Later, some of those same agents contacted Matt to see if they could get some of his business, but Matt wouldn't do it. Once it became a daily system, I would check my local relationships with other realtors and on-line listings for properties that met Matt's criteria. After doing a few, I knew exactly what deals he was looking for and would not waste his time unless it fit. If it did, we would have a quick phone call, get a price together, and it was back on my plate to call and make that polite but very low offer. We realized that we would get about 1 deal accepted per 25 to 30 deals we submitted, and that number has not changed since day one. This simply works.

In the next few weeks, we should literally be closing on our 50th deal or so. It has been wonderful and I am so glad I was open-minded to a new way of doing my job. It has paid off for both of us, and now it will help so many others who use it.

With 3 years under our belt, our new goal is to purchase or assign at least 100 properties in this upcoming year. By the way, Matt retired from his job three years to the DAY of starting our part-nership. The trust and loyalty that Matt and I have for each other is what makes our relationship so successful and profitable. If any-one says this technique does not work, show them what I just wrote, and if it still does not spark their interest, then find a new agent.

Best, Star

That's the kind of real estate agent you want as a partner.

The first step is to have your agent find up to 100 potential properties that meet your investment criteria, such as homes in a certain 15-mile radius or township, priced between $75,000 and $150,000, and offering two or more bedrooms and bathrooms.

Besides searching for physical criteria, I also tell my real estate agent to look for certain trigger words that indicate a motivated seller. This way I find not only the types of properties I want, but properties that someone wants to sell as soon as possible. Some examples of these trigger words include:

- Motivated seller (obviously)

- REO

- Bank-owned

- Short sale

- Pre-foreclosure

- Handyman special

- Make an offer

- Vacant

- On market for long time

- Selling price below average (indicates a motivated seller)

- Property that looks as if no one is maintaining it anymore

I also have my real estate agent look for lower-than-average property taxes, since this indicates that the owner has held the property for a long time. Long-term owners not only have properties with a lot of equity in them, but they are often motivated to sell because they wish to move and no longer want the property.

Finally, I instruct my agent to look for homes that have been on the market for at least 90 days or more. The longer a home has been on the market, the more motivated a seller will be.

Second, with as much of the information my agent can get from the above questions, I'll sort through this list of 100 properties to find 25 properties I want. There's no hard-and-fast rule for this; just find the properties you like. For example, you may only want to look at homes that include a swimming pool or homes that include over an acre of land, or homes in a certain location.

Third, have your agent submit offers to all 25 to 30 owners. To save time, submit these offers verbally or by e-mail. Always submit an offer 30% to 50% below the asking price. Go to **www.deangraziosi.com/agentscript**

to get the script my agent uses when talking to sellers. The worst that will happen is that the owner will say no. Out of 25 to 30 offers, you'll usually get one homeowner who will either accept your low offer or be willing to negotiate from that low offer. That's the property you want to pursue, since it allows you to buy a home at an incredible discount.

Fourth, take the time to examine the property yourself to check for obvious problems, such as cracked walls or broken windows. Also, check out the neighborhood at different times of the day and week to see if it's the type of neighborhood you like. By waiting to inspect only those properties that have already accepted your low offer, you can prevent wasting time driving around to look at properties that won't accept a low offer.

Fifth, once you receive an accepted offer and like the property, decide on a strategy to use:

• Use the bank's money to buy the property and rent it out for positive cash flow. I've done this with over 30 deals now.

• Use no money of your own to lock the property under contract (you'll learn how to do this shortly), and then assign the contract to someone else. This other person still gets a great property at a discount and you get to put cash in your pocket because you were smart enough to find such a killer deal. (In the next chapter you will learn exactly how that works.)

Remember, motivated sellers are the key to finding killer deals. For example, I once found a house that had four bedrooms and two bathrooms. The house was valued at $130,000, but I bought it for $73,000. The house was owned by an elderly guy who didn't have a lot of family. When he passed away, he gave several million dollars and his home to a great-nephew who lives in Colorado.

When this nephew suddenly got a call that he just inherited a million dollars and a house, the first thing the guy wants to do is sell the house and get the cash. He got a real estate agent, told him he wanted to sell it quickly, and put the home on the market for $120,000.

I put in a low offer for $73,000. The seller owned a house that didn't mean anything to him and he didn't want to pay property taxes on it. Since he wanted to get rid of it fast,he accepted my offer. I now own this home at a huge discount and have a rental income of $375 a month on it. Someday I'll sell if for a massive profit.

To give you an idea how to assign a contract, let me tell you the story of a 23-year old kid who came to me with no experience in real estate. He only made $20,400 a year while living in Southern California, which meant he barely made enough money to survive. He was so desperate to learn about real estate that he even offered me $10,000 to work with him for four days. I basically told him I'd do it for free if he could come out to visit me for a few days.

In four days, I taught him everything I knew, which basically consists of my 25:1 system, detailed in this book. This kid then took that information back to Southern California and within two weeks had his agent put out 90 offers and got 18 counteroffers.

He wound up buying a duplex for $48,000, which was less than half its fair market value. Then he found a single-family home and assigned that contract for $2,000 to another buyer for a quick deal. So out of 18 deals, he made money on 2 of them—and in Southern California, where home prices are so much higher than the rest of the country.

If you're putting in offers all the time, you're going to get those deals. Put in 25–30 low offers and you're bound to get one. It's the law of averages.

• • •

We have used Matt's story, along with many others throughout this book, to show that we should all be open to learning from other people. I have learned so much from students I taught because I know that none of us can know it all or discover it all on our own.

I know these marketing strategies may seem a little tough at first, but they're not,and you need to get it set up so it spits out deals for you automatically. But what excuse would you have not to get started with Matt's 25:1 strategy? None. Go for it!

At www.deangraziosi.com, we have literally thousands of people who visit the site every week. Many novices and successful students share their stories on how they did it, because success is addicting. Here's a fact: When you bought this book, you became a loner among your social circle. By stepping out of the norm, you have ventured into uncharted territory. Many times, even the people who love you may say you're crazy. Unfortunately, that's just human nature, since it's always easier to pull a person who is trying to climb out back in the ditch with you, rather than trying to climb out with him.

But by buying this book, you did something a little different. That's why we created a social environment for all of our students to talk to one another and share the same goals, the same desires, and the same risks to go into real estate investing. At **www.deangraziosi.com**, we are truly a family; sharing everything we can to help the next person.

What I am saying is that I know my strategies work. I know countless students who took my strategies and became insanely successful, and many of them find a niche or improve upon what I taught so they can create their own system. In this book, you get to benefit from my proven strategies as well as many others. And at **www.deangraziosi.com**, the wisdom never stops coming.

In addition, on my site you'll get my weekly video blog, FREE monthly live conference calls with me, monthly newsletter, and so much more. We are here to be the pleasant thorn in your side, letting you know you can do this and change your financial future forever. Plus, at any time you can call to talk to a consultant about becoming a student of my Real Estate Success Academy at 1-800-315-7782.

In the next chapter, you're going to learn how, after you've submitted offers and gotten sellers to say yes, you cash in. Ah, the million dollar answer to how you do that is just a few short pages away.

Summary

Let's review what we've covered in this chapter and the important points to take away:

- A killer deal starts with a motivated seller.

- Every seller has a different motivation for selling.

- You can calculate a fair market value (FMV) for every property using multiple sources (previously sold properties, appraisers, etc.).

- Physically examine a property before making an offer.

Action Steps

Now that you understand what makes a killer deal, let's get started finding them. Even if you don't have a real estate agent yet or even a property you might want to get, I want you to go through the following steps anyway. Think of this as training to get your mind thinking about real estate. The more you think about real estate, the more likely you'll take action and make it happen, so be a doer and make it happen for you!

- Find a property for sale (in the classified ads, on the Internet, etc.) and calculate a fair market value for it using the methods in this chapter. Do this for at least three properties in different parts of town where you might want to look for deals.

- Talk to at least three sellers and find out their motivation for selling.

- Examine at least three different properties. You can even examine your own house from the eye of an investor. Look for problems that could lower your home's value and think of ways to fix those flaws.

- Look in the newspapers at houses that have already sold. Using that sale price, calculate how much over (or under) the new buyer may have paid for that house based on what you believe the fair market value is for a similar house in that area.

Success Story #7: Elena Margaritis

Location: Tucson, AZ

Experience before taking Dean's course: Bought and sold a duplex.

How much profit on your first deal: $25,000 in two weeks, using the exact techniques Dean is sharing in this book. Oh yeah, I didn't use any of my own money to make that profit either.

Favorite part: Feeling like an empowered woman who can take charge and be in control of my own life.

Best quote: "A lot of people say real estate is a numbers business, but I really don't believe that. It's a people business."

Before I discovered real estate, I was pretty much living from paycheck to paycheck. I had just gotten off food stamps and was still pretty desperate. My mom had passed away so the property where I was living was going into probate. I had 30 days to vacate the premises. So with no savings and nowhere to go, I decided to look into real estate and discovered I actually had good credit, despite being a single mom with two teenage kids.

I managed to get a loan and buy a duplex. Now I had a place to live and a tenant paying part of my mortgage. A year later, I sold that duplex and made a profit of $40,000. When I got my inheritance from my mother's estate, I started to look into real estate investing more seriously. I bought tons of books and audio courses, but I found that only Dean's course made it real. The others had good information, but only Dean's books had stories of actual people, which made it real and attainable.

I took an old-school approach and started cruising around the neighborhoods and found a house for sale, but the owner was asking for too much. I knew the area was a good one, but I couldn't afford the asking price so I told the owner to keep me in mind if he didn't sell it. About a month later, he called me and dropped the price by $25,000.

It turned out that the house was now abandoned because the neighbors had petitioned to have the tenants removed since one of the tenants had set the neighbor's garage on fire. Sounds crazy, but that incident actually allowed this deal to happen. The owner lived out of state and just wanted to get rid of the house. I took over the house, did minor cosmetic work to improve the property, and within two weeks I assigned the contract to another person for a $25,000 profit. In my entire life, that was the most money I'd ever made in the quickest amount of time ever.

Other people could have bought that house, but I'm convinced the only reason I got it was because I had built a rapport with the owner. A lot of people say real estate is a numbers business, but I really don't believe that. It's a people business. You solve other people's problems. Treat people like you want to help them and solve their problem, and that makes a difference. As Dean talked about in his book *Be A Real Estate Millionaire*, find people's magic buttons and then push them. In most cases if you do it ethically, the buttons you push are letting them accomplish the goal *they* desire while you can make money.

Besides building rapport, the next most important lesson I learned was to always do your due diligence and examine a property before you buy to make sure it's a good deal. After my success in real estate, I started investigating tax liens. Not knowing what I was doing, I found that many states auction off tax liens over the Internet. I saw a picture of a house in Michigan and bought the tax lien.

From the one picture that I saw, the house didn't look too bad, but if you examine the picture more carefully, you'll see that it's really a dump. Since I was so anxious to get started buying tax liens, I just bought it sight unseen. To this day, I still haven't seen the house in person.

After buying the tax lien, I realized that I needed to sell the house somehow, so I offered it on eBay. I asked for a small, nonrefundable deposit to hold the property for any interested buyers.

The first time someone paid me a deposit, I was ecstatic ,since that meant I could get rid of the house. Unfortunately, when the buyer saw the property in person, he backed out and agreed to let me keep his deposit, which basically gave me my money back from the tax lien.

Two more buyers bought the house, put a deposit down, and then, after seeing the house in person, backed out of the deal. So far, I've sold this house three times, made a profit, and I still have the house, so apparently I'm not the only one who buys homes without due diligence. Now I call this property "the house that never sells."

Unlike many people, I never use a real estate agent since I haven't had a good experience with any of them. I think the key to a real estate agent is to find someone willing to grow with you, one who is willing to try anything. So far, I haven't found one yet who meets my criteria.

I'm still interested in tax liens and also commercial properties. I just want to study about them more before I go at them again. I think you need to find what fits you, I personally know that I don't want to be a landlord and I don't like fixing up and flipping properties either. I love doing wholesaling and assignments. I just like getting in and out as fast as possible with minimum risk. Control everything but own nothing, that's my goal. So far it is working like gangbusters and I love it.

Elena's Success Secrets: This course is the real deal because it brings the human element to real estate with real-life stories that make all the difference in the world. You've got to make mistakes and get through your fear. You're going to make mistakes anyway. If you think you're not going to make mistakes, you're never going to do it. Just do it. Chances are, nobody will ever know you're making mistakes, since they probably don't know any more than you do. Go make mistakes and get that experience because it will just make you more confident for the next deal. And don't forget, do your due diligence!

To see a video of Elena telling her story go to **www.deansmedia.com/elena**

CHAPTER 8

Get Your Deal Finalized and Make Some Money

The hardest part for me in writing this book is explaining what specific steps to take in each chapter. Even though this is my third book, I feel much more adept at teaching what I know by speaking. I feel if we had a few hours together, I could explain everything in this book, easily answer all of your questions, and send you on your way. My challenge in writing is to make sure that after reading each section and chapter, you can say to yourself, "I get it!" This is one of those parts. In writing this book, I want to make investing like following a recipe, but it's not as cut and dry as saying, "Put the water in first, then the flour, etc." Successful real estate investing is rarely this rigid, since every property can be different. Besides, I want you to learn along the way so you innately know how to respond in every situation you may face.

You see, each technique covered in this book is as important as the other. If I help you find a killer deal but can't help you sell it, what good is that? If you don't know how to complete a transaction without using any of your own money, or do not know how to talk to the buyers or sellers, it won't matter how good your ads are, because you need the whole package of capabilities.

I just shared all that with you for a reason. As you go through this chapter, you may scratch your head at some parts and say, "What's next?" I assure you, I'm not leaving any crucial facts out. Everything you need to know is in this book. If you get the impression that something is missing, I just may have chosen to elaborate on it in another chapter.

In the previous chapter, we left off at the point where you've made an offer and got it accepted. In this chapter, we are going to talk about "locking up deals." In other words, get properties under contract so you can put cash in your pocket.

The following five tips are the most common actions to take after your offer has been accepted:

1. If you have not already done so, go look at the property to make sure it fits all your criteria and that it isn't in worse shape than the seller described.

2. If you decide to keep the property, order a whole house inspection. If you plan to sell the equity in the contract (we will explain that shortly) or assign the contract to another buyer, then you can help the buyer order a house inspection. For a list of due diligence, go to www.deangraziosi .com/duediligence so you can help expedite the process and get money in your pocket faster.

3. Double check your calculations to make sure the equity you need is really there.

4. If you are going to "assign the contract" (hand it off to another investor or home buyer without taking possession yourself), contact the person with all your data, such as how much cash flow to expect from monthly rent, how much equity is in it, how big of a discount they'll be getting, etc.

5. If you plan to buy and hold (which you will eventually be able to do based on what you'll learn in the following chapters), prepare it for renters by advertising before it is ready to rent, if possible.

If everything up to this point looks as though you have a motivated seller, a property in good physical condition and in a decent neighborhood, and an accepted offer from the seller, then it is time to discuss one or more of the following agreements to make your no money down deal work:

• Investor Disclosure Statement and Seller's Acknowledgment

• Investor Purchase Agreement/Lead Paint Disclosure Notice (for pre-1978 homes)

• Property Disclosure Statement

• Discharge of Agreement to Purchase Statement

• Assignment Contract

Before we get to the nitty-gritty of contracts, let me explain the two different no money down strategies you can follow. Both strategies are similar in nature but have different advantages, depending on whether your buyer can pay cash (or has financing) or needs to go to a bank for a loan. Once you have a great offer accepted, it's time to get it on contract so you can make some money. I hope that after the next few pages you'll say, "I get it!"—but first things first.

First Things First

I have a lot to teach you in this chapter. You'll learn how to structure the deal using an automated system (much like a recorded message to find sellers in this down market), when you're going to pass it off to a home buyer, and the different classifications of motivated buyers, that is, buyers who have decent credit but were told "NO" by their bank.

You will be able to show them how to get funded, with no extra work for you, so they can purchase the home you found. We will also teach you how to find cash buyers that are actively looking for property to invest in but do not have the skills you're learning now to get the same great deals on properties. (These buyers will be knocking down your doors to get the great deals you can find for them). In fact, the beauty of the system you're learning is you will actually have buyers ready and willing BEFORE you get these homes on contract.

Obviously, a buyer is the last key to a successful deal and making a profit. Before you start learning how to find these motivated buyers, you need to get your deal wrapped up and ready to make you money with the seller. In this section we are going to talk about the techniques for getting a property under contract.

First, let me explain the concept behind these two no money down techniques. They are very similar in nature, yet with subtle differences to make them more efficient for the two types of buyers you will be attracting. These two "contract" or "cash out" techniques will make money in a win-win situation for everyone.

We'll call the first strategy our "Instant Equity Exchange (IEE)," which you'll use when you have a buyer who needs a bank loan.

Our second strategy we'll call the "Assignment," which you'll use if you have a cash buyer or investor who does not need bank financing.

In our Instant Equity Exchange or IEE technique you are going to use all the methods you have learned so far to get an offer accepted at a greatly reduced price. Once the seller says yes, you are going to lock this house up on contract, also known as a "purchase agreement." I suggest a pretty straightforward contract (see the examples below and at **www.dean-graziosi.com/ieecontracts**). One difference is that you will have the contract expire in 14 to 30 days or so. If you can get more time than that, great. You will let the seller know you intend to use your marketing skills to sell this house to another buyer within that time frame.

You will tell them the truth about the unique strategies you have that no one else does for attracting buyers. What will be different is that you will also include an extra 2 documents to be signed by the seller (below) that basically says that if you hand off this great deal to another buyer and back out of your contract you will get paid a pre-set amount upon the closing, which is money that comes out of the new buyer's pockets and doesn't cost the seller a thing. Please note that you are not selling this person's property for him. You are getting this piece of property under contract. At that point, you could purchase it yourself, but you are letting the seller know you may be selling the equity in that agreement and therefore the house may be sold to another individual. (I'll explain this in detail very soon.)

You'll hand this document directly to the attorney or "Title Company"[7] doing the closing, and you will be paid the agreed-upon amount at close of escrow if you pass it along to another buyer. That may have sounded a little confusing so to help you understand it, let's look at an example:

Using my automated system to attract motivated sellers, you run your ad in the local newspaper. You get lots of calls, and one caller is going into foreclosure on a house that has a fair market value of $150,000. After running all your numbers and talking with your real estate agent, you offer $100,000 to the seller. The seller owes less than that to the bank, and is willing to sell rather then lose it all to a foreclosure.

Now that the seller has agreed to your offer you tell him or her that you feel confident you can quickly resell the property, or the equity in the contract, in the next 30 days for $110,000. At this point, you write up a contract that expires in 14, 30, or maybe even 60 days with a sale price of $110,000. (The price of $110,000 includes the amount you will be making for the equity in the contract.) You also have the seller sign an "Investor Disclosure Agreement" (which I'll explain soon) that lists your

---

[7] A company involved in examining and insuring title claims, usually for real estate, on behalf of its customers.

exact intentions as a real estate investor and states very clearly that upon close, you will be paid the $10,000 for the equity you created in the contract. (As explained below, a real estate attorney or your real estate agent can help you with the contract or you can use one of ours.)

As soon as the seller signs all the paperwork, you quickly line up your buyer for that home. Ideally, you will already have a buyer (or even a list of buyers) ready to purchase the equity in your contract and therefore buy that home.

Remember, everything is transparent and out in the open. The seller knows you are doing this to make money. The seller also knows that traditional ways of selling in today's market do not work. You can be positioned as a beacon of hope, not the person stealing a home and simply making money.

You are not serving as a broker or advertising to sell their home for them. Rather you have legally bound this property up on contract, you are acting solely on your own behalf, and you are looking to sell the equity in the deal that you structured for your own benefit. If this sounds a little self-centered, the point to remember is if you didn't come along to do this, they would end up losing it all and killing their credit for years to come.

Now you have a buyer who is ecstatic about getting the home at such a discount. At this point, you let the seller know that their home is going to get sold. The seller will be ecstatic to finally be selling, because they NEED to sell. Just get the seller to also sign the **Discharge of Agreement to Purchase Statement**, (explained below) as a backup, which releases you from the Investor Purchase Agreement and clearly states the exact amount you will be paid upon closing. This may or may not be necessary but is a good idea to use as a backup, and it also doubles as an invoice.

You will keep this Discharge Statement and the Investor Disclosure Statement and submit it to the attorney or Title Company to get paid out of the escrow funds. In this case you would make $10,000 for your knowledge and effort. But this is how you can make $5,000, $10,000, $15,000, $20,000 or more with no money out of your own pocket. You are getting paid to rip up your contract and getting paid for the value in your actions, not for buying the home. (In a more traditional assignment deal, you would not be ripping up the contract at all, rather assigning that original contract to a new buyer for a fee. You will learn all about that very soon.)

To help make this easy to understand, this is what you'll be doing:

- Find a killer deal at 30% to 50% off FMV owned by a motivated seller.

- Lock that deal up on contract, Use the strategy you will learn in chapters 9 and 10 to pass it along to another buyer and get paid because you walked away.

- Deposit money in your bank account!

That's it.

How You Can Make the IEE System Work

Below is a list of the paperwork that would be part of this proposed IEE-type sale. When structuring a deal like this, you will need to have the following agreements signed by both you and the seller:

- Investor Disclosure Statement and Seller's Acknowledgment

- Investor Purchase Agreement, also includes Lead Paint Disclosure Notice

- Property Disclosure Notices

- Discharge of Agreement to Purchase Statement

Investor Disclosure Notice and Seller's Acknowledgment

The Purchase Agreement is the main instrument of the sale so I will explain all the terms and conditions of the sale so everyone is on the same page. But first, I want to explain and show you the Investor Disclosure Notice, which is one of the "extra" quick statements that explains your intentions to the seller and allows you to get paid for the equity in your contract.

Let's say you have completed your pre-screening discussions with the seller and your preliminary analysis of the property looks promising. Now is the time to review the Investor Disclosure Notice with the seller. The best and most successful approach in business is to be transparent and provide full disclosure about your intentions.

That is the purpose behind the Investor Disclosure Notice. It also serves as a sort of contract to make sure you get paid for your efforts. This disclosure clearly explains to the seller that you are an investor and binding this deal up on contract so you can make money. The by-product will be that their home could get sold in 30 days or less, and in some cases as quick as 7 to 14 days. This is why this Disclosure Notice is short and specifically outlines your intentions.

When talking to the seller, it's important that they sign this document. That is why—and I can't stress the importance of this enough—it is crucial that you make your intentions apparent from the start.

Since you have developed a relationship over the telephone, through a real estate agent, or e-mail, this is an appropriate time to review the Investor Disclosure Statement. You have previously discussed the concept of this program with the seller and the seller should know your intentions, so nothing will be a shocker. Seller will know by now and confirm with this agreement that you're an investor with fully disclosed intentions of getting his house sold. You have also told the seller there are some agreements required to sign in order for this process to work. So now is the appropriate time to sit down and review those agreements.

Always remember that you are doing more for most of the sellers you meet than anyone else. In many cases, without you they could lose their home and get nothing but bad credit for ten years.

This form along with others can be downloaded for FREE at my investor's resource website **www.deangraziosi.com/ieecontracts**. But let me show you now, and then I'll explain it more after you take a look.

Investor Disclosure Statement and Seller's Acknowledgment

Date _____

Investor hereby discloses to Seller:

It is understood by Seller that Investor intends to purchase Seller's property described below (hereinafter referred to as "the Property") with the full intention of immediately reselling the Property to another party. Investor will sell said Property to another party for approximately $_____ more than the amount for which the Investor purchased the Property from the Seller. It is further understood that Investor intends to earn a profit in this resale transaction.

This sale shall be contingent upon the Investor finding a Buyer that shall qualify for financing according to accepted criteria of _____ and its funding sources.

Seller agrees to sign any other forms that are required to close the transaction and generally cooperate with the Investor to effect the sale.

Seller will allow showings of the property by Investor and/or Investor's representatives at reasonable hours agreeable to both Seller and Investor.

Seller may not show the property or receive any other backup offers while there is contract in effect with Investor.

Subject Property:

Street Address_____

City_____ State _____ Zip Code_____

Legal description of the Property:

_____

Investor _____ Date _____

Investor _____ Date _____

Seller _____ Date _____

Seller _____ Date _____

You can see that this is a very straightforward document. The blanks to be filled in are self-explanatory. You are the Investor in this case and the property owner is the Seller.

In the first paragraph, you are disclosing the approximate amount of profit you are going to make from this transaction. This amount can be figured by all the due diligence you have done and what you think the market will bear, or simply the realistic fair market value that you have previously discussed with the Seller.

Finally, both parties (all owners of record for the house—usually, it's the husband and wife) will sign and date the agreement. I recommend you have two copies of this agreement, one for you and one for the seller.

This important document needs to be signed first, as it clearly outlines for the seller your intention as an investor in this transaction. Once you have reviewed and signed the Investor Disclosure Notice and Seller Acknowledgment, the next step is to complete the Investor Purchase Agreement, and then write up an offer to purchase the seller's property, as discussed below.

Investor Purchase Agreement

In connection with the Investor Disclosure Statement and Seller's Acknowledgment agreement, you will then review and complete the Investor Purchase Agreement or "contract." You can use a state-approved Real Estate Purchase and Sales Agreement or the Agreements online at my FREE investor resource site: **www.deangraziosi.com/purchaseagreement**.

Completing the Investor Purchase Agreement With the Seller

Before we go through this, remember that an experienced real estate agent will have seen hundreds of these agreements and have templates on file.

Also, if you are using an attorney for your deals, he or she will know these contracts as well, so don't get overwhelmed by the details. I know it may be a little boring to learn this, but do it anyway.

Take notes and be educated on the details, even if you never really draft a contract yourself (in most instances that is always the case). It is always good to be informed, but in most cases, this contract will be filled out by someone else after you express your exact intentions.

Let's discuss a few specifics of the purchase agreement. Remember, most of the rest of the contract is standard and won't need to be touched.

Your offer/contract to Seller has (but isn't limited to) the following key points:

• **Your name as Buyer and the Seller's name right at the top of the contract.**

• **The amount you are paying for the property and that your offer to the Seller is a cash offer**. (In many cases the new buyer will be paying cash, and if not you can explain the details of financing to the seller.

This will never be a deal breaker if the money is there on time.)

• **Earnest Money Clause.** The earnest money clause is an extremely powerful section of the agreement. It lists the parties, describes the property, the kind of deed, the price, the earnest money deposit amount, the terms of payment, and many other conditions. Some earnest money agreements provide that the buyer will lose his or her deposit by backing out of the deal, or even allow the seller to force the buyer to purchase the real estate. Yet we have a way to make this clause a very positive thing and serve as an exit clause for you.

• **Your offer expires in 14 to 30 days** (or whatever number of days you agree on). I'll explain how to wrap that in to the Earnest Money Clause and give you a strategic exit plan that will cost you nothing while explaining exactly your plan to the seller.

• **Most of the rest of the agreement is boilerplate standard.** Go over it with your real estate agent or attorney.

In the Earnest Money Clause, it will state that you, the purchaser, agrees to put up a certain amount of earnest money (good faith deposit) at the time of signing this agreement. (I'll explain more about earnest money in a little bit.) For now, write zero in the blank.

You'll go on to fill in the blank for the title company (for example, First American Title, or an attorney's name if you live in a state where lawyers handle this process). Next, fill in the blank for "Additional earnest money in the amount of" (and this is where you can write in an additional amount of money if needed to make the deal work—but not necessary). Generally, this amount is no more than 1 percent of the sales price, not to exceed $1,500, due 14 to 30 days later from the date you and the seller sign this agreement.

If you have to obligate yourself to some earnest money, try to set it as low as possible, such as between $500 and $1,500. Try to make it so the money doesn't come out of your pocket. Simply fill in the amount of earnest money you decide on that will be paid in 14 or 30 days—this should be the same amount of time listed on the purchase agreement. Therefore, no earnest money is due up front and you essentially have a grace period of 14 to 30 days before you have to come up with any earnest money. This notifies both parties that earnest money will be paid, just not upon signing. And if earnest money is not paid in the 14 or 30 days, the agreement becomes null and void. If all goes well, you will find a Buyer and receive earnest money from him, which can satisfy the earnest money requirement with the Seller without taking any money out of your own pocket. If for some reason you can't find a buyer, you can both walk away with no out-of-pocket costs.

A word of caution: Do not deposit your earnest money with the escrow agent unless you have an agreement with a Buyer who wants to purchase the home and has paid earnest money which you can then use as earnest money in 14 to 30 days with the Seller.

Otherwise, if you put up earnest money without having a signed deal with a Buyer to resell the property, you risk losing your earnest money. That's the beauty of the system: you never have to use your own money. You are using the Buyer's money to pay the earnest money to the Seller.

Once you make the offer, you need to double check that the contract states that you have a 14- to 30-day contingency. (Basically, if you cannot find a buyer to purchase your equity in the contract within that time period, the Purchase Agreement becomes null and void.) Remember, with today's tough circumstances for selling a home getting an extension from the seller is easier than ever. Especially when you are honest and keep in constant communication with the seller.

Once you have a signed agreement in place with the seller, you want to keep in touch with the seller during that period of time. It's crucial to keep the seller informed at all times to help him feel comfortable with the process. You want to avoid a situation where sellers feel like they just signed an agreement tying their house up for 14 to 30 days, and then they don't know what is going on. So, communicate often with sellers.

I recommend contacting the seller daily or every other day, or however often the seller wants to hear from you (by e-mail, text, telephone, or fax). Furthermore, stay organized. Even if you are a naturally unorganized person, stay organized with this transaction. I can promise you that just one of these transactions could make you as much money as many people make working a 9-to-5 job they despise for many, many months. When done right, this process can be completed in just hours of actual time.

Keep track of your communications with all parties during a transaction (from start to finish) by saving all e-mail and other written correspondence. Write down detailed notes of all telephone calls (even if you don't connect with the seller, make a note that you called and left a voice-mail message) and text communications. This is just a smart way of staying organized in business and documenting your good service. Think of this as a critical part of your successful business model.

Here is a snapshot of a traditional first page of the Purchase Agreement. They will all look a little different but all contain the same exact information. Not as difficult as it may seem.

Option To Purchase Real Estate Agreement

This Agreement is made on the [day] of [month], [year],
Between

[sellers full name]
of [address], [seller],

And

[buyers full name]
of [address], (buyer),

The Seller now owns the following described real estate, located
at [insert full property address] [city or town], [state]:

For valuable consideration, the Seller agrees to give the Buyer and exclusive option to buy this property for the following price and on the following terms:

1. The Buyer will pay the Seller $_____ for this option. this amount will be credited against the purchase price of the property if this option is exercised by the buyer. If the option is not exercised, the Seller will retain this payment.

2. The option period will be from the date of this Agreement until the [day] of [month], [year].

3. During this period, the Buyer has the option and exclusive right to buy the Seller's property mentioned above for the purchase price if $_____. The Buyer must notify the Seller, in writing, of the decision to exercise this option.

4. Attached to this Option Agreement is a completed Contract for the Sale fo Real Estate. If the Buyer notifies the Seller, in writing, of the decision to exercise the option within the option period, the Seller and Buyer agree to sign the Contract for the Sale of Real Estate and complete the sale on the terms of the Contract.

Property Disclosure Notices

A Property Disclosure Statement is exactly what it sounds like. It is the part of all real estate transactions in which the seller lets any prospective buyer know of any issues with the home, such as leaks, bad appliances, cracks in foundation, or whatever they know. To make it really easy to understand, I found an actual Disclosure from a closing I did in New York, and here it is exactly word for word:

PURPOSE OF STATEMENT:
This is a statement of certain conditions and information concerning the property known to the seller. This Disclosure Statement is not a warranty of any kind by the seller or by any agent representing the seller in this transaction. It is not a substitute for any inspections or tests and the buyer is encouraged to obtain his or her own independent professional inspections and environmental tests and also is encouraged to check public records pertaining to the property. A knowingly false or incomplete statement by the seller on this form may subject the seller to claims by the buyer prior to or after the transfer of title. In the event a seller fails to perform the duty prescribed in this article to deliver a Disclosure

Prior to the signing by the buyer of a binding contract of sale, the buyer shall receive upon the transfer of title a credit of $500 against the agreed upon purchase price of the residential real property.

"Residential real property" means real property improved by a one to four family dwelling used or occupied, or intended to be used or occupied, wholly or partly, as the home or residence of one or more persons, but shall not refer to (a) unimproved real property upon which such dwellings are to be constructed or (b) condominium units or cooperative apartments or (c) property on a homeowners' association that is not owned in fee simple by the seller.

I've included more on this in the auction section in chapter 11, but for a copy simply go to **www.deangraziosi.com/disclosurestatement**.

Discharge of Agreement to Purchase

Okay, this is the last piece of paper that you will get signed once you have found a motivated buyer who wants the property. You will go to the seller, who already knew your intentions, and let him know that you have a buyer. From my experience in buying and selling property in a down market, this is the point where you will see the happiness on the desperate seller's face when you let him know his home is going to be sold.

At this point you will be basically assisting the seller and the new buyer in drafting an all-new "standard" purchase agreement between them that matches what everyone has already agreed to.

Once the new contract is signed, you will be ripping up the original contract between you and the seller. You will keep the Investor Disclosure Statement and Sellers Acknowledgment Agreement signed by seller and get the seller to sign a Discharge of Agreement to Purchase statement that will also act as your invoice to be paid at closing.

No need to overexplain this because the statement below explains it pretty clearly.

Discharge of Agreement to Purchase Statement

Investor's name: Platinum Real Estate LLC

Address: 103 West 1st Avenue

City, State Zip: Anywhere, AZ 98765

Seller's Name			Invoice #:
	John & Mary Smith		Invoice Date
Address			
	123 N. Main Street		
City, State Zip	Anywhere, AZ 98765		

DATE	DESCRIPTION	AMOUNT	TOTAL
	Agreement Discharge Fee		
	Investor/Buyer, **Platinum Real Estate LLC** , releases, makes null and void an existing contract/option with **John & Mary Smith** (Seller) dated **(input date of the agreement)** . The fee for such services is $**10,000** to be paid at the closing of the sale of Seller's property located at **123 N. Main Street, Anywhere, AZ 98765** . Closing/Escrow Agent is hereby authorized to pay invoice directly to Buyer at the above address at the close of escrow.		
			$10,000.00
	TOTAL DUE		

Seller Signature: **John Smith & Mary Smith (both signatures of sellers)**

Date: **(date you and seller sign documents substituting final/end Buyer)**

At this point, you would basically hand the two "extra" agreements to the closing agent, title company, or attorney and be paid your agreed-upon amount at close of escrow or at the closing. That's it.

So to recap:

- You found a killer deal at 30% to 50% off.

- You explain your intentions to the seller.

- You locked it up on contract with a few extra pieces of paper with full disclosure.

- You use the strategies in the next two chapters to find a buyer for the property and get it sold.

- You match the seller up with a new buyer, you rip up your original agreement, hand the "extra" paperwork to the closing agent and get paid your agreed-upon amount at close of escrow.

- Done deal, move on to the next one.

I may have jumped ahead a little due to the last piece of paper to be signed, so let me briefly go over what you do once you have the agreements in place . . .

Now remember, if it is an amazing deal and you want to use the strategy of buying, renting, cash flowing, and selling when the market turns at a point before you find a buyer, you have the legal right to purchase that property yourself. If the no money down strategy fits your goals or makes you more comfortable, then you are on the right path for profits sooner than you might think.

These agreements also give you the right to resell the property and the equity in your contract. As outlined in the Investor Disclosure Notice and Seller Acknowledgment, you have clearly stated your intentions to re-sell the property. Now you can advertise for buyers in the same way that you advertised for sellers. You'll learn those techniques in the following chapters.

One great thing about this strategy is that you will soon learn how to find buyers in advance and make these deals happen super-fast, in fact, mere hours in many cases.

That's right! Hours.

Matt Larson always finds his buyers first and it works tremen-dously well. I will reveal what he shared with me when I asked him to describe his method of finding buyers in the next chapter.

By tying up the property with the seller, you have the legal right to resell the property even though you haven't closed on the property with the seller. In legal terms, this agreement provides equitable conversion.

Equitable conversion allows you to sign the agreement to purchase a piece of property while giving you specified ownership rights, including the right to resell the property to someone else for a profit.

Note: It has become incredibly difficult to assign properties to buyers who need a bank loan and get paid at closing because lenders are not experienced in allowing this practice.

This is a creative and legal way to avoid that issue with lenders. When the circumstances are right and executed properly, an "assignment" deal can be a quick way to put cash in your pocket and that is why it is strategy number two.

Remember, a Purchase Agreement is similar across the entire country.

What you have learned here is that through an attorney, your real estate agent, or you directly, you can tailor a deal and spell out all the pieces that protect you and the seller and explain exactly how this unique deal will work.

The Assignment

The "IEE" strategy that we just covered is a great strategy to use for buyers who need to go to the bank. The old-school way of doing this was to simply have a basic Purchase Agreement that has your name on it as the Buyer along with the phrase "and/or assignee."

Take a look at how simple this is:

SAMPLE REAL ESTATE PURCHASE CONTRACT (RESIDENTIAL)

STATE OF _____Arizona_____ ; COUNTY OF _____Maricopa_____

1. PARTIES: _Big Bob The Owner_ (Seller) agrees to sell and convey to ImaRichNow Properties, LLC by John Doe **and/or assignee** _____ (Purchaser) and Purchaser agrees to buy from Seller the Property described below.

2. PROPERTY: (a) *Land:* Address: _____ [insert full address] or more specifically described as: (Legal description goes here:)

You are simply assigning the contract of a great piece of property you found to a new buyer and getting paid an amount you think is fair for giving up your rights to buy that home. Although this is still a great strategy, it does not work with many banks. So that is why you learned the IEE strategy to avoid that problem (or else I would have you use this strategy all the time, since it is a bit cleaner and easier). So when a buyer or investor has cash, then let's go with the "Assignment" strategy.

Basically, people have been using assignment clauses for years, since they can be extremely profitable, especially with all the techniques you now know to find killer deals that most people don't know how to do. Now I am going to suggest that you use this strategy when you have a cash buyer.

I know I often repeat myself when I say you will soon learn how to find these cash buyers and non-cash buyers as well. And once you know how to do this, you will want to create a Master List of cash buyers and buyers who need funding. Then go through each list to decide how to structure the deal with the seller, whether you should use the IEE model or the Assignment.

To further promote Matt Larson as the poster child of someone following my strategies to a *T*, and actually tweaking and improving upon them to fit his needs, I am attaching the following story he posted at www.deangraziosi.com to help others, just like you, understand how to make assignment deals work. The greatest thing about success is that once you achieve it, it feels just as amazing to share what you know as it did structuring your first deal. I know that firsthand, and now so many of my students feel the same way. You're next! After you finish reading this, I will give you details on how to make this strategy work for you.

Matt Larson's Advice: The Best Scenario Possible When Assigning Contracts

Now that I have been assigning contracts, I have learned a ton from the entire process. I see a lot of people on Dean's website who want to assign contracts, but they are struggling to get through that first one.

By the way, once you get through the first one, it gets really easy after that. To get you started, here is a list of the ways to assign contracts with the least amount of resistance. Just follow these steps and victory is yours. Remember, it's not that hard to do and don't let anyone ever tell you otherwise.

1. Find your buyers first. The buyers who will pay cash should be at the top of your list. The reason is that some banks will not let their clients close on a contract that is not written in their name.

2. Lock up deals that are For Sale By Owner. If the house is listed with an agent, then make sure the house isn't bank owned. I'm not saying bank-owned properties can't be assigned; I am just saying that it is much easier to assign deals that aren't. All you do is sign your name and after your name you write "and/or assigns." The place you write this is on the line that says "Buyer" at the top of the page (which is right above the legal description of the property). You only have to write "and/or assigns" in this spot and nowhere else.

3. Get a real estate attorney in your area who is familiar with assignments of contracts involved with the closing. This is a must. A title company does not have "legal counsel" to be able to handle an assignment. An attorney does. Once you lock up a deal with "and/or assigns" and you have a Buyer in place, call your attorney and give him a copy of the contract and the phone number of the buyer. He will do the rest of the work for you and call you if he needs more information.

DO NOT USE A TITLE COMPANY TO HANDLE AN ASSIGNMENT OF CONTRACT. A title company's job is to make sure a clean title is delivered; they are not in the business to give "legal counsel."

That is why some title companies will tell you it is illegal to do assignments because it is illegal for them to change contracts since they are not lawyers.

I hope I am making this clear. At the point when the attorney starts getting the assignment put together, your new buyer will send a check to the attorney.

You can do one of two things:

• Have the check made out to the attorney and then the attorney will in turn write you a check (the best way).

• Have the buyer make the check out to you or your corporation, and the attorney can hold the check until closing.

Note: Some title companies will do assignment of contracts, but they are few and far between. It is only a matter of time before they won't handle them any longer.

I have met several people who used to do assignments and then one day, their title company told them they weren't allowed to do them anymore. When I explained to them why, they looked at me with a new sense of hope. Now, after learning what I taught them, they are off to the races.

4. Make sure you help your new buyer run through his due diligence checklist. The buyer needs to have the property inspected, get insurance ready, etc.

I hope all of you realize this is LEADING EDGE information. This isn't stuff I have read somewhere or stuff that someone else is using. This is information that I have learned as I have been doing assignments.

You will not find this information anywhere else. I have discovered several "mistakes" that the biggest gurus in the country were making when teaching assignments of contracts. I realized why so many people have failed when trying to complete one. Please use this information and go make money. I want you to make money, Dean wants you to go make money, and America wants you to go make money. Go out there and accomplish your goals and dreams. Get it done!

• • •

In doing an assignment deal, use all the techniques we have shared with you thus far to find killer deals. You may have found it through using our automated system, or by having your real estate agent flood your area with offers at 30% to 60% off FMV. Perhaps your neighbor or someone you met at the gym or at work might bring you a killer deal if they know you do real estate investing. It really does not matter where the deal came from. All that matters is that you found a killer deal! Most people can't find one, and now you are going to help someone else get a great deal while you get paid for exercising your newfound talents.

Working backwards, you will know which deals you can swiftly and painlessly hand off to a cash buyer. In this instance, you will simply do the same thing and get the property under contract (purchase agreement). You will use a similar purchase agreement as you learned about under the IEE strategy. You do not have to explain to the seller your exact intentions unless there is a need to do so. You need to put an exit clause in the contract, such as "contingent upon bank financing," or simply put an expiration date on it that says if you don't close by a certain date, the contract is void, giving yourself plenty of time to make the deal happen.

You can also push the escrow money off for 14 to 30 days as well, and if you don't give escrow money by a certain time, then it is void as well. This is very similar to what you learned for a purchase agreement with the IEE strategy, except this contract will simply have those magic words "and/or assignee" in the first part of the contract.

In an up market, when anyone can sell a house, people are less likely to do a deal like this. But in a down market, things are very different. When people are used to trying to sell a house themselves for months and months, or have been using an agent who delivered no results for them (because they simply stuck a sign in the yard and placed it on the MLS), they get tired of trying. These sellers are open to anything that can work, and this does work.

So you simply get the contract drawn up (see the example at www.dean-graziosi.com/assignmentcontract) along with the phrase "and/or assignee" in the appropriate place. Then you work out how much you want to make on the deal while still making it a great deal for the new buyer. Merely get a check from the new buyer to hand over the contract, or arrange it so he does it at closing through the attorney.

- So a quick recap for the "Assignment"-type deal:

- Find a killer deal using the strategies you have learned.

- Agree on price by evaluating the property and knowing what you can make on it.

- Get a purchase agreement signed with the words "and/or assignee" in it.

- Use an attorney to help make this deal happen, not a title company.

- Get a property disclosure statement signed, as explained in the "IEE" section.

- Assign the deal to a buyer on your list you have found from techniques you will learn in the following sections.

- Get a fat check for making this deal happen.

Now, take a moment to read a story from one student who followed what we told her and scored on her first deal. You will want to take notes, or highlight sections on how this real-life student put these techniques in place and cash in her pocket.

I Did It!!!!!
My First $10,000.00
Assignment

I have just done my first assignment for $10,000. I cannot believe it. I bought Dean's book 3 months ago and I am about to close my first deal.

Here's the kicker . . . the investor that I just assigned my deal to has set a goal to purchase 25 properties in my area. This assignment is #9 and he wants me to be his bird dog and find him 16 more properties. AHHHHHHHHH! I am so excited!!!!

I could have never have done this without my Dean Graziosi family, thank you everyone!

Here is what I did for this deal.

I called rental ads and asked the owner if he would consider selling the property if I could offer him cash and close in 30 days. He said that he would not only sell this one but he had 3 more he wanted to sell. I am telling you . . . call the "for rent" ads in your local paper. Most of them are people who cannot sell their house in today's market and are trying to rent so they can continue to pay the mortgage.

I also put an ad on craiglist that said, "Investor needed for multiple investment properties." You would not believe how many calls I got. I built my buyers list in leaps and bounds overnight.

My husband and I went to look at the properties that we inquired about in the rental ads. We did a cost evaluation (copy of one in Dean's book) on each one. Before we went, I researched the property to find out how much it was last sold for. This gave me a good idea of how much negotiating I could do on the price.

One of the properties was a four-unit quadplex for $249,000. We spoke to the owner and found out that he had to get the full amount because he had taken out multiple loans on the property and had to pay them off.

The ARV on the property is $439,000.00. (*That stands for After Repair Value: the value of the property after all repairs are completed —Dean*)

I had my realtor run comps on similar properties that recently sold in the area. The closest comp was another quadplex that was exactly the same, only it had garages for each unit instead of off-street parking. That property recently sold for $469,000.

I locked the deal in 3 days later for the full amount. No money down!

I added $10,000 to the price and called my investors and offered the property to them at $259,000.

I assigned the deal 13 days after I locked it, knowing I WOULD GET A CHECK FOR $10,000!!! I sold the property for $259,000. It needed approximately $30,000 in repairs, so after closing costs, etc., the investor will have approximately $139,000 in instant equity. The rental income on this property is $3,500 per month.

I still can't believe it's for real!

NO GUTS . . . NO GLORY!

Do not fear, for I am with you; do not be dismayed, for I am your God. I will strengthen you and help you; I will uphold you with my righteous right hand. Isaiah 41:10

Carol Stinson

• • •

After reading Carol's story, I hope you can see yourself in the same position. It's not magic. It just took me a lot of time, research, and trial and error to figure this out and provide you with a path and a plan to do yourself. If it seemed a little confusing, read it again or call one of our trained consultants at 1-800-315-7782 and see if you qualify to be in my Real Estate Success Academy.

I have no doubt that if left you on your own in a year or so of trial and error, you could figure out exactly what I just shared with you. But with the smart and tiny investment you made in this book, your learning curve just got put on steroids.

Summary

In this chapter, you learned specific steps to take so you can close a deal. I know a lot of these legal documents in this chapter may seem complicated and scary, but they basically protect everyone's interests so that everyone understands the deal. What I want you to take away from this chapter is:

Always examine the property yourself before committing to a deal.

Order a professional inspection at the expense of the seller

You can make money by either buying and holding the property yourself, or assigning the contract to another buyer.

Always be open and transparent about your intentions and goals.

Make sure you understand which agreements you need to use and when.

Action Steps

Whew! I know this chapter had lots of solid material involving agreements so if you don't understand something, go back and read it as many times as necessary, until it makes sense. If you still need help, feel free to call my coaching staff (1-800-315-7782) and talk to someone who can walk you through the steps and explain what different agreements do and why you might need them.

The point is that every deal needs agreements. That way everyone understands exactly what is happening and what they're getting out of the deal so it's a win-win situation for both sides. Since you might not have an actual deal in front of you right now, I want you to pretend that you do and take action on the following:

• Make copies of all the agreements listed in this chapter (or download free examples at **www.deangraziosi.com**).

• Read over each agreement so you clearly understand what it means.

• Give this agreement to a friend and ask him if he understands it. Have him ask questions to test how much you understand everything in that agreement.

• Explain in your own words the different No Money Down strategies you can use and the types of agreements you need for each.

• Make a cheat sheet for yourself that lists each type of agreement that you need for each No Money Down strategy.

Reward yourself for completing all these action steps. Treat yourself to a nice dinner out or your favorite dessert. You've earned it! (Believe it or not, just by knowing the information in this chapter, you already know more about real estate than many people.) Keep going! By the end of this book, I want you ready to take action and get results so you can start putting money in your pocket today.

Success Story #8: Anita W.

Location: Lancaster, California

Experience before Dean's strategies: None.

Net worth increase since starting: From $11.21 to $548,000.

Additional monthly income: $6,370 positive monthly cash flow.

Best deal using Dean's strategies: $14,000 on assignment with less than 10 hours of my time.

On April 5, 2008, I celebrated my birthday by being hospitalized, facing eviction, and finding myself deeply in debt with medical bills. I was broke and living in a house with the option to buy, but the owner had sold it away from under me. At the time, I didn't even know where I would find the money to pay my rent for next month. I was facing the toughest time of my life.

Wondering where to turn, I saw Dean on TV and felt that this may be an option. I ordered Dean's book. I was optimistic, but I was in some pretty serious financial trouble. I hoped Dean would provide me with answers and opportunity, but really, "Me? Now? Could I do anything?"

I got Dean's book and read it cover to cover multiple times. It made sense to me, especially the no money down sections. I had nothing left but hope and a strategy given to me by Dean and I went for it. Literally the next week, I signed a lease option on a house. The owner wanted $230,000 and I offered him $190,000. Since I carried Dean's book around with me like a second Bible, I read the book again and came up with some ideas that I thought would work to get my offer accepted and they did. I got the house locked up on contract for $190,000, and even though it was an amazing deal, and if I had more time I could have made much more, I needed money fast. So just days later, I reassigned the contract to someone else and made $1,600. Not a lot of money to most people, but it meant the world to me and paid my rent for another month. It gets a lot better, though.

Even though it was not much money, the confidence of doing my first deal inspired me to push on and push harder. My next deal was with an owner of three houses. Dean teaches us where to look, and in this case, it was a seller who had been trying to sell his homes for quite some time. Even though lots of people may have looked at those homes, I felt confident none of them had been armed with what I now knew and carried with me in Dean's book. At first I tried to get into one house with a lease option using the same technique that just worked for me. He wanted $1,500 per month and while I was in the middle of negotiating that price down he came out and said, "Do you want to buy all three homes?"

A little in shock, I played it off as calm and cool as possible and said I would be interested if the terms were right. He then asked me the question I knew would be next: "How much money do you have?" I told him, "None," and he just looked at me and asked, "Well, how do you expect to pay for this?" I was honest and told him how I got started with Dean Graziosi's techniques and there were several different ways I felt we could structure it to be a win-win for both of us.

One of Dean's techniques is simply to listen to people. Find out what their needs are or as Dean calls them their *Magic Buttons*. I was genuinely interested in what this man wanted since he was considering selling to me. I wanted to help him as I helped myself. What I found out from listening is that he didn't need all the money up front. He just wanted to retire and move to a new location and wanted out really fast. Another thing Dean will teach you over and over is DO NOT BE AFRAID TO ASK. So with the information I had, I made him an offer.

I repeated back to him what he had told me. That he had been trying to sell for a long time and could not. It was delaying his move to Florida and being with his family, and it was becoming a major hassle. He also wanted to enjoy the equity he had accumulated over the years, yet he didn't need it all up front. I told him I could be his solution to all of that. I told him I would give him his asking price, which was already reduced to a really fair price. But in return for that I needed him to hold the mortgages on the properties and let me take over the properties with no money down. Let me tell you after it came out of my mouth—I almost felt like saying I was kidding because I felt he would laugh. But he didn't.

Instead he looked at me real serious and asked me if real estate investing was something that I really wanted to do and I told him absolutely, positively YES, and so he said, "Let me think about it."

Leaving his house, I felt a little confident but was still thinking, "Could it really work as Dean said it can?"

The next day he called. I nervously said hello, waiting for his response. He said, "Somebody helped me out when I was getting started so I'm going to help you out because you've got to get started somewhere." I almost fell on the floor. Just weeks earlier, I was wondering how I could eat and pay my rent and now I was going to own three houses because I followed what some young-looking guy on TV told me to do in his book. Those properties currently bring me $2,050 per month positive cash flow. At the same time, they are building equity while I pay them off to the kind owner.

I used lease options, just like Dean explained in his book, and that's how I wound up buying three houses with no money down—and this was just my second deal since getting Dean's course!

This was only the beginning. It's not so much about accruing property, but about finding good deals and passing my newfound knowledge on to others. I have gone from thinking that I was a victim of my circumstances to knowing that I am a victor of my future. Dean and his staff have become the backbone of support that I lacked in my life. I now know that

I am part of something bigger than me. I am a part of a wave of success that leads others to financial freedom.

I am alive again. I see people and make deals and I am but a hop and a jump away from "Being a Real Estate Millionaire." Thank you, Dean, for making me feel like somebody again. Thank you for giving me the ability to support not only myself, but my two kids and my 80-year old mother. It's been a blessing for me and I only hope other people will receive it as the same.

Anita's Biggest Secret: Just do it. Stop procrastinating. You've been waiting this long and if you're still broke today, you're going to be broke tomorrow. You don't need to wait because you don't have any money. That's the whole point—to make money! I have a goal to have a million dollars and Dean's book makes it so simple that you've got to get it and just do it.

To see a video of Anita telling her story go to **www.deansmedia.com/anita**

Part Three

CHAPTER 9

Driving a Flood of Motivated Buyers to You

So far you've learned how to find a motivated seller, how to make an offer and how to lock up a property for a chance to sell it for a nice profit. I hope you're staying excited as you complete each chapter, because you're close to having every piece of this strategy that will put money in your hands.

Once we are done with this chapter, you'll be able to put all the pieces together and have a road map to real estate riches. Okay, that sounded a little cheesy, but seriously . . . you're almost through and ready to start implementing what you've been learning!

In this chapter, we're going to use the same techniques I've already taught you about finding sellers; we're just going to put a cool spin on those strategies to attract motivated buyers instead. We'll focus solely on finding buyers and meeting the needs of buyers wanting to purchase homes.

We'll talk about two kinds of buyers and what to do to find each. I'll also review a number of marketing methods—including flyers specifically targeting these prospective buyers—as well as classified ads, business cards, online advertising, and how to incorporate a 24-hour recorded greeting to pre-screen buyers. You will also learn traditional, but often overlooked, ways to find buyers right around your community.

First, let's go ahead and start with a quick review of the buyer for our first strategy, the "Instant Equity Exchange," and then we'll cover our buyer profile for the second strategy, "The Assignment."

Instant Equity Exchange Buyer Profile

The IEE Buyer is a person who REALLY wants to own a home but has not been able to for one reason or another. Often, these potential buyers think they have no options left, because they do not have enough cash for a down payment or their credit score is too low to get a traditional bank loan.

They might be self-employed, making it hard to get a traditional loan, since tax returns can be skewed. They may have been recently rejected for a loan from their local bank, leading them to believe they do not qualify for any home loan at all. Lots of people want to buy a home, but for one reason or another, feel it is impossible. Unfortunately, in many cases that is true, but for a huge number of people, it is simply not the case. Rather, they just do not know other options exist.

There are a few common denominators that can get this group of people approved for a loan when their local bank has told them no. One key factor is a quality mortgage broker. I am going to explain exactly what I mean in a moment and the importance of a key mortgage broker to help make the IEE strategy work. But first I want to share some of the characteristics an IEE buyer may have:

- Credit score in the 600s

- Less-than-average down payment money available

- Seasonal job

- Been turned down by the local bank where they have a checking account

- Transitioning from one specific type of industry into another so now they do not look like they have a solid job history

- Self-employed

- Commissioned income as a salesperson

Due to one or more of the above factors, these buyers may not realize they could qualify for a property. Basically, they have self-defeating beliefs that they do not qualify for a mortgage. They may not realize a good mortgage broker can help them improve their credit score and that just because their bank turned them down, it does not mean others will too.

Even though this seems as if it could be a small group of people, it's not. There are literally millions of people in this group. You just need to use our techniques to get them to poke their head out of the sand so you can get them into a house.

All banks have certain criteria for loans. They use job, credit score, down payment money and debt-to-income ratio as a foundation for their traditional loans. They also rely on countless other factors that are developed internally by that bank. So one bank may need 20% down and a 700 credit score while another may accept a 680 credit score and 10% down.

Here's a personal example to help you make more sense of this. Not that long ago, I bought a foreclosure for $60,000 in the little town where I grew up. The day I bought it, I immediately started the process of getting it refinanced. I knew the property had a boatload of equity and I wanted to pull the cash out for other deals. I went to the local bank for the loan and was denied. Why? I have a credit score around 800, more cash in the bank than I was asking to borrow, and a great monthly cash flow. I got denied because that particular bank's policy required six months of "seasoning" on any home, which meant that they could not fund a property that someone did not own for at least six months. I got denied a loan for no other reason than my situation didn't fit into their loan guidelines.

I then immediately turned to a friend, who is a terrific mortgage broker, and gave him the deal. He shopped the loan with several banks and literally within weeks we closed on the loan with an out-of-state bank. I refinanced that property for $193,000. I took back the $60,000 investment, used about $30,000 to renovate the property, and stuck almost $100,000 in my pocket. I now have renters in that property whose rents are paying the mortgage. The point of the story is that getting turned down for a loan happens all the time. With a robotic system, I can show you how to find those buyers who have been denied as one group, and, through what you are about to learn, how you can help get them a loan.

Finding the right buyers is the main key to your success with the Instant Equity Exchange program. Also key is developing relationships with performance-oriented mortgage brokers, who are resourceful enough to find lenders willing to work with your buyers. Ideally, you want to make the qualification process as easy as possible so they can get through that process with minimal pain.

Before explaining how to find buyers, it is important to talk about finding a mortgage broker. A good mortgage broker can get your prospective buyers approved for a loan, do it efficiently and handle the majority of all the work that goes along with it.

How To Find A Mortgage Broker

This is an excellent time to find a mortgage broker because the mortgage industry has really slowed down. Since mortgage brokers do not have the same business they used to have, they're more willing to work with people whom they might not have had time to work for during the up market.

You can find brokers by doing a search online in your area, looking in the newspapers, or just through word of mouth. Once you find a great real estate agent, ask your agent to recommend a good mortgage broker she can trust. It's essential to find a mortgage broker who has programs specifically geared toward people who may be unable to qualify for a traditional loan. Despite the collapse of the subprime market, there are still loans available. You just want to find the right broker who knows how to find them. Then you can help your buyers out in ways that most traditional lenders or mortgage brokers cannot.

Get a list of brokers online, from friends, real estate agents, or the Yellow Pages. Get an e-mail or fax number and send over a letter similar to the one below:

> REAL ESTATE INVESTOR LOOKING FOR PROFESSIONAL MORTAGE BROKER EAGER TO MAKE A LOT OF MONEY IN TODAY'S MARKET.
>
> Hi, my name is Mr. or Mrs. (your name) and I am an investor in the local area. Due to the current economic conditions, I have decided to ramp up my existing operations. I not only represent myself, but I also have several investors in and out of the area that I help find, rehab, rent out, and manage properties.
>
> I have a unique marketing strategy that attracts buyers on the edge of being qualified. Meaning that a local bank with one loan option may have rejected the buyers I attract, but with a quality mortgage broker with many options we could get a lot of approvals. I AM NOT ATTRACTING people with horrible credit and absolutely no money to invest.
>
> I have set the goal to buy and immediately sell 100 hundred properties within the next 12 to 18 months. Some of these properties I will buy and hold myself, but most of them I will sell to the type of homeowner I mentioned above.
>
> Regardless of the strategy I use on each property, I need an aggressive, ethical and honest mortgage broker to whom I can send 100 percent of all my buyers. Yes, you may have to sort through

a few who are not qualified, but the end result will be a huge influx of business for you. Also, before these people ever get to your doorstep, you and I will discuss minimal criteria these people need to start the application. This will be done in advance to weed out all people for whom we unfortunately would have no chance of getting financing.

I have not chosen a broker to represent me yet. The broker I choose will have to be available at all times to pre-qualify or jump on loans sent your way so an aggressive work schedule will be required. The upside for the broker I choose is that I will be a source of a steady stream of deals in a market where most people struggle to find one. We will close on properties every month. With the strategy I am using, I also want to create a system that allows us to close in the fastest amount of time possible. I know that may not be right away, but once we have a few under our belt, I would like to help us create an efficient system to expedite each deal so we can move on to the next.

All that aside, I am a professional and I expect to work with a professional. I want to make money and I want the broker I work with to make money.

I will be offering properties that fit the criteria below:

(Below you would replace these sample details with your own preferences).

Single-family homes,
3-4 bedrooms, 1-2 baths, at least 1,000 sq. feet.
No mobile homes at this time
No home built before 1950
No vacant ground
Located in zip codes 12345,54321,43434,23231,
only in low crime neighborhoods

We will be searching for people who:

• May have been denied by a local bank recently only due to certain criteria that did not allow them to fit

• Have a credit score that is above what we agree is the bare minimum

- Have some down payment money but may need to be creative

- Have a job

- Have not had a bankruptcy

- Are willing to wait and work on repairing credit to raise score

- Are able to move fast when we find a home that fits there needs

- If this sounds like something you are qualified to handle and eager to make money with please contact me at 555-555-5555.

Thanks for your time
Mr. or Mrs. (your name)

Make adjustments to this sheet to fit what you want, and then fax it to every mortgage broker you are considering. It will eliminate a lot of wasted interviews and discussions. This says it like it is and details what you are looking for.

When you get calls, simply confirm with the broker exactly what you are looking for, and make sure they commit to the things that you wrote in your fax. You may even ask them to respond to your fax with a one-page letter. From there, go with your gut feeling and pick someone you feel is easy to talk to, and who seems *hungry* too.

Back to the Buyers

Remember, attracting this type of buyer is a main selling point. Basically, you can promote your ability to get them into a home, even though a bank may have recently denied them a loan. In addition, with the right lending relationships, you can promote relatively quick transaction processing speed. Of course, you can often offer properties cheaper than average on a regular basis. These are compelling factors to finding buyers in a down market.

The lending approval process can take place within a relatively short period of time as long as you have all the pieces in place and supplied to the mortgage broker. Once you pick a broker and do a few deals, you can work on systems to expedite all actions, meaning profits sooner for everyone. Your chosen mortgage broker already understands what needs to be done. That way you should have a very smooth transition from point A to point B. Remember, he will be doing most, if not all of the work, once you get a buyer's name to him. Mortgage brokers will be happy to do so because that is how they get paid—by making deals happen.

You will do some pre-screening with your automated systems, so that the buyers you attract do not have to worry about being told that their credit score is too low or that they do not have enough money for a down payment, because you will be able to find programs specifically geared toward them. (More on that in a few paragraphs.)

The buyers are going to be able to move through this process quickly and easily. You do not even have to be heavily involved in the approval process. You can be an intermediary between the mortgage broker and the buyer to help them understand what is going on from time to time within the course of becoming qualified. You can emphasize this benefit on your flyers, business cards, and website, etc. The critical difference about this system is that, in addition to offering a house for sale cheaper than most people could offer it, you are offering a solution to buyers with financing problems, which isn't commonly available in today's market.

Again, and I know I have beat this idea to death, that is the real selling point here. Besides offering homes at a discount, you are also solving the financing problems of many Middle-American households. You may have to work a little harder to find the right mortgage broker/company; but this is where your creative efforts will pay you huge profits. You only need to find the broker once, and then the dividends can pay off for many years with no extra work to you.

Before we get into the exact strategies to find these motivated buyers, let's talk about finding buyers that fit into the "Assignment" strategy.

Assignment Buyers Profile

The Assignment Buyer can fall into a number of categories. It could be someone who just wants a terrific deal on a home or it could be an investor or group of investors. The difference is they already have the cash to pay for the property or they have financing set up and ready to go in advance.

You will use some of the same types of marketing techniques to find your IEE Buyers and your Assignment Buyers. The difference will be what you say in your promotions. Yes, we are going to be showing you exact robotic ways to get these buyers to come directly to you.

Before we get into that, I want to share with you what Matt Larson considers his two favorite "traditional" ways to find buyers: The first one is very simple: word of mouth. I talked about this early on. Let everybody know that you buy real estate and that you have properties at huge discounts, up to 30% below market value (you may be buying at a bigger discount but need room for your profit), which tends to bring a lot of people out of the woodwork.

Create business cards targeting investors or people looking for cheap homes and give them out to every potential buyer. Tell everyone that you are extremely lucky and keep finding these unbelievable deals. They don't have to know that you made your own luck by reading this book and applying these principles—they will just be happy to get a great deal.

You can also go directly to other investors by attending Real Estate Investment Clubs in your area. These clubs usually meet at a regular time every month and may or may not require a fee to attend, but it's usually quite affordable. Out here in Phoenix, a first-time attendee or guest can attend for a discount. Finding clubs is easy by going online and searching for "Real Estate Investment Clubs" in your area using a search engine like Google. I talked about this in the first two pages of chapter 6, and listed two websites to start with.

When you find a real estate investment club, get as much information as you can before attending a meeting. Essentially, you want to find out who is serious and if they are cash buyers and how many properties they are looking to buy. Finding out exactly what they are looking for is the key. Once you find buyers and know what they want, you can go out and target only those types of properties.

For example, if these investors are looking for single-family homes, then target and buy single-family homes. If they are looking for duplexes, triplexes, or whatever—that is what you want to buy. Once you determine what your future buyers want, go find those exact properties using the marketing systems in this book, which most people have no idea exist and therefore cannot find the killer deals that you can.

Find out how much equity these investors want, what they are looking for, and how much cash flow they need because that can determine whether or not you can create your profit margin based on what they want.

For example, if your investor wants a property with $30,000 equity and you find one with $30,000 equity before your assignment fee, there's no profit margin built into that deal. If you have an investor looking for lot of equity, then maybe he is not as high on your list as somebody who is looking for less equity.

How to Find Buyers with Automatic Marketing Methods

Now let's move into automatic marketing strategies to find both types of buyers. I'm going to focus the discussion of how to use these strategies primarily on finding IEE buyers because assignment buyers are very straightforward—they are typically cash buyers or are prequalified. IEE buyers are going to need help with getting qualified, so advertising for them has to be a little more specific. With what you are about to learn, you will see how easily you can modify each piece to fit assignment buyers by simply eliminating certain parts and attracting investors who have cash and want killer deals.

Remember, this is similar to finding motivated sellers by placing ads that get people to call a recorded message that provides information and asks questions to screen and qualify them in advance.

Flyers

Use a flyer to promote your 24-hour recorded message that tells callers about the homes you have for sale and the possible financing available for anyone who has recently been denied a loan. Use the tear-away pieces of paper on the bottom of the flyer to list your 24-hour recorded message phone number along with a promise that they'll get their questions answered.

Your free, 24-hour recorded message can let callers know of a particular property for sale, the types of properties you typically sell, and their possible loan options. Finally, your recorded message must ask them to take action and leave information to see if they fit your screening criteria. (An exact script will be presented to you later in this section.)

Let your callers know that you offer various options to help people qualify for a loan to buy a home or a particular piece of property. Someone who wants to buy a home but was denied a loan is more likely not to be picky on a house to buy. You can help them repair their credit and get them into a nice home, which are great incentives to get people to call and say yes to working with you. Creating that sense of urgency and the call to action is really important.

Another great use of flyers is to advertise the date and time you will be holding open houses (more on that later). Clearly, there are many excellent uses for flyers to communicate your messages that call buyers to take action and make a phone call or go to your website.

You can post flyers in many different public places, such as:

- Large apartment complexes

- Community bulletin boards

- Colleges and community colleges' bulletin boards

- Grocery stores

- Local dinners or delis

- Church message boards

- Lunchroom of larger companies

- Public libraries

Back in chapter 3, I covered the most important elements of creating your "marketing" ads. What was the most important aspect of any written piece? If you said the headline, give yourself a gold star. Some examples of flyer headlines to attract IEE buyers would be:

- "Have You Been Turned Down By A Bank?"

- "Do You Think Your Credit is Good But Your Local Bank Says No?"

- "Why Rent When You Can Own?"

- "Problem Credit Okay"

Your flyer needs to grab a buyer's attention and hit the magic buttons that touch on their motivation to buy and their pain related to renting. They would love to own, and you are helping them to understand how they can buy their own home.

You Can Own This Home

If the bank turned you down and you've all but given up your dream of home ownership, I would like to help. Imagine yourself in this home! It's a 2200 sq. foot beauty, with tons of upgrades and I have three more, (all different), one will surely be right for your family.

You could stop renting this Month!

Call the 24 hour pre recorded message below to see if our unique strategy can get you qualified for home ownership when others say no!

To see if you qualify call our FREE Recorded Message
Call anytime 24/7 **XXX-XXX-XXXX**

The flyer above pictures a specific house, but you could take the concept and use it dozens of different ways (you can download these flyers at **www.deangraziosi.com/ieeflyers**).

You could modify the wording to fit whatever type of buyer you want to target. Working with your broker will help you determine the minimum criteria that you can put right in your ad.

You may be able to say, "Does the bank say you need a 700 credit score to buy a home? We can get you into this home or one like it with a credit score of 620 or more. Call right away to see if you qualify." Just emphasize all the main bells and whistles to draw their attention toward you and what you can provide. This will take some effort on your part, but it is not complicated.

Here's another example of a very basic flyer.

FREE RECORDED CONSUMER MESSAGE REVEALS... HOW TO STOP RENTING AND START OWNING A HOME

CALL XXX-XXX-XXXX

FREE RECORDED MESSAGE
Call Now! Info Available 24 hours a day...

Now, if you were creating a flyer to target investors for an assignment deal, you could easily tweak this flyer to include words like:

- Below FMV

- Instant Equity

- Cash-Flow Property

- Better Than Bird Dogger

- Wanted: Real Estate Investors

Then your flyer would drive potential investors to a pre-recorded message that targets investors or buyers with cash, rather than home buyers in need of a loan. That makes sense, right? I knew it would.

Here is another sample flyer targeting investors.

ATTENTION INVESTORS
LOOKING FOR "BETTER" THEN GREAT DEALS.

NO ONE FINDS BETTER DEALS THAN WHAT WE HAVE. NO ONE!

If you are investor and would like the chance to buy this home and others like it at up to 40% off FMV then look no further. Call right now, before you miss out on a deal that you could flip in this market and still make a profit, or rent for massive cash flow and a ton of equity.

FREE RECORDED MESSAGE CALL ANYTIME 24/7 XXX-XXX-XXX

Recorded Message Revisited

As you can see from these examples, and the process to find sellers, I'm a big fan of the 24-hour recorded message (go to www.coaphonesolution.com to learn more about a service that I use as my recorded message). As a tool, it allows you to robotically attract buyers (or sellers) at all hours of the day. Let me share with you a statistic that should reinforce why this is such a powerful tool: "Over 80% of people are more likely to call a recorded message than call a number where they may have to talk to a live person." This is especially true for sellers who might be in a tough situation or buyers who feel that their options are limited and don't need another sales pitch. Callers don't want a confrontation, to be sold to or asked a hundred questions, or having to deal with an uncomfortable situation. That is why the recorded message is such a critical tool. It allows them to get the information and then, if they are interested, the message prompts them to leave their contact information along with any other facts about their current situation.

The 24-hour recorded message helps you automatically weed through the callers, leaving you with only the potential buyers best suited for your deal. Plus, it helps validate a buyer's feelings, addresses their fears, and reduces hesitation. The message also answers questions as to why they may not have been able to qualify for a loan in the past such as lack of job history, self-employed, not enough money down, if they have a commission-based income, high debt-to-income ratio, low credit score or a number of other different factors.

Your message reassures them that there could be a solution because you have a mortgage broker who could possibly help people in their situation qualify. To get them qualified for a loan, your mortgage broker will need their information for you to help them out.

At the end of your recording, you can either tell them what information to leave on their message, connect directly to you, or provide them with another phone number where they can reach you. Again, all this is done to pre-screen buyers who are really motivated to take action. It can also let you know if these buyers have a good chance of getting qualified or no chance at all. You want to attract the right buyers and repel the ones you can't help.

Picture This

Imagine you are now chatting with a prospective buyer. Your mortgage broker gave you minimum criteria that you included in the message so you know you are talking to someone who could likely get a loan. You described the house and location as well as the price of the home. Your recorded message has literally pre-screened potential buyers so now it is worth your time (and theirs) to further screen the caller with your questions. (Also, if you would rather take everything I teach about using recorded messages and do it live, it will surely work too. Just be aware that people are more likely to call a recording as it is completely non-threatening). Whether you are dealing with an Assignment caller or an IEE caller, you need to know exactly what their time frame might be, the types of property they want, the location they are looking for, and the monthly payment they can afford.

During this call, you might provide the caller with information about an open house that you have scheduled (date, time and address). Or you might just become a valuable reference to the caller who later decides to buy a property from you.

Remember, you will know what questions to ask based on the minimum lending criteria that your mortgage broker gives you, such as at least 10% down, 620 credit score, job for 12 months, etc. Whatever it is, cite it on your message or in person so you are not wasting anyone's time, especially your own.

When talking in person, explain how you can help the buyer through the qualification process, how quickly the transaction can take place, and how you will follow up with him in the future.

As the relationship develops, record the buyers' contact information. If they do not qualify right now or they are not quite as motivated to buy the current property in inventory, then you have their contact information for future properties. (You may also push them along to your mortgage broker to give them a path and a plan to repair and improve their credit score, so they are ready to buy as soon as six months from now.)

Some of the motivational cues will be easy to pinpoint with some of the following questions to ask, such as:

• What type of home are you looking for?

• How long have you been looking for a home? This is a key factor to identify their true motivation.

• Where are you living now? This gives you an idea where they like to live or maybe where they do not want to live.

• How much are you paying per month? This gives you an idea of what they can afford for rent and how long they have been there. They are probably going to be able to afford that amount and maybe a little bit more.

• Have you tried to qualify for mortgage before? This helps establish some of the obstacles to overcome with this individual and maybe why he has been turned down in the past.

• How much money could you put down as well as also how soon you do need to move?

- How quickly are they looking to have their housing situation resolved and move on with their life?

- What is their current credit score?

Again, a lot of this can be placed in your recorded message or you can ask parts on your message and some in person. The information you capture will allow you to say, "Sorry, I don't think you will fit at this time" or "I am going to put you in contact with my mortgage broker who can help you from here with the loan options and process. As soon as we know you are eligible for a loan I will let you know more about the house or houses that I have available. If I don't have a house ready to go right now, I will aggressively search for the right house to fit you."

Once your mortgage broker says the buyer is preapproved, then you are off to the races, and with what you know from this book, it's almost money in the bank.

Here is a script that asks for information robotically, and can be all or part of the message you create. Feel free to modify and use it to attract the exact buyer you want.

Sample Recorded Message (also can be downloaded at **www.dean-graziosi.com/buyermessage**):

> *Hi, and thanks for calling. I've got a gorgeous house in (the name of the city/town) and I'm willing to work with you to make you the proud owner, at an extremely low price in comparison to all homes like it in the surrounding areas.*
>
> *If you've tried to buy a home before and were turned down, this may be a great opportunity for you. With our unique system I may be able to help you get approved.*
>
> *If you have a great credit score or are preapproved already then you will still want to listen to this message and leave your information at the end since this is an insane deal that you will not want to miss. But if you have been denied or told your credit score was too low, or that since you are self-employed you cannot get a loan, or denied for a number of other factors then you will surely want to continue listening. We may certainly be able to get you and your family into your own home when others can't.*
>
> *In a moment I'll describe the house and give you details about*

how you may qualify to own it, and give you a website address where you can see pictures. But before I do, let me be completely transparent with you and tell you why I'm offering this house at such a terrific price.

First of all, I'm not using a realtor, which has allowed me to drop the price thousands below its appraised value. That's like giving you instant equity! Second, the market is slow right now. That means it could be a while before the house is snapped up under regular conditions. Frankly, it's far too nice to be sitting there empty. I'd like to make sure someone enjoys it.

Last but not least. I want to do my part to make the dream of homeownership a reality for someone who has really been trying to make it happen.

Okay, so now you know why I'm making you such a great deal, now let me describe the home.

THE BELOW DESCRIPTION IS ONE I USED ON A PROPERTY I BUILT. OBVIOUSLY YOUR DESCRIPTION WILL BE UNIQUE, BUT THIS IS A SAMPLE OF WHAT TO SAY AND HOW TO SAY IT.

As you pull up to the house, the professional landscaping accents the color and trim of the house. The front porch is lined with eight smooth columns that give the home a very regal look. You pull down the driveway to your 2-car garage with a door for each bay. Once inside the 2,200 square feet home, you'll see it is beautifully painted. There are 3 spacious bedrooms with closet space and nice windows, and you won't have to fight your kids for bathroom time with the home's 3 full baths. That's right, not half or 3/4, 3 full baths.

It doesn't stop there. You also have a den with the same beautiful Brazilian cherry hardwood floors that fill the rest of the home, except of course for the bathrooms and laundry room, which I've attractively floored with high-grade tile.

If you like food, you'll love the kitchen. I've filled it with top-of-the-line stainless steel appliances, upgraded cabinets, a gas stove, and plenty of counter and cabinet space.

To make sure you get the warmth you need, I've installed a gas hot-water heater, and gas furnace, and in the summertime you'll keep nice and cool with the central AC. Moving outside 'through pane-styled Arcadia doors, you'll step out onto a spacious deck, where you will spend many hours enjoying the fresh air and a terrific view.

Let me tell you, this will make a beautiful HOME for someone. It is a really nice, high-quality house and I'm only going to ask $XXX,000 for the house—which is a killer deal!

Now, if you are interested I want you to know that I have some top-notch pros that could get you qualified for this home, under good terms with no funny business, even if your local bank has said no. You see, each and every bank has its own set of criteria that can get you approved. If you work with just one bank you have to go by their rules. When you work with a professional mortgage broker who has relations with many banks and knows many different lending options, your chances of getting a loan rises dramatically. Well, we have the best of the best standing by ready to use his knowledge to get you in a home of your own.

Like I said earlier, if you have good credit or are already preapproved and you simply want to get a killer deal on the house listed, then leave your name and contact information at the end of this message and I will get back to you right away.

On the other hand, if your credit is not the best or at least you were told that, or you have been recently turned down for a loan or have very little down payment money, then take a listen to this real quick. We may be able to get you approved if you have (here is where you could put minimum criteria given to you by your mortgage broker). You will need a credit score above 620 (if you don't know it, then call us), you will need to be employed for at least XX months and have at least 10% to put down.

If you think you are even close to these standards, then make sure to leave your name and information because, trust me, you don't want to miss out on this house . . .

One last thing—if you think with a little help your credit score could be improved, then also leave your information and your situation and we will get back to you if we think we can help you reach your goals.

Now, if this sounds interesting, and without making any commit-

ment, what you need to do next is simply leave your name and contact phone information at the end of this message.

Speak slowly and clearly, spelling out any unique names or e-mail addresses, basically anything that might be difficult for me to spell, and I'll make sure you are called back within 24 hours.

There is absolutely no obligation from leaving your information and I will keep your info strictly confidential. I will only contact you to communicate with you about the home.

Oh, if you have Internet access, you can go to www.yoururl-here.com to see photos of what your potential new home looks like (include if you have a website set up).

Thanks for calling and I look forward to speaking with you soon.

Name

This audio message can be tweaked to fit just about any type buyer you are looking to find. You can get very specific or leave it a bit more generic and explain the details on the phone. Test both ways and start building your buyer list. (We will talk about building your buyer list a little later on.)

Back to Placing Ads

You will want to consider carefully placing ads due to their costs. I recommend taking a similar approach as we discussed with finding sellers. Determine your target population, who the readers are, and place the ads where the renters and prospective home buyers will be looking for places to live. Typically, those are the people who are renting or living with friends or family members. Right now, they would love to have their own place and contribute toward ownership of their own home, but believe they do not have any chance to purchase a home.

Where will they see your ad? Do these people typically have access to the Internet or is it something that they are going to read in the newspaper? Whether you use the mail, post flyers, or use classifieds, it is important to check out and understand where your media will go. Before putting an ad in a printed paper, find out what the circulation of the paper is and where it goes. Does it hit areas where there are a higher percentage of renters?

I recommend looking for the small, local newspapers that offer free classified ads. You can find these freebies in grocery stores, outdoor distribution boxes and other various locations depending on the state and city where you live, such as *The Penny Saver, Thrifty Nickel* and other such papers available for people to pick up and thumb through. Plenty of people look for freebies all the time, and that is why I like free classified ads. (This is why I am also a huge fan of the free online classified ads at Craigslist.com. I explained how craiglistworks in chapter 3. Use that same FREE strategy to place ads for buyers and investors.)

Here are some additional examples of classified-style ads. Keep in mind that you can modify these ads and use them in any media you wish. From a flyer to a postcard, you can use the marketing messages to communicate with potential buyers in as many ways as you can imagine (these ads can be downloaded at **www.deangraziosi.com/buyerads**).

Are You Ready For Your New Home!
Bank said no, we can say yes! In (city)
2200 sq ft many upgrades priced to sell at
$XXX,000 call our 24hr recorded message
to see if you qualify. XXX-XXX-XXX

You CAN Own Today!!!
Did the bank say no? We can say yes!
EZ Qualifying—All Credit Situations Welcome
24-hr recorded info XXX-XXX-XXX

BANK SAID NO! WE SAY YES!!!
Stop Paying Rent! EZ Qualifying
Call our 24-hour FREE recorded
Message to qualify xxx-xxx-xxxx

Here is one targeted at other investors or assignment deals:

Deal For First-Time Investor
Brand-new cash-flow property
will rent for $1,800-$2,000 mo.
24hr recorded info XXX-XXX-XXX

Investors Look No Further
Simply the cheapest prices on great
Investment properties. No one has
better deals then me. Call to get
discounts of up to 40% off FMV.
Only two properties left. Call today at:

Placing paid classified ads in local newspapers is also a great option. In some newspapers it will cost more than others—like running an ad in a metropolitan paper versus a community edition. Many papers also offer the option of putting your ad online to coincide with the printed ad you run. Ask about that option, and be aware that there might be an additional cost to list your ad online.

Remember, your ad must grab a reader's attention. The way that you use words within your headline can actually generate certain types of leads. Some examples of attention-grabbing headlines are:

- Easy qualifying

- Low down payment

- You can own today

- Bad credit okay

- Why rent?

- Get pre-approved today

- All credit situations welcome

- Own your own home today

All of these headlines touch emotion points or pain points that will get people to take action by contacting you.

Here is an example of the classified ad message that you can expand upon when you have catchy headline:

"Why rent? I can help you own your own home. You need to call today for a free, no obligation, 24-hour recorded message."Make sure the message is to the point and gives them enough information to get them to take action today:

- "Do not delay! Do it now!"

Here is an example of a display ad from a newspaper that could also be used as a postcard.

Local Resident Creates Amazing System That Allows People to Stop Renting and Buy a Home

When searching for a mortgage lender, most people contact traditional lenders. However, these lenders first and foremost focus on conventional loans. To acquire a conventional loan you must have a credit score of at least 640. This score fluctuates according to lenders. In some cases, lenders require a score of 660. Furthermore, you must have a down payment. Standard down payments range from 3% to 20%. If you do not fall into this category, you won't get the loan. There are other obstacles too. People who are self employed or who have gone through a divorce or a bankruptcy can also have a very difficult time obtaining a mortgage loan. But one local resident (your name here) has a system that is solving this problem for people who otherwise could not have become homeowners. For people who have been told no by lenders in the past, and felt doomed to stay stuck in the annoying position of renting, (you name here) is proving that the America Dream of home ownership is indeed achievable. (He/She) has set up a 24 hour free recorded message that explains it all at XXX-XXX-XXXX. Now there is hope for individuals truly seeking home ownership.

Business Cards

I would recommend printing different business cards, depending on the individuals you want to target. With hope by this point you already have cards targeted and geared toward your sellers. Now let's talk about the cards geared toward your buyers. Identify the key points to motivate buyers to take action. You can have one card specifically targeting certain types of buyers or it can position you as a resource for buyers. (You can view sample business cards at **www.deangraziosi.com/buyerbizcard**)

Did The Bank Say No? I Can Say Yes!

YOU CAN OWN A HOME TODAY! We want to help you where the banks failed to. I find houses for people that meet their needs, in nice neighborhood at prices you can manage! Stop Paying Rent and Start Owning!

EZ Qualifying - Call my FREE 24 hour
pre-recorded message now to see if you qualify.

XXX-XXX-XXXX

John Doe, Professional Provider of the American Dream

Your contact information, phone number, e-mail, website, and mailing address should all be included. The back of the card should include the lead generating message that promotes your free 24-hour message. Make sure that they know where they need to call if they have specific questions regarding your buyer's program.

Distribute your business cards by posting them on bulletin boards and handing them out to strangers, friends, family, colleagues, and other buyers and sellers. You might consider handing out cards to contacts and offering a referral fee if they refer buyers who qualify and purchase a home with you. Leave your business card on doors and rental properties. Attach it with mailings you send directly to those individuals who are currently renting. Make sure you carry your business cards at all times. Cards are absolutely vital to making this business start working for you and to have the success you deserve.

Finally, always remember to offer your ten-second verbal commercial to anyone you meet in the elevator, on a bus, at a family event, or while out with friends. The more people know what you do, the faster and easier it will be to start making money.

Matt's Coaching Story

I've only been investing in real estate for a few years, yet many people have now started asking me if I would coach them. Usually the first question I get from people is, "Sure Matt, your system might work where you are, but it won't work in my hometown." It's crazy to think how my life has evolved from where I was just a few years ago. I know Dean asked me to contribute to this book because of how far I've come—and now I am getting similar questions. That blows me away, while at the same time I am honored and proud all at once. So after speaking directly with Dean about this, I've decided to take a certain portion of my time and allocate it to visit people in their hometown and help them find and locate good deals right in their own backyard.

For three days, I show people everything I know and how to implement my 25:1 system in their neighborhood. I show people what to look for and how to do it, and then they can see for themselves whether these strategies work or not.

The first time I did this was with a husband and wife team. The husband was excited about real estate and knew a lot, but had little confidence and was afraid of making a mistake and losing a lot of money. His wife was even more skeptical and didn't think real estate could ever be profitable for them, although she was reluctantly willing to investigate the possibilities some more.

An hour and a half before meeting this couple, I decided to look in the newspapers for that area, and I quickly found several promising properties with words that indicated motivated sellers such as "Motivated to sell" and "Willing to look at all offers."

Then I looked on Realtor.com for properties in that area. Even though this information is out there for anybody to see, most people aren't looking for these types of deals. Anyone could have seen what I saw, but I took action and I found a 1,200 sq. ft. home for $20,000.

The house looked just fine, and even more remarkable was that similar homes in that same area were priced at $60,000 to $100,000. I've long ago stopped trying to figure out why people list properties low, even when they are clearly below fair market value. The moment you find property priced below average you know instantly that the seller is motivated, which means you can put an even lower offer in. You can always work your way up, but you can never work your way back.

I was doing all of this from thousands of miles away, and based on the pictures alone—this house looked fine, and when we went to look at this property in person, everybody's jaw dropped. The couple's real estate agent had never seen a deal like this and neither the husband nor the wife knew about this property, even though it was within a neighborhood the couple knew about.

Even if they had paid the asking price of $20,000, they could have rented it out for $500/month with positive cash flow of at least $200/month. The house just needed new carpeting and paint.

Seeing this incredible bargain flipped a switch in the skeptical wife's head. When she saw that it was possible to find houses priced below market value, she said, "Even I could have made at least $20,000 on this house." Despite being on the market for several weeks, someone else had already submitted an offer just days before

Despite this obstacle, I told this couple that not every offer closes, so they should put in an offer anyway. That way if the first guy's falls through, they'll be next in line to grab the property at the bargain price.

This one deal showed both the couple and their real estate agent that incredible deals are for real and that if you get up and look for properties every day, you'll find bargains. To find this particular deal took me less than fifteen minutes on the Internet.

In the three days I spent with them they learned some real "Dean" strategies in real life that blew them away and also some techniques that could be unique to them. But the main lesson the couple learned was that they missed one deal, but they didn't have to miss the next one. This is the same mentality that I use when looking for properties. I expect to find the best deals out there so I find them. It kind of goes along with the laws of attraction. You always find what you expect to find. Some people think that real estate investing is a lot of work. I don't think like that. I think that I'm always going to find houses that don't need any work and still get them at 50% below value, and as long as I look long enough, I do.

Summary

The main point to remember from this chapter is that you need to find buyers for your properties. Rather than put out a **For Sale** sign and wait for results, I want you to take action and market your properties to find your buyers ahead of time, and have them come to you. When you get to a certain point, you can be like Matt Larson and have buyers fighting to get the deals you find.

By now, you should understand the importance of an automated system that contains the right message targeted to the right target at the right time. There are only a couple more pieces to learn and we'll be done. You're about ready to start knocking them out of the park!

• There are two types of buyers: IEE buyers who want to own a home but may not qualify for a loan, and Assignment buyers who have cash and want a good deal.

• Establishing a relationship with a mortgage broker can help you screen and qualify people for a loan.

• An automated system can deliver your message to the right people and screen them in advance to save you time.

• Use business cards, classified ads, flyers, and any other form of advertising to drive people to call your recorded message.

Action Steps

Take action now and don't stop. Remember, if you get off track or need guidance from a seasoned investing professional, don't hesitate to call one of our consultants and see if you qualify to enter my Real Estate Success Academy. Call them anytime at 1-800-315-7782.

Now, to get things working and moving for you, here's what I want you to do:

• Design and print a set of business cards specifically targeting your buyers.

• Record a 24-hour message geared toward answering questions from buyers.

• Create and put up some flyers focusing on buyers.

• Consider sending out direct-mail pieces to individuals who are currently renting property.

• Research what your classified ad options are and consider placing some classified ads.

• Research online places to advertise like craiglist, Kijiji, and other classified ad sites.

Success Story #9: Laura J.

Location: Middletown, New Jersey

Experience before Dean's strategies: None.

First thoughts of Dean: Beyond skeptical. Okay, I just rolled my eyes.

Feelings toward Dean today: So glad to admit I was wrong. Dean and his techniques have changed my life forever.

First deal profits: $22,000 in 6 1/2 weeks.

Regrets: Not seeing Dean's infomercial on TV years ago.

Message for others thinking about real estate: I made $22,000 on one deal and I work at a job where I make $17,000 in a year. Need I say more?

While visiting my boyfriend one night, we sat on the couch and watched Dean's infomercial on TV. I at first rolled my eyes and kept my mouth shut since my boyfriend wanted to watch it.

Within fifteen minutes, however, I was on the phone and ordered the book. I judge people by my gut instinct, and for some reason, the infomercial struck me that Dean was a real person. (Boy was I right!) I ordered the book for my boyfriend, who had always talked about investing in real estate, but I mistakenly had the book sent to my place instead of his. From the time I got it, every spare moment I was reading it, taking notes, and beginning to search for houses. I just devoured that book and got more excited every day about getting started.

From being a skeptical person who knew nothing about real estate, I was now working with different realtors, and while driving around, looking at properties, I spotted a house that I knew would be my first deal. The lawn was overgrown with weeds, the siding was falling off, garbage was piled up, and old newspapers were left in the driveway. In the window was a tiny sign that read For Sale By Owner along with a phone number that turned out to be in Florida (the house was in New Jersey). It was exactly like one of the stories Dean had written about in his book, and I knew I was on to something. Armed with the right information I had the confidence to pursue my newfound instincts.

I spent the next week calling and leaving messages and finally I got a call back. It turned out the house was an estate sale and the owner gave me the code to get in, which was perfect because my boyfriend and I could then take all the time we needed and really check out the house.

The house was a complete mess. The second floor was gutted, the kitchen had no cabinets and the appliances needed to be replaced. The bathrooms were way outdated and the flooring was only half finished. Apparently the previous owner was a do-it-yourselfer who didn't know what he was doing and never finished anything.

The owner was asking for $275,000, but after running the numbers to see how much it would cost to rehab, I came up with an offer of $235,000. I was terrified to make the call, but Dean's coaching support told me that the worst that would happen was that the owner would say no. So I picked up the phone and decided to offer $225,000, and the owner said, "How soon can you close?"

I nearly fell out of my chair. I used all that Dean teaches and leaned a bit on the mentors and closed on the property. Scared but excited we pushed forward. My boyfriend, who is a handyman, and I did most of the work ourselves except for the sheet rocking and the carpeting. I was shooting to get the work done in a month, but it took us six and a half weeks.

Let me be honest, I did get a little scared when we went over budget on the repairs. I spent many sleepless nights wondering, "What did I just do?" and "How can I get my money back?" When we were finally done, we put the house back on the market at a lower price than every other house on the block, and sold the house in two days.

I made $22,000 in six and a half weeks on my first deal! What's more amazing is that my part-time job as a secretary pays me only $17,000 a year. I faced my fear head on because I kept what Dean taught me and his voice in the back of my head. You have to embrace change as something new and not be scared. If you are buying the property at the right price, knowing exactly what you have going into it, using all the determining factors Dean teaches you, the end result will inevitably be amazing. But believe me, the first one is not easy. When I say not easy, I mean controlling your emotions and the doubt that pops in your head. The actual buying, fixing up and making money was a lot easier then getting the fear out of my head. That is what is great about Dean—he provides the strategies and the motivation to take action and keep taking action.

I would suggest you read every e-mail Dean sends you, visit www.dean-graziosi.com often, take advantage of his monthly live calls and whatever else he provides. Once you see how much work he puts into helping us achieve you will know that he is a man who wants to make a huge impact on all of our lives. Trust him, trust yourself, and go for it.

I also fulfilled my dream of buying land in Maine. My best friend and I found beautiful lots right next to each other near Bar Harbor in a town called Surry. Thanks to my confidence and knowledge from Dean, we offered to buy two lots for the price of one and have the owner pay half the penalty to take out the tree growth, and he went for it! Now we own them where similar lots are already selling for $20,000—more than what we paid for our lots.

So thanks to Dean, I have now made two real estate investments in five months. Now I'm putting in offers for bank-owned properties. Each time I look at a house, I'll take lots of pictures along with detailed notes that explain the repairs that might be needed and the estimated costs to fix them. That way I can justify asking a lower price. I figure the banks have so many properties that they don't even know their condition.

The banks have told me that my offers are the most detailed they've ever seen. While I've submitted several offers, I haven't gotten a good deal yet, but I'm still looking. It can get frustrating to keep putting in offers and watching great deals go to someone else, but I'll keep at it, especially when I know the amount of money that can be made on just one deal.

The only regret I have is not meeting Dean or seeing him on TV earlier in my life. Other than that, I love the new path my life is on because of what Dean taught me.

Until I read Dean's book, I was desperate for something to come my way to help me gain financial independence and freedom and let me wake up excited every day to get going, and this is IT!

Laura's Success Secrets: One of the most important strategies I got from Dean is that you make it a win-win situation for everyone. Without Dean, I would never know where to start and thought real estate was beyond my means to ever understand. Dean taught me to just do it. His book, mentorship and all the people on the website changed my life a thousand times.

I love the fantastic feeling of being in charge of my own future and knowing now that there's something I can control to make my life and my family's life better. It's that awesome feeling of discovering something I love to do.

I really did take a leap of faith and I know I'm going to be successful in real estate. I also know I'm going to be a greater success story a year from now.

Also make sure to talk to one of Dean's advisors to see if you can work with his coaches in his Real Estate Success Academy. It is worth every penny if you get accepted.

To see a video of Laura telling her story go to **www.deansmedia.com/laura**

CHAPTER 10

Locate Buyers Right Around You

In this section, I want to teach you other great ways to find buyers, in addition to the automatic marketing techniques you learned in the previous chapter. These techniques may not be as "creative" or "cool" as the others, but I can't pass over any ideas that have made me small fortunes in the past.

I'm going to start with some brief suggestions on how to take advantage of the Internet and then we will move on to other ideas.

Profiting with the Internet

Nowadays having a website is about as common as having a business card. However, just like a lot of business cards I've seen, some websites do nothing for their owners.

Don't get me wrong, every business needs one, but it has to do more than just sit in cyberspace. When you decide to build a website for your investing business, define what you want your website to accomplish.

Start by determining your target. Will you have one website for everyone or different websites for buyers and sellers? What will the main message of your website be? Make it crystal clear to visitors what they will gain from spending time at your website. Use the same concepts that I have already taught you about using headlines and focusing on the hot buttons of the people you wish to attract.

You'll also want to think about technical considerations. You may want to post pictures, sound recordings, or video on your website. All of these things play into the cost of not only creating but hosting your site. Probably the most important question to ask yourself is how much you wish to budget for a website.

My suggestion is to keep it simple. However, at the bare minimum, your website should do the following for you:

Provide compelling information about what you do that others can't. Your site should follow the same style as your advertising. You want to grab your visitor's interest, create desire for what you can offer, and cause them to take action.

> • For example, your site could say that as an investor, you create win-win situations for property owners and home buyers. By using unique, little-known methods, you can help property owners sell fast and help people who have had trouble buying a home in the past become homeowners.

Provide educational information that is relevant to your visitor's needs and wants. Your website can sift, sort, and screen out the best prospective deals. You can provide simple "reports" or articles that appeal to many interests, all of which point to your assistance as the solution. Some suggestions might be:

> • How to sell your home when others can't.

> • What to do if you're facing a foreclosure.

> • How to purchase a home for less than renting.

> If you are driving people to your website via classified ads, flyers, or signs, remember to make it connect with your ad media. So if your ads promised low-cost homes, your website should also promise low-cost homes.

Provide a way to capture your visitor's contact information. No website should be without a method of capturing visitor information. You can ask them to subscribe to your property alert list, which could be nothing more than an e-mail that you send out when you have the property that meets their specifications. On the website be sure to have a place where people can fill in all of their information. I like to use surveys because it makes the buyer or seller take action and provide you with all of their information while you are providing them with a tool—a "customized analysis." You'll learn more about the importance of capturing visitor information when I talk about "building your buyers list" in just a few moments.

Provide a way for visitors to contact you. Make it easy for interested parties to contact you. Timing is everything, especially in a down market. If a motivated buyer or seller is interested in talking to you but can't get hold of you, you miss out on potential profits. I'm not saying you need to post your personal phone number all over the site. There are many options to make yourself available. You may request that visitors listen to or read information available on your site and tell them that once they've done that, they will be given a means of communicating with you directly. Whenever possible, you should always offer an e-mail option to contact you, along with a promise of a specific response time. This will help create confidence in the visitor.

If you don't know how to create a website or have no desire to learn, you can always pay someone to create your website for you. Also take into consideration the activation of that website through web hosting, which puts your website on the Internet for everyone to see it. Finally, you need to optimize your website so that others can find it on the Internet. When somebody types in "low money down," "buyers program" or something like that, you want to make sure that they see your website in the search results.

A website can be a great tool, but it isn't mandatory. Like a recorded message, a website can be working for you 24 hours a day, 7 days a week. The most important part about having a website is that it provides a professional look that adds instant credibility for you.

NOTE: *Okay, I got done writing this section and said the heck with it. I feel it is so important that you have a web presence that I contacted my team and told them to build you one. To get your very own website that can help you with exactly what we talked about, go to* **www.dean graziosi.com/freewebsite** *and get your site set up. No catch. No cost. Go get it!*

Once you take a few minutes to set it up you will be able to tweak the site to include what you desire. You're welcome!

Traditional Ways to Find Buyers

Although I love what I've learned over the last twenty years to create effective, automated marketing methods, I also want to talk about attracting buyers through more traditional, and sometimes time-intensive methods.

1. Work with large companies in your area that are moving people in and out. When I was growing up, there was an IBM plant nearby. People were regularly moving in and out of that area for their jobs with IBM. This gave me the idea for a strategy that capitalizes on that need for housing. First of all, find all the large companies in your area. Any of these companies might have an ongoing need to find housing for employees who have relocated. If you find a few companies who do relocate, let them know that you have a system to find and sell houses fast, and that you are enthusiastic about helping them. For companies that relocate employees, keep in touch on a regular basis so they don't forget about you. Put them on an e-mail list so you can send them regular updates, or make a call to a specific person once a month to see if they need any houses to be sold or found.

2. Identify hospitals or places where families who just had a baby would visit. Targeting families with a new baby often means finding a family that needs a larger place. How do you find these families? Think about all the places where new parents might spend their time. Are there Lamaze classes in your area? What about baby stores, clothing, furniture, maternity stores, secondhand toy and clothing shops, hospital pediatric units, OB-GYNs and local pediatricians? There are plenty of different places where you could take a flyer or other material and ask if you can post something on their announcement board. You could even provide materials that could be included in brochures, or take-home packets that hospitals or others pass out to their patients/customers etc.

3. Find retirees. If you live in one of the southern states, consider targeting retirees who are moving south to spend their golden years. Also think about targeting "snowbirds"—meaning people who live in the South part of the year to escape brutal winters up North. This may take a little more effort than some of the other methods because people come from not only northern states but Canada as well. It is possible to place classified ads in smaller papers, on craigslist, even Canadian papers. Think about other places where you could use your advertising tools to attract the attention of such people.

4. Target couples who are coming and going: I'm referring to newly married and newly divorced couples, both of whom may need to buy or sell quickly. Obviously, you would target newly married folks through places like bridal shops, wedding planners, catering services, travel agents, jewelry stores, etc. Newly divorced people can be found a number of ways. There are many local support groups in your community as well as in your place of worship. Divorce filings are public record and can be found at your county courthouse or website. There are countless websites dealing with divorce, such as www.divorce360.com. These could be good places to test online advertising.

5. Give bird-dog fees to friends and relatives who bring you a buyer. The term "bird dog" refers to a person who finds properties and brings them to the attention of a real estate investor. Earlier in this book, I mentioned how you should tell everyone that you invest in real estate. That way if they happen to run across a tremendous deal, you'll pay them a fee for letting you know about it.

These are just a few ways that can bring additional buyers your way. You can probably think of more, and if you come up with a new one that works for you, come share it with the other investors in the forums at **www.deangraziosi.com**.

Creating a Buyers List

As you market any properties you have under contract, you're going to generate a list of buyers. Your buyers list is a precious resource. Go back to the people on this list and offer them new properties as you find what they want. So, right from the start, create a way to build and organize your list. (This is the same system or list you should build for sellers and properties you have locked up—you want to always be able to see in a glance what homes you have and which buyers might be interested.)

You can do it dirt cheap and simply by writing each person's details in a composition book, which you can buy for about a buck. Dedicate at least one sheet of paper in the notebook, front and back sides, per person. That way if you need to, you can add notes later on.

If you want to get fancy and sophisticated, keep your list electronically on your computer. There are plenty of different options such as using a database, spreadsheet, or even a word processor.

If you keep your list in electronic format, you can contact buyers by e-mail. Keep your list updated with what you are doing. In the beginning, you may only have one property but twelve potential buyers.

Only one of those buyers will get the property, so the other eleven will still be looking. They may be folks who did not meet the qualifying criteria previously but now they do. Maybe this wasn't the best property for them in that location or it didn't have enough bedrooms. Keep in touch with that list of buyers and contact them on a regular basis with updates and new properties through e-mail, text messaging or a good old-fashioned phone call or letter. Put all notes of communication in your book or your electronic format. If you get your buyers pre-qualified, you can concentrate on finding properties that fit their needs—and you've got a slam-dunk deal! Take notes, keep track, and make your list make you money!

A Favorite Buyer-Finding Technique

Talking about the buyers list reminded me of a technique Matt and I consider one of our favorites because it is so counter-intuitive. Put ads either in the newspaper or on yard signs (also called bandit signs—those signs you see stuck in various locations on the side of the road).

Your ads or signs need to read, "House For Sale, Must Sell, Great Area, $20,000 Below Value" and that will bring out buyers. Matt Larson shared his simple newspaper ad that works well to find sellers AND buyers too, which says:

"I buy houses any condition!"

Local investor looking for properties

Call (phone number)

Matt says people will constantly call that number looking to sell a property they have. A lot of time other investors will actually call to find out who their competition is, and at that point, put them on your buyers list! That is exactly what Matt has done, so that it makes them part of his team too.

Holding an Open House

You probably have a general idea of how an open house works. Basically, it's a public invitation to attract drive-by attention of people interested in purchasing a home. In the next chapter, I'm going to cover an auction technique using the open house concept in a different way. Once you read it, you may decide to come back and apply parts of it to what I'm about to tell you. Either way, I'll use this as an introduction to the process and explain how to use it to find a buyer.

As you might imagine, in this technique you promote the open house to find buyers. I will cover effective ways to promote an open house in the following chapter. Right now I want to talk about one of the most important things that must be done prior to holding an open house, and that is staging the home. That means arranging it to look its absolute best, much how food photographs on magazine covers display some tantalizing, delicious-looking entrée.

That plate of food was staged to look its absolute best, and if your mouth has ever watered by looking at a photograph, there's your proof the staging worked. If you're going to hold an open house, make that house look as irresistible and inviting as possible.

Here are some tips to do that. Make sure the home is bright and clean. Don't overlook the little things, like built-up dust on ceiling fans or air vents. Make the home smell good, but do not overdo it—some people are sensitive to even pleasant smells.

To the greatest extent possible, check that the seller has addressed any glaring items that could create negative first impressions. Make sure the property exhibits some sort of curb appeal.

A few years back I created a video with specific techniques to get a house looking it's best for little to no money. You can check it out at **www.deangraziosi.com/maximize**.

Use those ideas to make the house look the best it can. You never get a second chance to make a first impression. Some areas to consider include:

- **Yard**—Mow the lawn, remove dead plants, remove junk lying around, clean grease marks on driveway, weed or plant flowers.

- **Home exterior**—Sweep or wash sidewalks and driveway, clean gutters, clean walls and roof.

- **Windows**—Clean all windows inside and out, add fresh coat of paint to trim, make sure all windows open and shut easily, replace loose screens.

- **Front door**—Clean door inside and out, polish handles, make sure doorbell works, oil hinges if necessary to stop squeaking.

- **Interior**—Paint if necessary, repair cracks and holes in ceiling and walls, clean draperies and open them to let in more light, clean floor and carpets, remove magazines and books from tables to avoid clutter, position furniture to showcase the size and space of each room.

- **Kitchen**—Set the kitchen table, clean countertops and sinks, fix dripping faucets, clean oven and stove, remove all magnets and clutter on the refrigerator door, reorganize pantry to make it appear spacious, repair or replace cabinets if necessary.

- **Bathrooms**—Check that sinks and drains work, repair leaky faucets or toilets, clean sinks, put in a new shower curtain, remove grout and stains from tile, and invest in matching towels.

- **Added extras**—Put air fresheners in each room, bake a fresh batch of cookies in the kitchen, discard dead plants, throw away magazines and other clutter.

I have bought houses for pennies on the dollar simply because people never mowed the law, trimmed the shrubs or removed the broken-down car from the yard. I even got a deal on one property because they had a dog that pooped all over the front porch . . . A little effort goes a long way here.

Home staging has become a new business in recent years, and in a down market people who specialize in staging homes may be kept very busy. However, it may be in your best interest to seek out a few of these professionals in your area and see if they would be interested in being part of your team.

You could offer them a larger than normal fee for staging homes for you, but only if the home sells. That way there is no money out of your pocket up front, and the person staging a home as an incentive to provide services without up-front compensation.

Ideally, set the proper mood for prospective buyers by arranging for everyone to arrive at the same time. This creates a sense of urgency with buyers. However, this is difficult to do if you only have a few days' lead time and are holding an open house because you need to find buyers immediately or the deal won't happen.

The reasoning behind this is if a buyer couple arrives at the house and likes it, they will be much more motivated to take action if they see three or four other families checking out the house than if they are the only ones there.

If you create this atmosphere of excitement, there will be some sense of competition and/or motivation for the prospective buyers. Human beings often become more interested in having something once we know someone else might be interested in it as well.

Make sure you have an adequate supply of prequalification forms. (You can find example forms at **www.deangraziosi.com/prequalform**.) If an interested buyer completes the form, make sure there is enough information for your mortgage broker to pre-qualify these individuals. You will take the form and fax it to your mortgage broker so that they can go ahead and start the qualification process. If possible, arrange with your broker and your seller to send the information over during the open house.

Out-of-Town Open Houses

Here's a technique to use if you want to attract buyers when you haven't had or don't have much time to prepare or market.

If you don't live in the same city, or the home is a great distance from you, then you need to arrange with the seller, or possibly the real estate agent you are using, a time that they can host an open house. If you and your seller plan on holding one of the two open houses on a particular day during the week, try to arrange the open house to start after normal workday hours and hold it open for around two hours. I also encourage sellers to hold open houses on Saturday and/or Sunday for four hours.

Provide sellers with credit application ahead of the open houses. If a prospective buyer shows interest in the house, then have the prospective buyer fill out a credit application (which is pretty basic and asks applicants to list the name, address, how much the house is, job information such as length of employment and income, and signature of the applicant). Then your mortgage broker can pull their credit report and determine what type and how much of a loan can be extended to this buyer or what corrective action needs to be taken by the prospective buyer to improve his/her credit score.

If you attend the open house, then have buyers complete the application right there. If you cannot be present at the open house, then the seller can hand out the credit applications with your business card attached.

If you don't have a business card, then the application should list your name, e-mail address, website (if you have one), and fax number on the top of the form. The interested buyers (for example, either an individual or husband and wife) will complete these forms and get it back to you. Once you have the credit application, you either fax or e-mail it to your mortgage broker to determine if financing can be arranged.

The person will either be qualified or not. If the mortgage broker can qualify the buyer with the right financing amount, then you contact the buyer and arrange for him to sign the Real Estate Purchase Agreement between you (as seller) and the buyer (as purchaser).

At the open house, you will also need to educate prospective buyers on how this system works, as well as confirm that they are motivated. You can create a flyer that emulates what your pre-recorded messages say so they get all the information they'll need by reading a few pages. In many cases you advertise in a similar way to get people to the open house.

If they complete the form, then you know they are fairly motivated. A good sign of their motivation is if they are asking questions about how soon they'll hear back from you or the mortgage broker. Comments like that demonstrate they have a vested interest in the information that you are providing, as well as an interest in follow-up from you.

Once Your Buyer Is Pre-qualified

Qualification may require a little extra work, but with the right mortgage broker, you can help people qualify for financing all the time. A 600 credit score is about as low as you can go, although it depends on how good your broker is. Fortunately, even credit scores below 600 may not be a problem (it's common to find errors on credit reports). Through your killer mortgage broker, a prospective buyer can make significant improvements to someone's credit score, allowing that person to buy a home from you if not this one.

Once the mortgage broker has pre-qualified the buyer, then the mortgage broker can notify you of the good news. You should give the buyer a call, congratulate him or her, and confirm their motivation in terms of your agreement.

You want to confirm the desire to go forward with the transaction to purchase this house, at the previously agreed-upon purchase price, as well as what the closing date would possibly be. Arrange a time to meet with the buyers again and sign the Purchase and Sale Agreement. Once the agreement is signed with the buyers, you contact the seller and let them know you have one more document to complete.

As we covered in previous chapters these documents do the following:

- It releases you from both separate Real Estate Purchase and Sale

Agreements with the (1) Seller and the (2) Buyer, and makes these two agreements null and void;

• It creates a real estate agreement to sell the property directly from the Seller to the Buyer, and;

• It includes a provision for you to get paid the amount of money (your equity essentially) at closing from the original agreement you had with the Seller.

• The net result is that now you are left with one contract between the Buyer and Seller that includes a provision for you to get paid for backing out of the transaction.

• And if it was a Assignment deal, then you are simply assigning the contract to a new Buyer for a fee.

In the next chapter, I'm going to discuss a strategy that I did NOT invent, called the 7-Day Auction. It has been amazingly effective in selling homes for many people in down market times with entire books written on that strategy alone. You will pick up additional ideas for promoting an open house once you read the auction strategy, so I will not be redundant by describing them all here.

Matt's $20,000 profit in Less Than Two Hours Using No Money at All

As I mentioned in the beginning of this book I have been a real estate investor since 2005. I got in during the end of a hot market and now am seeing a market at its worse. I am so glad it is right where it is right now. This so called "bad" market is going to allow me to be a multimillionaire. Just saying that out loud from where I started feels so good. And I hope that I did my service to you throughout this book and inspired you to take action.

I also had the option of 100 percent financing when I first started, which has since gone away. When the 100 percent up-front financing went away I then went on to purchase really cheap houses for cash and then refinanced in 30 days, pulling all my money plus some back out. That became my new strategy.

But the evolution that is more exciting then anything is the exact strategies you are learning from Dean right now. And that is locking up great deals at 30% to 50% off fair market value and then assigning that great deal to another buyer for a fee because you/me/we were smart enough to find such a great deal.

In just the few weeks before writing this section for Dean I have done 4 deals using the exact "No Money" strategies Dean is teaching you and I shared with you in this book for a profit of $37,500 . That's zero money out of my pocket and literally a handful of hours to get all 4 deals done. And that is only the beginning: I have 9 deals currently locked up that average 45% off FMV price. I intend to make a small fortune on those without using a dollar of my own money and making people happy along the way. I help get properties sold, and I help people get great deals and get paid in the middle. Please know that once you dig in and start using these techniques you will discover there is no shortage of great deals and no shortage of buyers who want great deals. Luckily, you are somewhere in the middle making money.

One deal that I completed recently really stands out. Let me share that with you:

One day I got a phone call from a guy who was looking to rent a house. He had just gone through a divorce, and although he had a pretty good job, he also had to pay child support for his three children, so that cost alone ate up most of his money.

Of course, this guy didn't tell me this right off the bat. Just by using Dean's strategies to find a person's "Magic Buttons," I learned to listen and ask a lot of questions, because I am always trying to find an opportunity to make it a win-win for everybody.

So I asked him how much he could afford as a monthly rent payment and he said $1,250 per month. When he told me that, I realized he could actually afford to buy his own house for around $125,000. Then I asked him why he didn't just go out and buy his own house. That's when he told me that the banks would only qualify him for $100,000. When he started looking for homes, he didn't like any of the houses he could buy for $100,000 and all of the houses he did want to buy were priced in the $130,000 range.

That's when I asked him, "If I could find you a $130,000 house that would only cost you $98,000, would you be interested?" Naturally, this guy's face lit up and he said, "Absolutely!"

Rather than me doing all of the work to find him a house, I just linked him up with my real estate agent. Together they started looking at houses until they found one that he really liked. This house had been on the market for a while and someone had even put in an offer, but the bank had turned it down.

Since this was a foreclosed property, the bank had already priced it low enough to sell, but it still needed some minor repairs before anyone would want to live in it. Beyond some problems with the roof and a few windows, most other repairs were minor cosmetic details.

I wound up buying the house for $48,000 using the exact methods I have shared with you throughout this book and then got estimates for how much repairs would cost, which wound up in the $25,000 price range. That meant combining the cost of repairs ($25,000) with the price of the house ($48,000). My total cost was $73,000.

I sold the house to this guy for $98,000, which gave me a profit of $21,000 after expenses and real estate commissions. Everyone wins. I made a nice profit, my real estate agent made a profit twice on the same house, the bank got the foreclosure off their books, and the new homeowner got a house he loved at a bargain price.

By you being "out there" and in the game opportunities like this are everywhere. But you have to be in it to win. Get started, follow what you have learned, make a few mistakes and reap the benefits of your accomplishments. I don't know about you but $21,000 is a lot of money to me, especially when I only had a few hours of personal time to make this entire deal come together.

Summary

In this chapter, you learned all about finding buyers for your properties using a variety of methods that many people will never think about. Even though they require some extra effort on your part, they can produce significant profits for you. As you progress in your experience as an investor, you will undoubtedly discover more resources and ideas to locate other buyers.

- A website must present a clear, focused message that educates and informs visitors and explains what your service will do for them.

- Every website needs a way to capture a visitor's information by providing a free report or other information.

- Large companies often need to relocate employees. You may be able to help them buy and sell houses.

- Young couples starting or growing a family may need larger houses.

- Newlyweds and divorced couples are great sources of buyers and sellers.

- Retirees often need to sell larger homes to move to smaller ones or to homes in warmer climates.

- Holding a special event, like free hot dogs or cookies, at an open house can attract multiple buyers and create competition among them.

- "Staging" a house to make it look its best can increase the chances of attracting a buyer.

- Provide the proper paperwork (loan forms, agreement forms, etc.) for all potential buyers at an open house.

Action Steps

To get you started making money right away, I want you to set a deadline for when you will complete the following tasks:

- Get your website set up. Either go to the web address **www.deangraziosi.com/freewebsite** and get set up or call my office at 1-800-315-7782 and tell them you want your free website.

- Think of traditional ways you can easily create a system for people to know what the heck you are doing now and all the great services you provide.

• Attend at least one open house a week for the next month. Look for ways that the house has been staged to look its best. Look for ways you could improve its appearance.

• Decide on the type of buyers you want to target and look for places (both online and in your neighborhood) where you can place flyers or business cards for free.

• Decide how to build, keep, and update your buyers list (notebook, computer, loose-leaf binder).

In the next two chapters, you will find out how putting everything together allows you to cash in.

Success Story #10: Grady and Kathleen C.

Location: Eunella Springs, Arkansas

Real estate experience: Owned and rented three properties before getting Dean's course.

Feeling when ordering Dean's book: Very skeptical.

Feelings now toward what Dean teaches: Extremely grateful we took action and ordered his book. Life-changing.

Profit on first deal using Dean's techniques: $12,000 in less than 5 weeks

Deals since starting with Dean:

So many success stories involve people who were nearly broke and changed their life around by investing in real estate. That wasn't our situation. We were financially solvent and enjoying a nice standard of living, but real estate has become our vehicle for accelerating our wealth building and cutting in half the time till we can retire and travel.

Before Dean's course, we had bought a couple of properties, fixed them up, and rented them out, enjoying positive rental cash flow for several years. We had bought two apartment buildings and had other people paying our mortgage. Then we picked up another house for $20,000, fixed it up, and got some cash flow. That's when we started to see how real estate could work for us.

We listened to Robert Kiyosaki's audio course and that got us excited about real estate investing as a plan for an earlier retirement. We knew about the possibilities of real estate, but we didn't know how to do it. Then around January, we saw Dean's infomercial. Not sure if it was the real thing, we took a leap of faith and ordered Dean's book and just went from there. Besides the amazing new skills we learned in his book, his constant cheerleading and enthusiasm helped us set a solid path to our goals and our lives have changed for the better, forever.

Our first deal using Dean's techniques happened when I was putting letters around at houses, looking for properties to buy. I met a man who was sitting on his porch, recovering from a lengthy illness and heart surgery. When he heard we bought houses, he told me he wanted to sell his house.

After talking to him to learn his "magic buttons," as Dean had taught us, I learned that he wanted enough money to travel. We offered $82,000, which he rejected, so we walked away from the deal. A week later, he called and we offered $87,500. After talking to him some more, we found that all he wanted was $18,000 down to pay off his RV. Then we would take over payments for one year with no interest, renovate the house and pay the mortgage.

We put $13,000 into fixing up the house and five weeks later, sold it for $112,500, earning approximately $12,000 profit.

We did this by finding our own buyer, which was a Mexican family that didn't speak much English. We accompanied them to the bank and found they could only qualify for 90% of the purchase price. We decided to think a little different and wrote a promissory note for the other 10%. That way they got the house and we got the price we wanted.

This was just the first deal of six we have done so far using Dean as our cheerleader, guide, motivator and so much more.

At first, I was really short of confidence and the whole thing overwhelmed me. Now I work 8 to 12 hours a day and am excited to do it. I have the time to devote to it while my wife has a full-time job. She loves to do the staging and the fix-ups with veto power on the decorations. She has a great eye for what makes a house look good to increase its curb appeal.

We aren't trying to be greedy. We just do comps for an area to find the fair market value, calculate the cost of fixing up the house that will give us at least a $10,000 profit. Then we make an offer. To us, a good deal is a win-win for everyone.

We went through several agents until we found one who was friendly to investors. The first three or four agents we met wouldn't even let us talk to the seller. We finally found someone willing to be creative, think outside of the box, think of creative deals and creative financing, and was able to build a rapport with the seller. Listen to Dean and make sure to build a team with the right players. Once you do it right ONCE then you will get to reap the benefits for many years to come.

Now we're trying to do something really nice for other people. We were comfortable financially before we got into real estate. To be honest, we needed something to focus on, and everything I could see convinced me that real estate was the way to go. We are grateful for everything we have learned from Dean.

Grady and Kathleen's Success Secrets: It can be done. If someone says, "I can't do it," I will say, "Yes, you can. If you follow the steps correctly, you can be successful." It may be hard work, but it's all about the journey. Once it all comes together and makes sense, it's very much fun. I'm thankful and grateful that I saw the infomercial, got excited the way Dean presented and sold the program, and took that first step buying the book. The book led to phone calls from Dean and the offer to do the mentoring program. We paid the money and signed up, and, under seven months, we had done five deals. Sometimes I would get shaky and feel like I lost my way, but Dean's cheerleading kept me going. I gained a lot from the things he had to say that made me believe I could do it if I just followed the steps. Don't be afraid to jump in and try it. Use the advisors and mentoring. Start out with the basic program and just go. Take a look at this as being your own boss. You'll feel proud doing it and have a lot of creativity and flexibility.

To see a video of Grady and Kathleen telling their story go to **www.deans media.com/gradyandkathleen**

CHAPTER 11

Sell That House in Seven Days

I want you to picture yourself on the first day that you've officially started your life as a new investor. Excited and a bit nervous, you go about your daily routine, proudly carrying your first batch of business cards in your pocket. You stop for a cup of coffee, and just to get some practice doing it, you pull out one of your new cards and proudly hand it to the girl behind the register, and say:

"Keep me in mind if you know of anyone with a property to sell."

That went pretty well, right? You're feeling good that you got your first card out, even though you know it's a throwaway...until she chirps back:

"Wow, that's pretty cool, you're an investor? I know where there's a house for sale. It's owned by a little old lady. She's just down the street from where my parents live."

The girl says it has been for sale a long time, gives you the general directions and off you go. (Tip: Don't prejudge people since you never know where your next deal will come from.)

Later that day, you decide to check it out. To make a long story short, let's just say you do the things I've taught you in this book, and lo and behold, the house ends up fitting all of your criteria. The owner is motivated, the price is well below FMV (fair market value), and it's in great condition and located in a popular area. Turns out, the owner has been trying to sell it for months, but she's using nothing more than an FSBO sign in the front yard. That might have worked in most cases, but because the home is tucked away on a cul-de-sac, it doesn't get a lot of drive-by traffic. Consequently, almost no one has seen the "For Sale" sign. You figure that is the only reason it hasn't been snapped up, so you're excited.

The owner is willing to let you put the house under contract, but only wants to give you ten days. You see, her newly widowed friend, Lucille from Pocatello, has convinced her to finally call a real estate agent and list the house. The owner plans to leave the state and join her friend in Pocatello. You think: "Ten days! I don't even have a buyers list built, what am I going to do?" Normally that would be a problem...but not for you... because you remember that THIS chapter, chapter 11 of this book, gave you a strategy to sell that beauty with three days to spare!

What you're about to learn can be used to sell just about any property, whether you've locked it up under contract and don't have a buyer for it or you're holding properties of your own to resell. You can save time selling the home and substantially reduce the costs associated with the sale. Best of all, you can use this great technique in an up or down market because it will attract buyers of all kinds and sell your house fast. Since you are ideally going to lock up most of your deals for 14 to 30 days, the 7-day sale method is perfect for achieving your goal within your allotted time period.

First, I have to give a small disclaimer. This is the only strategy in this book that I have never personally used. However, I would use this method for sure (and may do so in the future). The only reason I haven't used it is that I have been so amazingly lucky with everything else I've shared with you in this book.

So this section borrows advice from others who have used this strategy successfully. I had heard of a number of the techniques in this method from associates of mine in the marketing field. However, before I wrote about it I had to go do some hard research to get the facts straight. In my research, one of the books that I thought was written extremely well, with practical advice, was called, *How to Sell Your Home in 5 Days* by Bill Effros.

Although there are a few variations of the auction, Mr. Effros's book is great if you want a more in-depth guide to this strategy. I even found people you can pay to teach you this technique, and others who do nothing else but apply this strategy and get massive success each time. There are also websites I found that sell pre-made signs (using the same marketing techniques I've taught you), except the signs are strictly geared toward the "auction" strategy.

As we go through this method, I'm going to describe it in a way that will show you how to use it in any market, under any circumstances, and make it super-easy.

How It Works

The 7-day sale method is based on the auction concept, which again, has been the subject of numerous books and courses. The basic idea is to allow interested buyers to bid on your property in a very strategic and calculated open bidding forum. This helps determine the true fair market value of the home that buyers will actually pay—not just the perceived value or the desired value.

If you've ever been to a live auction or an auction website like eBay, then you know how the bidding process creates excitement and competition, which usually results in a higher selling price. When you sell real estate at an auction, you usually wind up with both a significantly shorter time holding a house on the market and a much higher selling price at true market value.

Perhaps you've seen TV or newspaper ads promoting foreclosure auctions in your area? Recently, an insider at one of the biggest auction companies in the country told me that with all the thousands of homes sold, the excitement of an auction causes them to sell on average 97% of fair market value. WOW! 97% of fair market value! In most cases, these buyers are even experienced real estate investors getting caught up in the excitement and spending too much. Auctions work. Now you can use this strategy on the homes you want to sell.

This method can be perfect for a home that you know is a killer deal, yet do not have a particular buyer lined up yet. Using this 7-day sale program can help you find a buyer and sell a house before your contract runs out. In addition, it also eliminates having to show a lot of people the home at different times. This is especially attractive for the owner who is living in the home you have under contract.

Now let's go back to you and the great house you found. You have ten days to figure out how to make some money on this baby, what do you do? First, make sure the house is ready to show. Second, use smart marketing to advertise, and then hold an open house. Interested buyers will come, look over the home, and submit bids or offers to purchase for a particular price. Third, once you've collected a few dozen bids or so, contact the final few interested parties and complete the final phase of the bidding process. This will ensure that you get the best price at that time in seven days (or less)!

Now, the beauty of following this method is that until both the seller and the buyer have signed a Real Estate Purchase and Sale Agreement, neither party is committed to anything. There is total flexibility right up to contract signing!

Two Ways to Make the Most of the 7-Day Sale

You have two paths you can take with this program. One is to basically sell a property (which you have already locked up on contract by using all the techniques you have learned in this book) through the 7-day auction process. You have it locked up, you have 14, 30 or more days on your contract to close, and now, in comparison to many other methods, you can sell it really fast.

The second—and new—option I am introducing is to be a Marketing Consultant. You assist a seller through the process of getting their home sold through an auction platform, which they most likely could never do on their own or without this information.

As a marketing consultant, you are paid a marketing fee for your services if the sale is successfully completed. This fee can be negotiated between you and the seller. You may consider a flat fee, or a percentage of the sale price, if the home is sold to a party that you brought in during the 7-day process.

Since being paid to be a marketing consultant is a new area of reference, I am going to assume in this chapter that is the strategy you are going to follow. But remember, all the steps are exactly the same if you have the property locked up on contract. You still want to sell it fast, the difference is one strategy is used when you are selling someone else's home and the other is used for a home you have on contract.

The Marketing Consultant Agreement Method

In situations where you agree to act as a marketing consultant, you will not be taking ownership or locking up the property. The process from start to finish goes like this:

- Sign the Marketing Agreement

- Preparation of the property

- Hold the Open House

- Facilitate the Bidding

- Complete the Closing

Step 1: Signing the Agreement (Day 1)

If you're going to act as a marketing consultant, then use the "Marketing Agreement" included below and also downloadable at **www.deangraziosi.com/marketingagreement**.

This agreement lists the services you will provide to the homeowner to sell their home. You will simply be a consultant to the seller. As a result, you are not "locking up" the property. You are only providing consulting and marketing services to organize and assist the seller through the entire process. (Again, property you do have locked up already would be a similar process minus the marketing agreement.)

You can explain to the seller the following advantages of your 7-day program:

• The property will be bid upon by buyers within one week.

• The sellers are not tying up the property with a long-term contract, as they would with a typical real estate broker listing agreement.

• The sellers do not have to accept an offer below their "reserve price" (minimum acceptable price). In fact, until the final Real Estate Purchase and Sale Agreement is signed by both buyer and seller, the sellers can cancel at any time, providing the sellers with total flexibility.

• You, as the consultant, are only paid at the closing of the property. If it doesn't sell, you will not be paid.

As a marketing consultant, you would normally charge a flat fee for the service. You need to discuss what the seller's lowest possible sale price would be for their house. This will become the minimum "reserve price" and no offer will be accepted below this price. If there are no buyers willing to pay this amount, the sale is canceled and the home would not be sold. The sellers are not forced to accept an offer below their minimum.

In addition, the seller's "reserve price" is not discussed or disclosed to anyone. It is not public information, and no buyers will ever know what that amount is.

In helping the sellers determine the reserve price, have them allow for the closing costs, your consulting fee, and perhaps a commission to the buyer's real estate agent, that is, if the buyers are represented by an agent. If offers are higher than the reserve price, let the buyers know that the reserve price has been met and there will be a sale at the end of the specified time period.

Just a word of caution to save you time: If the sellers are unrealistic about the value of their home and have set an extremely high reserve price, politely back out of this arrangement. If at a later date the sellers become realistic about the value of their home, you can decide whether you would like to work with them at that time.

If the sellers are not realistic, you'll both get frustrated. The bidding process will not be a success, and both you and the sellers will have wasted each other's time. Sometimes sellers get emotional about their properties and cannot look without bias at current market conditions. Also, we often tend to see only the pluses and not the minuses of our homes (especially if we have lived in it for many years).

So Step 1 is to make sure you have the proper paperwork filled out and signed so that you're both clear on the agreement. Whether you're acting as a marketing consultant, or using the instant equity exchange (IEE) method of locking the property up under contract use this form:

Marketing Consultant Agreement

This agreement dated_____ , is made By and Between _____(owner name)___, whose address is_____, referred to as

"Owner", AND _____You_____ whose address is referred to as "Consultant."

1. Consultation Services. The OWNER hereby employs the consultant to perform the following services in accordance with the terms and conditions set forth in this agreement:

The consultant will consult with the OWNER concerning matters relating to the marketing and organization of an auction, desired by the OWNER, designed to facilitate the OWNER selling his/her own property.

2. Terms of Agreement. This agreement will begin_____and will end_____.

3. Time Devoted by Consultant. It is anticipated the consultant will spend approximately ____7 days_ in fulfilling its obligations under this contract. The particular amount of time may vary from day to day or week to week. However, the consultant shall devote a minimum of____days/hours____ to duties in accordance with this agreement.

4. Place Where Services Will Be Rendered. The consultant will perform most services in accordance with this contract at_____location_____In addition the consultant will perform services on the telephone and at such other places as designated by the OWNER to perform these services in accordance with this agreement.

5. Payment to Consultant. The consultant will be paid at the rate of $ _____per_____for work performed in accordance with this agreement, and provided the efforts are successful. The OWNER will pay the consultant the amounts due as indicated within ten (10) days of closing.

6. Independent Contractor. Both the OWNER and the consultant agree that the consultant will act as an independent contractor in the performance of its duties under this contract. Accordingly, the consultant shall be responsible for payment of all taxes including Federal, State and local taxes arising out of the consultant's activities in accordance with this contract, including by way of illustration but not limitation, Federal and State income tax, Social Security tax, Unemployment Insurance taxes, and any other taxes or business license fee as required.

7. Confidential Information. The consultant agrees that any information received by the consultant during any furtherance of the consultant's obligations in accordance with this contract, which concerns the personal, financial or other affairs of the OWNER will be treated by the consultant in full confidence and will not be revealed to any other persons, firms or organizations.

8. Employment of Others. Both the OWNER and Consultant may from time to time request the arranging of services of others. All costs for those services will be paid by the OWNER but in no event shall the consultant employ others without the prior authorization of the OWNER.

9. Signatures. Both the OWNER and the consultant agree to the above contract.

Witnessed by:

OWNER

_____(14)_____(15)_____

By:

_____(14)_____(16)_____

CONSULTANT

NOTICE

The information in this document is designed to provide an outline that you can follow. Due to the variances of many local, city, county and state laws, we recommend that you seek professional legal counseling before entering into any contract or agreement.

Step 2: Preparation (Day 2)

Once the agreements are signed, it's preparation time. There are two areas of preparation you need to get done. The first is the preparation of the home and the second is the preparation of the marketing materials and documentation.

You should recommend that the seller obtain a home inspection performed by a reputable, independent, professional home inspector. Be sure he or she is an independent party. (It can't be Uncle Johnny who just happens to be a general contractor. Only a licensed and bonded home inspector will do in this case.)

The cost of a home inspection is generally about $250 to $450, depending on the size of the house and amenities (outbuildings, pool and spa, etc.). If the homeowner throws a fit about doing this, let them know that a buyer may require it, and without an inspection, they could lose a good deal.

The inspector will prepare a detailed report outlining the scope of the inspection, and all the findings of defects. This allows the buyer to review the report and be aware of any issues raised. It will also make the seller aware of any issues with the home they may want to repair prior to the sale. It's always better to correct significant issues or obtain an estimate of the cost of the repairs, especially in a slow real estate market.

• Pest Inspection—This usually costs around $100 and will eliminate any concerns potential buyers may have about termites and other pests.

• Seller's Property Disclosure Statement—Have the sellers complete the Property Disclosure Statement. This should be available for potential buyers to review at the open house. It gives the buyer additional information about the home, and will be a valuable tool in their assessment of the home. It is important that the seller discloses all items and be truthful in completing this statement.

• Home Warranty Plan—Discuss with the seller the option of purchasing a Home Warranty for the buyer, which costs about $350. Buyers will often ask for this as part of a negotiation. It would most likely cover items for a one-year period that would require repair or replacement such as furnace, air conditioner, appliances and other items. Check with a local real estate agent or Title Company for recommended companies that offer these warranties.

• General House Preparation—Some of these items may be obvious, but I will review them. Sellers should thoroughly clean their home. Remove clutter, have closets tidy, floors waxed, carpets cleaned, windows washed, potentially offensive items removed and stored (i.e., posters, magazines, etc.). The yard should be mowed, plants and trees trimmed, driveway swept and front entry made to look inviting. Remember the street appeal (or curb appeal) and front entry create the first impression for a buyer.

You only have one chance to make a first impression so make it a great one. Touch-up paint could be helpful in making the home look fresh and clean. Valuable items that may be stolen should be removed from the premises. Encourage the sellers to examine the home carefully for such items. (Remember to check out my video or send the seller to check out my video at **www.deangraziosi.com/maximize** for ideas for a great showing.)

Step 3: Promotional Preparation: (Day 3)

Obviously you're going to need to advertise the open house, so determine what types of advertising will be most effective to attract qualified buyers such as advertising on Craigslist.com, placing ads in the local newspaper, distributing flyers in the community, posting notices on bulletin boards (such as grocery stores), sticking signs in the yard, and probably most important of all, planting bandit signs around the surrounding area that direct people to the property location.

(Examples for this can be found at **www.deangraziosi.com /7daypreparation.**)

This is a critical step because you need to attract as many buyers as possible to the open house. The earlier you start the advertising, the more exposure you'll have for your sale.

If you use online or classified methods to promote the event, chances are good you'll receive a lot of inquiries, and this is exactly what you want. You can direct these calls to a recorded message or take them live. Just remember that any prospect could be the final buyer, so treat them like gold.

I cannot overemphasize the importance of getting the word out about your sale. People must know about the home and the sale in order to attend it and submit a bid.

I suggest you go to a local print shop and have signs made for the open house and get them up right away. The more people who see the signs, the more people will attend the sale.

If you direct the people to a 24-hour recorded message, you could let that message explain exactly what's going on. You can include the dates and times you will be holding the open house, the property address, the opening bid price and phone number to contact you if they have more questions.

Make sure the signs are large enough so people can read them when they drive by. A brightly colored background may attract more attention, but signs have to be easy to read.

We have spent a lot of time in this book showing you the concept behind good advertising and marketing. Use all those skills here. In your classified ads, bandit signs, and flyers use powerful headlines to grab people's attention along with short, powerful statements. Below are just some quick examples that could get people to take action and call you.

Classified ad example:

Best Bid Sunday Night Wins My Home
Must Sell 4B/3B Beauty This W/E
View Sat & Sun 10–4 Best Bid Wins Sun 5 PM

FREE RECORDED INFO 24 HRS XXX-XXX-XXXX

HOME TO BE SOLD SUNDAY NIGHT

Situated on top of President Hill in the heart of any town, USA, our home is a breathtaking site. This 3500 sq. ft. Contemporary design has a 4 car garage and a full basement, perched atop the prettiest hill in any town. Convenient to schools, shopping and the Freeway, it is a quiet retreat that makes you forget how quickly you can get to the big city, or the local shops. If you can find a better house, pinch yourself because you'll be dreaming.

With 4 bedrooms, 3.5 baths, a formal dining room, a living room with fireplace, a gourmet eat-in kitchen, office, den and 12-Foot high ceilings on the ground floor, you'll never be at a loss for space. Our outdoor swimming pool is heated and can be enjoyed year round.

We have owned our home for 24 years, and during that time most homes in Any town have appreciated by more than 8% a year. You'll have instant equity.

OPENING BID 50% of CURRENT MARKET VALUE

Our Home will be Open for Inspection 10 to 5

Saturday and Sunday Only

No Appointment Required

Bids Accepted From People Who Have Visited

It will be Sold to the High Bidder Sunday Night

TO HEAR FREE 24 HOUR RECORDED INFORMATION CALL

XXX-XXX-XXXX

Bandit sign example: Note that bandit signs can be illegal in some areas. Check your local city office as some cities may enforce stiff fines. You have a better chance of getting noticed (and even excused/warned instead of fined) using a handwritten sign versus a pre-printed sign.

Make sure everyone who comes to look or bid on the home knows how the bidding process works. Of course, we will give you the basic bidding rules sheet that you can customize in the Resource Center located at **www.deangraziosi.com/all-forms**. In fact, we have all the forms on our website you will ever need, available for you to download or copy and use.

HOUSE TO BE SOLD SUNDAY

Simply customize the bidding rules to set the ground rules for submitting bids at the open house. Explain what information will be available to all bidders, the length of the open house, what happens once the open house is over, and finally, what will happen during the final bidding process. This can be customized for your specific seller's needs and for specific properties.

The actual form can be downloaded , but just so this makes complete sense to you, here is a sample of the "Bidding Rules" sheet. The actual sheet we've included on the website for you has many additional numbered points.

BIDDING RULES

This home will be sold on Sunday evening to the highest bidder. This home is being sold "by owner." This is **not** a "buyer-in-distress" sale, short sale, foreclosure sale, repo sale, tax sale, HUD auction, or any other type of auction.

1. Bidders (or their agents) must attend the open house on either (day) or (day).

2. Bids will be accepted at the open house on the bidding sheets. You will need to include your name, phone number and bid on the bidding sheet.

3. The bidding sheets will be available for viewing during the open house hours.

4. The final bidding process will take place starting at 5 p.m. on Sunday.

5. During the open house hours, bids will be accepted in $500 increments.

6. Bidders may call in bids after submitting their initial bid until the open house ends on Sunday at 4 p.m. After that time, bidders must wait to be called in the final bidding process.

7. The bidding sheets and information will be available for all bidders to view.

8. Every bidder will be able to submit a bid higher than the previous bid until the highest and best bidder is determined. The owner shall

determine the highest and best bid at the owner's sole discretion.

9. When the final round of bidding begins, we will call you at the number on the bidding sheet starting with the highest bid. The next highest bidder will then be called. This process will continue until all bidders have been called.

Bidders will have three options when they are called each time: (1) Increase their bid to at least $1,000 higher than the current high bid, (2) Stay at their current bid, and (3) Pull out of the bidding process.

Prepare a bidding packet to give to all potential buyers attending the open house. The following items ought to be included in the bidding packet:

- The Bidding Rules—Review the rules, and be really familiar with them in order to answer any questions potential buyers have when viewing the home. Make sure you can explain how the bidding works, as this will eliminate any confusion when you get to the final bidding process.

- A Detailed House Description—Specify items included with the house such as appliances, washer, dryer, etc. Also list any items not included in the sale of the home that are "attached to the home," such as a chandelier or particular light fixture, that won't stay with the home. Keep in mind that this could be viewed as a negative by prospective buyers. This description should be printed·on a separate page inside the packet.

- The Seller's Property Disclosure Statement—This is the form the owner of the property has completed that addresses the history of the home.

- A Home Inspection Report—This is a report prepared by an independent third party. This provides credibility to the selling process. No house is perfect. It is always a good idea to make full disclosure on anything that you or the sellers are aware of that may need repair or replacement. (The buyers can certainly hire their own home inspector who may find items that aren't on the first inspector's report. If this happens, there should not be major issues. If there are repairs the seller is not willing to make, have an estimate of the cost to repair them. This will enable the potential buyers to include that amount along with the purchase price to their actual cost for the property.)

- Plot or Neighborhood Map—This map shows where the property is located.. Find this on the Internet, often through the local county website. The title company can also provide this information to you upon request.

- Home Owners Association (HOA) Rules—If the property must follow HOA rules, include these items in a summary format. You could also have a complete copy of the HOA documents available at the home for bidders to review. You can get these from the HOA itself.

- A copy of the Pest Inspection—The more information you provide a potential buyer up front, the more likely it will save you potential issues after the completion of the bidding.

- Home /Description should be very detailed and include all of the information you have on your sample description. You may want to add a photo of the home at the top. (sample below)

Be sure to present these items in a professional manner. No items should be handwritten (unless from a third party) and all items should have a consistent format to ensure a professional look.

- Area Map—Include driving directions from all areas of town. You can get directions by going to mapquest.com or googlemaps.com.

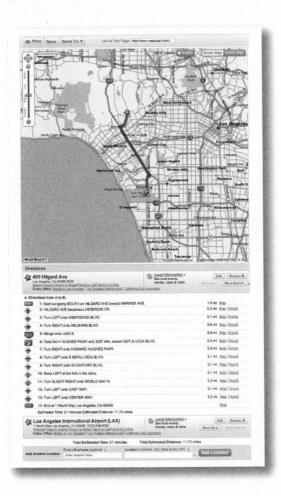

- Pricing of the Home—Obviously you must discuss the price of the home with the seller. We covered ways to determine the fair market value of the home in chapter 7.

Use all of those strategies to come up with a price that is exciting for a potential new buyer while still allowing you to make a profit and keep the home owner satisfied with the selling price. Remember, you are going to want to know the price they would really like to get, all the way down to the rock-bottom "I'll sell it at that price if I have to" price.

Remember, every home is different, so take your time and make sure you know the true value. In many or most cases, you will be educating the seller as well. They may be hoping for a price simply out of emotions rather than facts and what is going on in the market around them.

Once you come up with the amount you hope to get (as well as the rock-bottom bare-minimum amount), start the bidding of the home at about 50% to 60% of whatever you determine to be the fair market value. This will be the amount you advertise as the opening bidding price on all of your printed materials.

Step 4: Placing Ads (Days 3, 4 & 5)

By now, your signs at the sign shop should be ready, so pick them up and start getting them out. Now is also a good time to harness the power of the Internet by placing ads on Craigslist.com. As I've mentioned before, the ads you place on craiglist are free! And I don't need to tell you how large an audience you can reach.

You'll find craigslist is a fantastic place to list homes for sale. When you go to the site, find your city on the right side of the home page, and then click on your city. If you don't find your city, look for a nearby city. Next, click on the "Real Estate For Sale" link. That is going to bring all the real estate offerings posted for that day. Post your ad and get ready to field a lot of e-mails. I have posted an ad and literally gotten calls and e-mails in response within 15 minutes! I recommend placing your craigslist ad as soon as you have a decent photo of the exterior and you have enough information to post a great description of the home. So post an ad on Day 2 and then freshen up the ad and post another ad on Day 4 or 5 so your posting reaches the top again.

Here's a sample of a craigslist ad:

Must Sell— House to Be Auctioned, Make An Offer
Open House followed by Open Bid Auction on (days and dates) Public AUCTION. Custom home: by (builder) 2x6 Construction with lots of upgrades. Upgraded features including: 36' Raised panel Maple upper cabinets; Granite countertops in kitchen w/ all appliances included; Recently installed hardwood flooring; Oak tambour stain-grade front door; Laundry room w/ Washer/

Dryer, storage cabinets and sink; Extended garage with built-in storage; Bay window in oversized Master; energy-efficient heat pump; Epoxy finish on Driveway, garage, patios. Immaculately maintained. All offers subject to seller approval.

All HIGHEST & BEST OFFERS to be submitted to seller at (date) @ 5 PM. Rapid decision and ability to close fast. NOT LENDER OWNED.

Bedrooms: 3
Bathrooms: 2
Parking Spaces: 2
Square Feet: 1,796
Year Built: 2003
Floors: 1
LOCATION Click to view map: 123, Anystreet, Your City, Your State

If you have your own website, advertise the home for sale, with many photos and detailed descriptions about the great features of the house.

Placing classifieds in local newspapers is an effective advertising option. Depending on your budget, run your ad from Day 3 through Day 7. Remember, you're advertising and promoting your open houses; these are great homes with attractive opening bid prices. If you can't afford to run the ad all 5 days, do it as many days as you can. But don't miss running the Saturday and Sunday ads (Day 6 and 7). Second, after you place your ad, thoroughly review it the first day the ad runs.

It does you no good to place an ad with incorrect information. If you place classified ads through the customer service person, be certain the ad-taker carefully and clearly reads the ad back to you. Pay attention to detail (address, telephone numbers, open house times, etc.). Here is an example of a classified ad you can run:

PICK YOUR PRICE!!!
HOUSE MUST GO THIS SUNDAY
4 br/3 bath newly remodeled, pool, 2-car gar, large yard
This is going to be the deal
of a lifetime for someone!
OPEN INSPECTION SAT & SUN 11–4
WILL BE SOLD SUNDAY NIGHT TO THE HIGHEST BIDDER
Call 24 HR FREE RECORDED MESSAGE
for All the Facts 123-456-7890

If you haven't done so already, place your bandit signs in select locations directing people to the property.

Step 5: E-mail and Telephone Logs and Rosters— (Days 3, 4, 5, 6 & 7)

As soon as you place your first ad, you'll start to receive calls and e-mails about the home and people will want details surrounding the bidding process. Naturally, you want to be prepared. An exciting thing is that you never know which one of these folks will be the successful bidder. You can also use the same strategies we have already covered and send people to a pre-recorded message that explains everything along with time and date of the open house. Here is an example message to entice and excite people to come to the open house and bid on it:

> *Hi, this is Pat. Thank you for calling about the house to be auctioned off this weekend. In just a moment I'm going to give you details about this fabulous house and the opportunity you have to get a steal on it. So grab something to write with and be prepared to take some notes. The house, located on a lovely cul-de-sac off Adams Street, is a three-bedroom three and a half bath, 2,000 sq. ft. home with a large backyard. There is plenty of grass to play on, a play center, and a storage shed. The two-car garage also has a mini workshop and full-size custom cabinets for storage. There are pull- down stairs that allow you easy access to the attic from the garage, an extra-large laundry room complete with shelves. The kitchen has an eat-in breakfast bar, a double sink, dishwasher double ranges, all stainless steel appliances and they are included in the sale of his home. There is an eating nook in the kitchen, a formal dining room, a den and each bedroom has its own bathroom. The front room has a large picture window looking out on a beautifully landscaped yard with lovely full-grown shade trees. You can come see the home for her yourself on Saturday between 10 AM and 5 PM and again on Sunday between 1 and 4 PM. Bidding will begin Sunday and ends at 5 PM. This will be an open bidding process, meaning you will be able to see other bids. Pricing on this home will begin at $92,000 which is 50% less than the current market value for the home. We invite you to come and take a look at this lovely home and tell anyone you know about the event. Refreshments will be served both days so please plan to come. If you have further questions you can reach me at 555-555-1234 or e-mail me at Pat@blah.com.*

> *Remember that you can come see the home for yourself on Saturday between 10 AM and 5 PM and again on Sunday between 1 and 4 PM. The home is located at 123 Opportunity Avenue in Smart Town USA*
>
> *Thank you for listening. Again, this is Pat and I look forward to seeing you at the auction this weekend.*
>
> *If you need to reach me for any further information please leave your information at the tone and I will give you a call back promptly.*
>
> *Thanks again and mark your calendar for this great event.*

You can see how the right script can save you a ton of time explaining the same things over and over again.

Every inquiry should be treated with respect and all questions answered. I suggest keeping a log of names, telephone numbers, e-mail addresses and comments. It will be difficult later if you don't. Keep track of this information, including how you answered callers' questions.

That suggestion may sound strange to hear at first, but as you learn more about a caller's situation and/or the house, you might modify your standard answers to questions. Therefore, it is important to keep track of what you talk about. For e-mails, create a separate folder named after each property and save all communications there.

Step 6: Open House (Days 6 & 7)

Have everything ready long before the actual time of the open house. You don't want to be running around trying to get things ready with potential buyers standing around waiting. (Also, remember that the auction process takes 7 days from start to finish, but in most cases you have a lot more preparation time and it won't seem rushed. After your first one, you can create a system to do this so it will be a piece of cake.)

All the information packets should be ready and set up on a table. You should have at least 50 sets of the bidding packets ready to hand out to each potential buyer. (You can print these yourself or go to your local Kinko's or office supply store to make them fairly inexpensively.) Have a

bidding sheet set up on the table and some chairs around the table so potential buyers can sit down and chat with you about the home and details
of the sale.

Make the home as inviting as possible. Your guests should be comfortable and interested enough to write a bid on the bidding sheet. When
people start filing in, greet them warmly and hand them a bidding packet.
Explain to them there is information about the property in the bidding
packets, and show them how to bid. Encourage people to place bids on
the bidding sheet you have placed in a fixed location. It can be on the
table with you, or a wall in plain view. Sometimes people are afraid to be
the first one to place a bid, but if they see that others are placing bids, others will be more likely to do so. Let them know they can bid any amount
higher than the last.

A good strategy for bidders may be to increase the bids by a substantial
amount to let others know they are serious about buying the home. You
want as many people bidding as possible to raise the price to its fair market value.

Depending on the part of country that you live in, you should hold your
open houses on Saturday and Sunday from 10 or 11 a.m. to 4 p.m. You
can vary the start time and begin the open house at noon or even 1 p.m.
But keep it open for 4 or 5 hours. Whatever you choose, keep the times
consistent for the entire open house.

If possible, do not have open houses on holiday weekends where prospective bidders or buyers might travel out–of-town or have family visiting.
Don't compete with Thanksgiving, Christmas, etc.

Step 7: Bidding Process

The Bidding Process will occur during the open house. It will begin as soon
as you open the doors to the home and prospective bidders begin to inspect the home.

Carry a notepad or clipboard containing the Bidding Rules and the Bidding
Roster. As people walk around the home, they'll probably have questions
about specific features of the home. If someone seems interested though
reluctant to submit a bid, it might be a good time to review the bidding
process with him. You can explain there is no obligation during this phase,
and that someone can submit a bid if they have even the slightest interest in purchasing the home.

This is a no-pressure situation. With an opening bid of 50% of the market value, you will receive bids. Prospective buyers know value when they see it, and those who are serious about buying will submit bids.

Step 8: Final Round of Bidding

The final round of bidding will begin on Sunday at 5 or 6 p.m. Whatever you decide is fine. When it begins, call the bidders from the bidding sheet at the phone number they listed, starting with the highest bidder. The purpose of calling the highest bidder first is to let the person know he is the highest bidder at the beginning of the "final bidding process" and that you will now begin to call the remaining bidders. The next highest bidder will then be called. This process will continue until all bidders have been called.

Bidders will have three options when they are contacted each time: (1) Increase their bid to at least $1,000 higher than the current high bid; (2) Stay at their current bid; or (3) Pull out of the bidding process.

This process continues until there is only one bidder left. That person will be considered the high bidder. You will then offer the home to the highest/best bidder at their highest bid price.

If the highest/best bidder is unable to meet the conditions of the terms of sale or does not provide the necessary means to purchase the home, the home will immediately be offered to the next highest and best bidder at their final bid price.

Be mindful of the fact that bids are not legally binding contracts, and they may be canceled or withdrawn at any time prior to executing a Real Estate Purchase and Sale Agreement.

Here's an example of the conversation that you might have with the final bidders. The key is to make it consistent (same wording to everyone). Write down what you are going to say and then just read it each time to the bidders:

> *Hello, my name is _____. May I speak with _____, he is bidding on a home I have for sale. We are now entering the final phase of bidding. I will be calling all bidders until we end up with one high bidder. During this final phase of bidding, any increases in your bid must be at least $1,000 higher than the current high bid. The procedure that I will follow is that I will call each bidder to determine if they are interested in*

*increasing the last bid. This process will continue by telephone
until there remains one highest/best bidder.*

Bidders will have three options when you are called: (1) Increase your bid
by at least $1,000 higher than the current high bid, (2) Stay at your cur-
rent bid, recognizing you would be in a backup position, or (3) Pull out of
the bidding process. The current bid is $_____, and there are _____
remaining bidders in the final round of bidding. Would you like to increase
your bid?"

Continue this process until only one high bidder remains. You may want
to allow between five and ten minutes between calls to see if the previous bidder calls back to increase his bid. Occasionally a bidder will call
right back and want to raise his bid.

On the rounds after the initial round you could say something like "We
have now entered the _____round of bidding. There are ___ bidders remaining. The current high bid is $_____. By how much would you like to
increase your bid?

Now on to the Real Estate Purchase and Sale Agreement. This will be completed by the seller and the successful high bidder after the final round of
bidding. Complete the agreement and have all parties sign the agreement,
while providing copies to all parties. You will need to keep one copy to
give to the closing agent along with an earnest money check, which
should be payable to the closing agent.

Step 9: Paperwork, Earnest Money and Closing Agent

After the Final Bidding Process is complete and the sellers have selected
the highest bidder, all parties are ready to meet. Sign the Real Estate Purchase and Sale Agreement, collect earnest money and turn the Real Estate
Purchase snd Sale Agreement along with the earnest money check over
to the Closing Agent, payable to the closing agent's company name.

For example, if the closing agent is First National Title Company, then the
earnest money check is made out to First National Title. People often ask
how much earnest money is acceptable. My response is generally 1% of
the purchase price of the home. Thus, on a $200,000 home, the earnest
money would be $2,000.

This is also the right time to have the seller or sellers sign the Payment Authorization, which are their instructions to the closing agent to pay you for your services during closing. This is a critical document authorizing you to get paid. It is fairly obvious, but don't forget this form. Again, all the forms are listed online.

Once the owners/sellers select the highest bidder, it's best to meet either that same day or not later than the next day following the completion of the final bidding process. If the meeting occurs on a Sunday night to sign the agreement and deliver the earnest money check, then I recommend that you and the seller deliver the agreement and earnest money check to the closing agent on the next business day. If you meet with the highest bidder on a weekday, then I recommend you meet at the closing agent's office, sign documents and deliver the paperwork to the closing agent.

The closing agent will deposit the earnest money in their bank account and hold it in an escrow account awaiting completion of this transaction. Transactions will take between two weeks for an all-cash deal to 30 to 45 days for a sale where the buyer is getting a mortgage (the most common occurrence).

In the event the selected bidder does not show up for the prearranged meeting, then this will result in the selected bidder being eliminated as the selected bidder. If the highest bidder fails to deliver the agreed-upon earnest money, then this is also a sufficient reason for the seller to eliminate the selected bidder. The owners will have the right to (1) select the next highest bidder and offer the home to purchase; or (2) cancel the bidding process altogether.

Unless otherwise specified in the Real Estate Purchase and Sales Agreement, the selected bidder or purchaser shall pay the usual and typical closing costs associated with closing a real estate transaction. Certain expenses, such as real estate property taxes, will be prorated up to the date of closing.

Title insurance is becoming more expensive. It is an essential element for demonstrating clear title for the purchaser, and therefore is part of the closing costs. Normally, sellers pay for the title insurance fee as the seller is ensuring that good title is being passed on to the purchaser.

Closing & Consulting Fee Payment: Complete the consulting fee payment form and obtain the seller's signature once the deal is completed. This form is to be given to the closing agent. This is very important, as this form instructs the closing agent to pay you for your services.

Matt's Best No Money Deal Down Ever

One Saturday night, I was hanging out with some friends when I got a call from my property manager, who told me about a commercial building that went to foreclosure and was now owned by the bank (REO). Now, most people might have stayed with their friends, but I decided to leave and check out this property. It was a medical building, a little over 8 years old, and appraised for $2.4 million. Yes, it was $2.4 million! At this point I had never bought a home for over $100,000. But I remembered something Dean said, and that was, "The same amount of energy and wisdom goes in all deals no matter the size. And if it can be structured as a no money down deal with no downside risk, then why not go for it?" So I said what the heck, and went and looked at it.

Once I looked at it, I was haunted by it in a good way. I couldn't stop thinking of the money that could be made. I even found out that it had tenants already in place.

With no downside risk because I used the same strategy you are learning in this book, which I have used countless times on less expensive homes, I made an offer of 1.4 million dollars.

They said no to $1.4 but accepted $1,596,000. A little nervous but excited I said, "Let's do it." Again I used all the same no money down strategies you are learning and got a contract drawn up where I could own the building with no money out of my pocket. With a little back-and-forth negotiations with the bank, we signed the contract and now were just awaiting a closing in 30 days or so.

Three days after we signed the contract , the bank called me and said somebody else offered to buy the building for much more than I was willing to pay. So the bank asked if they could pay me $50,000 if I would tear up the contract and walk away. I acted on the phone as if I was calm and cool about and said I would get back to them. Once I hung up I jumped up and down and said YES!! Next level, here I come…

The reason I wanted to buy this property was because I knew that banks are hurting in today's down market, so I knew they would give me killer terms, a great price and let me buy it with no money out of pocket. I also knew that I could make $500,000 or more in three or four years off that

building while collecting rents each month and making money from that, so I told the bank that $50,000 was too low. Instead, I countered and asked if they would pay me $75,000 to tear up the contract and give me a line of credit for $500,000. Then I could go out and buy more properties to make up the money I would be losing from the profit in the medical building. I asked the bank if that sounded like a good deal that could be a win-win for us both, and the bank said yes. Talk about a good day.

So as I write this section, I am working with the bank on the best strategy to back out of the deal, get my $75,000 and also my line of credit. In less than 3 or 4 hours of work I was able to structure this deal because a few years ago I took action and decide to try real estate. I went at it full guns a'blazing, but look where I am now. I hope this inspires you to see what is possible. I have to pinch myself sometimes. And what is even better is that this down market created these opportunities. This is the time to get rich. I'm on my way, are you coming with me?

One more thing to consider is to expect to find good deals that don't need a lot of work. Some people look for deals that take a lot of work, but I don't because I want to spend my time buying properties, not fixing them up. Initially, my goal was to have one deal a month, which I did for 2.5 years. Now I'm up to nine deals a month, which I can do by partnering with other investors.

By myself, I could get 100 percent of a small pie, but teaming up with partners, I can now get 50% of a much bigger pie. Even though my share is only 50%, that piece of the pie is ten times bigger than anything I can do on my own.

It all boils down to confidence. Start small and build your confidence. I started buying small houses and worked my way up over time. It all comes down to your confidence level. After reading this book and getting a little experience, you'll find your confidence level shooting way up, but it all begins with taking that first step. Just do it and you'll find that first step will boost your confidence far more than you might ever thought possible, and then you'll be on your way.

Summary

Buying a house or locking one up under contract is just half the process to making money in real estate. The second half is selling the house. In this chapter, you learned about the 7-day auction process for selling a house at the highest possible market price.

• Auctions are a great way to drive the price of a home to its true market value.

• Even experienced real estate investors get caught up in the bidding process to outbid their competitors and raise the home price, typically within 97% of fair market value.

• You can make money as a marketing consultant by helping sell a house for a price agreed upon by the seller.

• You can also make money by locking it up under contract using the Instant Equity Exchange techniques.

• Advertise an open house auction by posting signs and flyers around the neighborhood, or by advertising on the Internet and in newspaper classified ads.

• Prepare the home ahead of time to look its best.

• Create a bidding packet for everyone who shows up at the open house.

• Assure the seller that he or she can always cancel the bidding process at any time and are under no obligation to accept any bids.

Action Steps

Once you understand how the auction process can drive a home's price up to at least 97% of its fair market value, you'll see how auctions can help sell homes in 7 days. Before running your own auction, this is what I want you to do:

• Scour the newspapers, look for signs, and check the Internet for any auctions near you. Make a point to attend one.

• Make a list of all the places where you've seen auctions being advertised. Chances are good that you'll be able to advertise in those same places too.

• When attending another auction, look for how the auction is being run and ask yourself how you might improve upon it, or borrow some techniques that seem to work particularly well.

• Write up a short description that emphasizes the highlights of a property, such as one you have under contract. If you don't have any houses under contract, practice writing an appealing description of your own house or a neighbor's house. The point is to practice looking for the major selling points of a home.

• Examine your own house or a neighbor's house and look for flaws that a buyer might notice or object to. This will give you practice examining a house from a buyer's point of view so you'll know what to look for ahead of time.

Success Story #11: Mike S.

Location: Sterling Silver, West Virginia

Experience in real estate before getting Dean's book: None

Net worth increase as a college student: $165,000

Monthly cash flow: $700, plus I get a place to live for free

Coolest thing about real estate investing: Letting tenants build my net worth. Or maybe it's just being 24 and on my way to owning a Million Dollars in Real Estate.

Age: Currently a 24-year-old college student, but bought first house as a freshman.

I was a first-year student at Georgetown University when I saw Dean's infomercial on TV. It stoked my interest so I bought his book, read it cover to cover, and it really opened my eyes. Now, I'm not a big reader, but it was actually the fastest I'd ever read a book. I guess when you find something that interests you, you definitely stay on it.

What I really liked about the book was learning how a guy like Dean could make so much money in real estate. His book really gave me the instruction and confidence to get started and made me believe that anyone could do it. Besides motivating me, it educated me about the whole real estate process. Dean taught me to just stay persistent and have a goal. Dean's book gave me a lot of different ways to purchase a house, find the right location, and just get started.

After getting his book, I made my first deal a couple of months later. My older brother, Matt, gave me a gift of approximately $15,000 as a down payment, money he got from refinancing his first rental property. I myself signed all the paperwork. Dean always said in his book that the three most important factors in real estate are Location, Location, Location—and I found my house approximately 1 mile away from the university, where my father and brother had purchased their first rental property. Since I was going to school, I noticed that the university never offered enough housing so there was a high demand for rentals in that area. I needed a place to live, so I decided that my first house would be near the college campus.

There were not many problems that I faced when pursuing my first deal. I just stayed confident, persistent and motivated on making sure it became a success. With help and advice from my family, I negotiated for the seller to pay all closing costs, which saved me a lot of money. The only money that was spent was the down payment and approximately $2,000 to $3,000 in refurbishing and maintaining the property and a total of 35–50 hours of labor between my dad, brother and I, landscaping, painting all the rooms, plumbing, installing and cleaning. Now I had a place to live while going to school, but I still needed to rent the other rooms.

Next, my brother and I printed a bunch of business cards at Kinko's that showed a picture of the house and how many bedrooms it had. We took this stack of cards and plastered them everywhere we could—on parked cars, on doors, and all over the campus. The next day, I had four students who wanted to rent.

I don't plan to sell this house unless the market comes back and I can make a boatload of cash. Otherwise, I'll just hold on and keep renting it out. I might refinance it or sell it, but it's still earning me $300–$400 cash flow a month and paying my mortgage, which is the main thing.

Since getting that first house with the help of my dad and my brother, I've gotten four more houses. My long-term goal in real estate is to keep buying more houses. In ten years, I want to have 20–30 houses. I'd like to have a bunch of different types of properties such as apartment complexes, condos, and regular homes. I do like houses because of the land, but there's also the yard work and maintenance to worry about too. I'm looking forward to the future. I would also like to help people make money in real estate like Dean does. He changed my life forever and I would love to pass it on if possible. Maybe you will see my book hit the shelves in a few years!

Mike's Success Secret: Stay positive, stay confident, and stay away from all the skeptics out there who say it's harder than it seems. It's a process. You just need to be educated and know what you're doing. Anyone can do it. As long as you stay motivated on task, you can achieve a lot of things. I've been blessed with some opportunities and letting everything work out. I encourage students my age to look into real estate because it can definitely open a lot of doors out there.

A lot of people are shocked that I bought my first house at such an early age, but I just tell people, "Look at this book by Dean Graziosi. It will definitely open your eyes and give you a lot of advice."

I really believe that anyone, at any age, can purchase a house and make money off it. It's a great way to make money and have a lot of dreams. I didn't think I could do it either, and I'm still in college.

After I graduate in spring, I plan on buying another house (like a graduation present to myself). That will keep me busy on the weekends fixing it up. Although my major is government, I don't want to work for the government. Now I can make my real money in real estate.

To see a video of Mike telling his story go to **www.deansmedia. com/mike**

CHAPTER 12

Take Action and Start Putting Cash in Your Pocket

All right, my friend. Strap yourself in; the finish line is in sight! This is the twelfth and final chapter. Truthfully, I couldn't be happier that our journey (for now) will end this way.

Twelve is a good number. Think of all the terrific things that come in packages of twelve. There's the ever-famous bouquet of a dozen red roses, you probably have a dozen eggs in your fridge right now, and surely, at some time in your life, you must have purchased a dozen donuts! Well, to that happy list, you can now add one dozen chapters, simple-to-read printed pages that will change your life forever . . . that is if you let them.

Are you excited or scared? Where are you today, right now, compared to where you were when you started reading this book? Are you encouraged and excited about what happens next, or are you struggling to keep your chin up with tough circumstances all around you?

Ten chapters back, I wrote about the economic turmoil that ushered in the 2007–2008 recession. I told you what caused the down real estate market and how that contributed to the despair that started to hit the country hard in the last months of 2008.

You have some options and some choices to make right now.

You could let uncertainty and panic paralyze you with fear, and you'll end up doing nothing. However, doing nothing changes nothing. Do nothing and your situation will only get worse in the years to come. If you have debt and you worry about money, but you don't do anything, you can expect to get more of the same. If you have money sitting in a bank, getting the minimal amount of interest, or in mutual funds not having any idea where it will end up, you can expect more of that as well.

The other option is to open your eyes and see how the real estate market has created a huge window of opportunity for you—an opportunity to make incredible amounts of money. By using the unique, no money down systems in this book, you'll have no limits to the amount of success you can achieve. If I have done my job well in writing this book, and I feel that I have, then you are equipped with proven techniques to profit in today's market, and you should also be inspired to take action with real estate—right now. You may not feel "ready," but don't wait around until you "feel" ready.

How you feel about moving forward isn't really that important, because feeling ready has nothing to do with actually being ready. You could spend the next 18 months waiting to feel ready, or you could spend the next 18 months making a change, doing something different, learning how to make money easier than ever . . . It's your choice!

Remember a favorite saying of mine, quoted earlier in this book: "Paralysis caused by overanalysis."

I may have flooded you with information in some areas, maybe I even wrote something a little confusing. If so I apologize. I did my best to make it easy as I could. But don't you dare let that stop you from getting started and taking action. So much more is learned with action than from analysis. If you have fully read every page, then you have more knowledge than you can imagine.

This book is not meant to spit out $100 bills. It is not meant to be your life-long business plan. It is meant to give you an exact strategy that works, a foundation for success, and then get you out there to make it happen.

While you are out there in the real world "doing it," you will learn so much more than anything I can share with you in a book. But you will have the foundation for success built inside of you from the pages you just read. For more help, I have support systems in place at www.dean-graziosi.com, or you can become a student in my Real Estate Success Academy.

However, you already have everything you need to get started, I promise you. If you feel a little nervous, then read the book again. But I promise that getting started and getting out there is the best way to change your life and become a successful real estate investor.

You have a choice to get in the game or sit on the sidelines and watch others score touchdowns. It is time for you to be the star in your family and in your own life.

It's an awesome privilege to have choices. In a few short pages, you will have to make a choice, or, more accurately, you will get to make a choice.

You have been introduced to a way of finding properties for 30% to 60% off their fair market value. You now have the blueprint and the templates for a marketing system that can find both buyers and sellers. You have the knowledge of how to profit from two different kinds of deals, the IEE and the Assignment, and you know how to find buyers and sellers for both.

I've done my best to flood you with more than enough information to succeed. I've included example charts, full contracts, a free website (where you can connect with other investors), and real-life inspirational stories and videos from other students just like you. I added all that and so much more, just so you would gain extra knowledge and motivation to do what you couldn't do before picking up this book. I didn't hold anything back, because I want you to succeed! The question for you is: Are you going to hold back?

You can finish this chapter, set this book down and start a new life, your new life! Was there anything super-special about me, Matt, or all the success stories from other students in this book? I don't think so. I think we all wanted more, took a risk, found new wisdom and gained new capabilities that were proven to work. Then we just went for it. Are you ready to go for it too?

If you have taken some or all of the action steps in the book you may never even get to read this chapter, because you're already busy making money. That's not unlikely at all if you took the action steps included at the end of each chapter.

You may have skipped through the book, reading only what most interested you, and then went out and applied what you read. If so, that's great. In the event that you don't feel ready, or that you have gotten through every chapter and are still waiting for the magic formula, I want to reassure you that you already have it.

You are equipped to be a problem solver who will get paid handsomely for your solutions. To prove it, I'll take you through a quick summary review of what we've covered, and then I'll give you a checklist of what to do first, from beginning to end, so you have everything you need to get going.

The Seller's Problem

In a down market, and especially in a depressed economy, selling a house is a major headache for anyone who doesn't understand all of the available options in the real estate market.

Many folks in today's economic environment don't just wish to sell their homes, they NEED to sell their homes. By now you know that most sellers rely on real estate agents, but just listing a property through a real estate agent is no guarantee the agent will ever bring you a buyer. That's why so many people get frustrated trying to sell their properties using the traditional real estate agent route, or they try to sell their homes by themselves. Neither option produces consistent results in today's market.

That's why my system works! Because you start by focusing on those sellers who either list their homes For Sale By Owner (FSBO) or have had their home listed on the market by a real estate agent for a minimum of 90 days. FSBO sellers have either had unhappy experiences with real estate agents or are attempting to save the commissions normally paid to real estate brokers. In addition, FSBO sellers usually have specific reasons for wanting to sell their homes for a particular price, such as having an independent appraisal for a certain amount.

With the homes that have been on the market for 90 days or longer, you can assume that either the real estate agent doesn't have the skills needed to market a property properly or just doesn't have the time (or motivation) to find a buyer as quickly as the seller would like. This combination of factors spells an opportunity for you.

Of course, there are also all the other potential deals I've listed: the people facing foreclosure who have no way out, are scared and are going to get stuck with a HUGE black mark on their credit if the foreclosure goes through. That's a problem you can solve for many of these folks. Real Estate Owned (REO) properties are owned by a bank, and when a bank takes a property back, it becomes a liability. That's a problem you can solve for many banks. Banks want to sell these properties off as fast as they can, to generate cash or establish a new mortgage loan, and turn the property into an asset. The list goes on from probate properties, to abandoned properties, to divorce properties, to the relocating employee. There is no shortage of opportunities—and there never will be.

Just remember, all of them are more than just "properties." There are real people with real-life problems and feelings behind each one of the potential deals. I've tried to convey a message that you can create a win-win solution for them. I don't advocate being a predator and I don't focus on techniques that require you to make money by taking advantage of another's misfortune.

Kicking your fellow man when they're down may put money in your pocket, but I've always been a believer in "what comes around goes around." I think that folks who prey on people and make heartless decisions are going to pay a huge price in the end. Besides, why in the world would you want to take advantage of another person, especially when you don't need to? You can get very wealthy, in a few years' time, by creating win-wins AND you'll sleep like a baby, knowing you have hurt no one in the process and created no enemies.

Using the marketing techniques you now have and seeking out sellers with problems you can solve will make you a lot of money in the current market, and in any market, once you have a little practice.

The Motivated Buyer

Some of the buyers you find will seek you out because you can supply homes cheaper than most anyone. Everyone loves a deal, and when you can make money providing others a great deal it is a home run.

In other instances, just as sellers have problems selling their homes, in a down market, buyers are having problems qualifying for loans. With banks and other financial institutions cutting back their loans, even previously qualified lenders cannot borrow the money they need anymore. Maybe their credit scores are too low, or maybe they can't afford a traditional 20% down payment. Even worse, maybe the bank or banks they previously dealt with have stopped offering loans altogether, or even gone out of business. When this happens, it locks out a huge segment of the population that in the past would normally have qualified for a loan.

Whatever the case, many buyers still want a house, but they simply do not have the information or connections to get the right financing. These are good people, often motivated and trustworthy, with a unique set of circumstances. Most banks have stopped offering a variety of loans needed to fit these individuals, such as 100 percent financing loans. Most subprime loans have all but disappeared. Yet with what you have learned in this book, you know that many of these "on the edge" people have options they do not know about, and you will be able to make a difference for them!

In the past, it was much more common to find sellers who owned their home, with no mortgage, who would be willing to offer you their own financing (known as "seller–financing"), but this is now exceedingly rare. (It does still exist, however, and if you find one don't pass up on the opportunity to ask the seller to hold the mortgage.)

Most Americans not only don't own their homes outright, they have second mortgages or HELOC (Home Equity Line Of Credit) loans, acquired when interest rates were so attractive. In many cases, these debts have made it so they owe as much or even more than the home is worth. In this case, it's time to try a short sale.

Financing strategies that worked in the past don't work in today's turbulent climate. Fortunately, what you have learned does work. With the right broker on your team, you can make money by making the dream of home ownership a reality for people. Also, because you know how to find homes at such steep discounts, people who may have not qualified for the same home two years ago will easily qualify now because the price has so significantly dropped. Trust me, there's a world of difference between trying to get a $100,000 dollar loan and a $200,000 loan. Today, many houses are priced at half, or less, of what they were worth a few years ago, in some cases, even one year ago.

Your Solution

It's not rocket science! Use the techniques in this book to find the Buyers and the Sellers. Match the buyers with the seller and take your profit from a number of different contract types, while helping both sides in the process.

Since sellers are desperate to unload their properties, they will gladly accept less than their asking price. Historically, homes sell for around 90% of the asking price, which means if a home has been appraised at $100,000, the owner will typically sell it for $90,000. Yet, that $90,000 price tag is buying you a house that's worth $100,000. You can even interpret every house you see with a For Sale sign out front as another sign that reads "Sale! 10% Off!"

This 10% discount ($10,000 in our above example) is your potential profit. YET, in today's depressed real estate market, homes selling for 90% of their value are the exception rather than the rule. Selling for 30% to 60% of their value is more realistic, and you know how to find these deals, making your profit potential even higher. Let's break it down into short, succinct actions:

• You are going to find a motivated Seller.

• You explained your intentions to the Seller and they agreed to sell you the property way below fair market value.

• You both sign the appropriate paperwork, which was addressed in chapter 8.

• The Seller knows that you have a certain number of days to make a deal happen and if not, you both walk away with no downside and no money out of your pocket.

• The ideal outcome is that the Seller gets to sell his home for a price he is satisfied with, a new buyer is happy to get a home at a discount, or get financing he did not know he could get, and you get to put profit in your pocket for putting it all together. That's a pretty big payoff for just taking the time to learn this strategy of investing, wouldn't you say? Through reading this book, and your desire for a better life, it can happen—over and over and over again.

The Seller knows that because you are acting solely on your own behalf, you have the leeway to resell to another Buyer. The Seller knows you will make a profit from the difference between your purchase price and the net sales price for your new Buyer.

As I've reiterated in the bulleted points above, you have a specific number of days that your Seller agreed to for making a deal happen. Either you buy the property yourself, sell your equity, or hand off the contract to another buyer.

In the unlikely event that you don't accomplish any of those things, both you and the Seller get to move on. If that Seller wants to hire a real estate agent after that, at least you had a shot at it, and the Seller has not lost anything besides a few days' time.

If you do make a deal happen, you were able to sell it in a shorter period of time, which probably ends up saving the Seller money in the process. That is one of the benefits to promote when you go to talk to these motivated sellers.

Let me back up a little.

Once you find a Buyer of your equity, or someone who wants you to assign the deal to them, you use the "Investor Sales Agreement" or simple Assignment clause added to a basic purchase agreement.

This, along with the standard Real Estate Purchase and Sales Agreements between you and the Buyer, is all you need to make it happen. Basically, we discussed two ways to complete this deal once you have a qualified willing Buyer.

Option #1 : Sell Your Equity in the Contract

By tying up the property with the seller, you have the legal right to try to resell the property even though you haven't closed on the property with the seller.

What this agreement provides in legal terms is "equitable conversion." Equitable conversion allows you to sign the agreement to purchase a piece of property and gives you certain ownership rights, including certain rights that allow you to resell the property to someone else for a profit.

You utilize this legal right to resell the property for a profit or, as we have stated, sell the equity in your contract. You back out of the original agreement at the end to allow the seller and buyer to complete the transaction, and that is how you get paid.

The steps to sell your equity in a deal are:
  1. Find a Seller
    a. Be completely transparent with your intentions, and if the seller agrees to go ahead, you use the Investor Disclosure Notice and Seller's Acknowledgment

    b. Sign the Investor Disclosure Statement and Seller's Acknowledgment agreement (it's one agreement). This is the document used between you and the SELLER. It makes everyone aware of your intentions (the real estate investor) and also shows what amount of money you will make.

    c. Get the purchase agreement signed and tweaked to match your offer. This is the basic sales contract between you and the seller with tweaks to fit this specific deal.

    d. Get the seller's residential Property Disclosure Statement filled out and signed. This tells you anything that is wrong with the property, from leaks to liens.

2. Find a Buyer (before or after you find the seller)
Have the original seller and your buyer sign a new, more traditional purchase agreement between them that fits their deal. You tear up the original contract between you and the seller. At this point when the seller is ecstatic about what you have provided for him or her, you also ask them to sign the Discharge of Agreement to Purchase Statement. This is simply an additional piece of paper showing that you are backing out of the deal and you are getting paid for that. It also shows the amount you will be making and it doubles as an invoice.

3. Get your Investor Disclosure Statement and the Discharge of Agreement to Purchase to the Title Company or attorney handling the closing and collect your check at close of escrow.

I recommend you stay involved at all stages to make sure that all the documents are delivered, and any questions are answered quick, fast, and in a hurry so you can bring this deal to completion.

Make a copy of the documents signed by the buyers to the sellers for their records.

Meet the sellers at the closing agent's office so you or they can deliver all documents, including your Discharge of Agreement, to the closing agent and arrange for closing.

I recommend attending the closing session where both seller and buyer sign final documents and keys are handed over.

You want the signing to go as smoothly as possible, so it's best if you're there to make sure. You can also arrange with the closing agent to provide you with a check or have it mailed to you.

If you think it is feasible, you can ask the seller to pay you directly for canceling the sales contract, instead of using the Discharge of Agreement Statement.

Basically, what this means is that you will pull out of the deal and allow the new buyer to purchase the property from the seller. The seller must pay you the amount you intended to earn to cancel the contract.

Obviously, this can only work when the seller has the capital to do so. But, things can be simplified by doing this, because you don't need the invoice, and it saves you a lot of steps and time.

Option #2 : Assign the Property

When you find a buyer who wants the home you control, have him or her complete an assignment contract with you, so they can take over your position, based on the terms and conditions described in the contract. This is easily done because in the original deal with the seller you put the statement "and/or assignee" in the purchase agreement.

An assignment fee will then be collected from the new buyer prior to closing. This fee can be whatever you feel is allowable for the deal, acceptable for both the seller and buyer, so you can make the money you deserve.

Depending on how far below fair market value you get the property on contract, you can allow yourself to make a wide range of money. Matt has ranged from $2,000 to $20,000 and he is currently working on an assignment where he hopes to make $75,000.

Work with an attorney for this transaction since title companies are not qualified and can sometimes make it a much harder transaction than it needs to be.

That's it. You've just tied up a property, assigned the contract, and got paid prior to closing.

If at any time you do a deal for a person you know, you trust, or you feel 100 percent comfortable with holding some paper on the amount you made, then you can always do a promissory note like the sample that follows. (*This should only be done if you have run credit and payment history on the person along with references.*)

DEMAND PROMISSORY NOTE

Date: _____

FOR VALUE RECEIVED, the undersigned jointly and severally promise to pay to the order of _____ [insert your name], the sum of_____ dollars ($_____.00). The entire principal and any accrued interest shall be fully and immediately payable UPON DEMAND of any holder thereof.

Upon default in making payment within_____ days of demand, and providing this note is turned over for collection, the undersigned agree to pay all reasonable legal fees and costs of collection to the extent permitted by law. This note shall take effect as a sealed instrument and be enforced in accordance with the laws of the State of _____ [state].

All parties to this note waive presentment, notice of non-payment, protest and notice of protest, and agree to remain fully bound notwithstanding the release of any party, extension or modification of terms, or discharge of any collateral for this note.

NOTICE TO BUYER: THIS IS A DEMAND NOTE AND SO MAY BE COLLECTED BY THE LENDER AT ANY TIME AFTER _____(date immediately after closing).

_____

[Maker's signature]

_____

[Maker's typed or printed name]

NOTICE TO CO-SIGNER: YOUR SIGNATURE ON THIS NOTE MEANS THAT YOU ARE EQUALLY LIABLE FOR REPAYMENT OF THIS NOTE IF THE BORROWER DOES NOT PAY.

_____

[Co-signer's signature]

_____

[Co-signer's typed or printed name]

Witnessed:

_____

[Witness's signature]

_____

[Witness's typed or printed name]

Let's recap your available wealth-building strategies:

Step #1: Find Motivated Sellers

Locate sellers who are eager or even desperate to sell their property. This will result in discounts of up to 60% off the fair market value. We have covered solid unique ways using my marketing strategies to automatically have sellers come to you, as well as great traditional ways. And there's Matt Larson's 25:1 deal, which works like gangbusters with the right real estate agent.

Step #2: Find Motivated Buyers

As with sellers I'm quite sure I've covered how to use smart marketing to find buyers, as well as great old-fashioned ways, so I'll keep this reminder brief.

You can find motivated buyers when you post flyers, run ads, and use robotic techniques (like the free recorded messages) and direct-response strategies. You'll attract both investors and everyday people who have been told they can't buy.

Put your ad in grocery stores, birthing centers of hospitals, and wedding shops—wherever people are going through life changes.

Emphasize the benefits of being a homeowner on flyers, business cards, ads, and even a website if you choose. You can direct people to a recorded message that gives them more benefits and explains in a compelling way how you can help them.

Once you find potential buyers, either through the above methods or the many other ways we covered, direct them to your broker if they need a loan and see if they will qualify.

Step #3: Put the Seller and the Final/End Buyer Together

I bet most of that is still fresh in your mind from a few pages back. I hope so! You have completed the transaction with the original seller in Step 1. You have found a final/end buyer in Step 2 (and, where necessary, coordinated their qualifying with the mortgage broker). You will use any of the two main ways (the IEE method or the assignment method) to complete the deals you find and cash in on the process.

What you now have in your hands is a powerful wealth creation system that requires little or none of your own money.

If you have funds to start your real estate investing or you want to do a buy, rent, get positive cash flow, hold and sell when market turns strategy, then it's your time to increase your net worth, pay off bills, or simply start living the secure, prosperous life you deserve.

Frankly, this will take time and work on your part. It's not as easy as snapping your fingers or changing the TV channel with your remote. But with a little work and follow-through, you will be able to create a large enough bank account for down payments on other types of property deals. This could be the start of an entirely different life for you.

Whenever you doubt yourself, or allow others to put doubt in your head, go back and read the student stories, Matt Larson's story, or go to **www.deansmedia.com** and watch videos of regular people, just like you, who made it in real estate. These people didn't succeed because they were smarter, richer, or free of all problems and insecurities. They succeeded simply because they got in the game, learned as they went along, and used what I taught them as their guide to make it happen, in spite of any obstacles. Why can't that be you? Why can't you live the life you know you deserve? There is no reason in the world, because nothing can stop you except you.

There's a quote that says, "Obstacles are the things you see when you take your eyes off the goal." So set your goals, get inspired, take the wisdom, confidence, and capabilities you just learned, use all we offer to assist you, and go get your American Dream, whatever that means for you.

Now I'll end this chapter the same way I started it, talking about choices. The way I see it, you now have three possible choices.

Choice #1 You can choose to do nothing from this point forward, and you will simply have read just another book.

Choice #2 You can choose to use SOME of what you've learned or put forth a halfhearted effort, or even give up when it gets tough.

Choice #3 You can choose to use what you have learned in the previous eleven chapters as the foundation to change your life and become a successful real estate investor.

C'mon . . . what's it gonna be for you? My hope for you is that you choose

#3. That you will take action, and if you choose to take action, it's my belief your life will change forever.

I want you to know beyond a shadow of a doubt that you can do this. You don't need anything else to be ready—all that's left for you to do is start.

In any market, you only have to get out there and try. The results of your actions will speak for themselves.

It has been my absolute pleasure to share with you techniques that can change your life. Real estate changed mine, and now it's your turn.

I wish you great success!

Resources

Originally I was going to add all types of forms and documents here for you to copy. But what I quickly saw was that there were a lot of forms. And I didn't want to limit the information by squeezing it into a book. So, for a master list of everything mentioned in this book and a lot more go to the Resource Center at **www.deangraziosi.com/allforms.** You will be able to print clean copies from there as well. Enjoy!

Index

Acknowledgments

Originally, I was going to write this book and publish it sometime in 2009, but with the crazy state of the economy, I felt obligated to get it done fast and give people a true way to prosper and find financial security in these insecure times. I mention this because it took eight weeks to write this book from cover to cover. It wasn't easy, at least for me, to get everything in my head, everything I have learned and some outside research on paper and in a format that allows people to learn and apply what you share. But we did it.

I say "we" because I could have never have done it without a great core group of people who assisted me. Tony Policci and Wallace Wang were my personal editors, helping in every area possible to make this a great book from start to finish. They busted their humps to make sure we got this book done fast so people could start changing their lives. Ryan Patten and my in-house staff, or should I say my extended family, do all they can to assist me in all ways possible so I can take the time to get this information down in a book and share it with you. It could not be possible without their support. I am blessed to have a team, all with the same vision I have, to provide people with the wisdom, capabilities and direction in real estate that gets results and changes lives forever. I thank you all for your dedication.

I thank each and every person in this book who took the time out of their busy lives to share their story and help inspire and teach others how to succeed. You are a testament to all that America was founded on. Success and sharing with others. Hats off, a deep heart felt thank you from me and I am sure hundreds of thousands of others who will read this book. Thank you to Matt Larson, Dawn Lutter, Mike Shotwell, Anita Wilson, Lorina Krisak, Bob and Debbie Bouchard, Laura Johnson, Greg Murphy, David Lessing, Kathleen and Grady Corbin, Carolyn Gronseth, Elena Margaritis and Carol Stinson.

Thank you to the entire **www.deangraziosi.com** family. You guys rock! When we first started the website, I never dreamed it would become so powerful. Because of each and every one of you who visit that site to share your experiences, your wisdom and inspiration, lives are changing by the thousands each week. Keep it up and thank you.

I kept the best for last. Thank you, Jonelle, for being an amazing partner in my life and even a more amazing mother. You have watched lots of transformations in my life since we have met, and you have stood by my side through all of them. Thank you for allowing me the freedom to work so hard on my passions. Your unselfishness in return will help countless people change their lives all over America, and for that I thank you.

And to my children, Breana Jewel and Brody Dean Graziosi. Words can't express the love that parents have for their children. Words are shallow in comparison. All I can do is hope that some day when you have children of your own, you will look back at this book and remember that Dad loved you like you will love your own children one day. I love you both dearly and thank you for choosing me as your father. I am truly blessed.

Final Thoughts

I just wanted to say thank you for trusting in me enough to read my book. I hope you see that I didn't hold anything back and gave you everything I know, every tool I could think of to inspire you to take action and start making money in Real Estate Right Now.

This is not a time to be paralyzed and stand still; it's a time to take action and change your life forever. This is the greatest time in history to prosper and profit from real estate using the right techniques for these changing times.

What you hold in your hands can be the starting point of a new life for you and your family. But for any reason—if you get off track, want further assistance, or would love the opportunity to be in my Real Estate Success Academy like many of the students who wrote success stories for my book—then call us anytime, toll-free, at 1-800-315-7782.

Your Purchase Also Made a Difference in Someone Else's Life As Well

There are so many wonderful people and organizations that could use financial help, and I'm sure you already do your part to help others who are less fortunate in one way or another. Well, I wanted to let you know that by simply purchasing this book, you did it once again. A portion of every single sale of this book will be donated to Richard Branson's Virgin Unite charity for helping homeless children here in America. It is a huge growing problem and Virgin Unite is doing their best to make a difference. I had the great pleasure of spending a week with Richard Branson and discovered that he personally pays 100 percent of the costs to run this charity. So 100 percent of the money that Virgin Unite receives goes directly to the people they are trying to help. It's a great cause and now you have helped too. Thank you.

—Dean Graziosi